Violence and Democracy

In this provocative book, John Keane calls for a fresh understanding of the vexed relationship between democracy and violence. Taking issue with the common-sense view that 'human nature' is violent, Keane shows why mature democracies do not wage war upon each other, and why they are unusually sensitive to violence. He argues that we need to think more discriminatingly about the origins of violence, its consequences, its uses and remedies. He probes the disputed meanings of the term violence, and asks why violence is the greatest enemy of democracy, and why today's global 'triangle of violence' is tempting politicians to invoke undemocratic emergency powers. Throughout, Keane gives prominence to ethical questions, such as the circumstances in which violence can be justified, and argues that violent behaviour and means of violence can and should be 'democratised' – made publicly accountable to others, so encouraging efforts to erase surplus violence from the world.

John Keane is Professor of Politics at the University of Westminster. Born in Australia and educated at the universities of Adelaide, Toronto and Cambridge, he is a frequent contributor to radio programmes and newspapers and magazines around the world. Among his books are *The Media and Democracy* (1991), which has been translated into more than twenty languages; the prize-winning biography *Tom Paine: A Political Life* (1995); *Civil Society: Old Images, New Visions* (1998); a biography of power, *Václav Havel: A Political Tragedy in Six Acts* (1999); and *Global Civil Society?* (2003). He was recently Karl Deutsch Professor of Political Science at the Wissenschaftszentrum Berlin and a Fellow of the influential London based think-tank, the Institute for Public Policy Research. He is currently writing a full-scale history of democracy – the first for over a century.

CONTEMPORARY POLITICAL THEORY

As the twenty-first century begins, major new political challenges have arisen at the same time as some of the most enduring dilemmas of political association remain unresolved. The collapse of communism and the end of the Cold War reflect a victory for democratic and liberal values, yet in many of the Western countries that nurtured those values there are severe problems of urban decay, class and racial conflict, and failing political legitimacy. Enduring global injustice and inequality seem compounded by environmental problems, disease, the oppression of women, racial, ethnic and religious minorities, and the relentless growth of the world's population. In such circumstances, the need for creative thinking about the fundamentals of human political association is manifest. This new series in contemporary political theory is needed to foster such systematic normative reflection.

The series proceeds in the belief that the time is ripe for a reassertion of the importance of problem-driven political theory. It is concerned, that is, with works that are motivated by the impulse to understand, think critically about, and address the problems in the world, rather than issues that are thrown up primarily in academic debate. Books in the series may be interdisciplinary in character, ranging over issues conventionally dealt with in philosophy, law, history and the human sciences. The range of materials and the methods of proceeding should be dictated by the problem at hand, not the conventional debates or disciplinary divisions of academia.

Violence and Democracy

JOHN KEANE

CAMBRIDGE
UNIVERSITY PRESS

HM
886
K43
2004

PUBLISHED BY THE PRESS SYNDICATE OF THE UNIVERSITY OF CAMBRIDGE
The Pitt Building, Trumpington Street, Cambridge, United Kingdom

CAMBRIDGE UNIVERSITY PRESS
The Edinburgh Building, Cambridge, CB2 2RU, UK
40 West 20th Street, New York, NY 10011–4211, USA
477 Williamstown Road, Port Melbourne, VIC 3207, Australia
Ruiz de Alarcón 13, 28014 Madrid, Spain
Dock House, The Waterfront, Cape Town 8001, South Africa

http://www.cambridge.org

First published 2004

Printed in the United Kingdom at the University Press, Cambridge

Typeface Trump Mediaeval 9.5/15 pt.   *System* LaTeX 2_ε [TB]

A catalogue record for this book is available from the British Library

Library of Congress cataloguing in publication data
Keane, John, 1949–
Violence and democracy / John Keane.
    p.   cm. – (Contemporary political theory)
Includes bibliographical references and index.
ISBN 0 521 83699 9 (hb) – ISBN 0 521 54544 7 (pb)
1. Violence.   2. Democracy.   I. Title.   II. Series.
HM886.K43   2004
303.6 – dc22   2003067574

ISBN 0 521 83699 9 hardback
ISBN 0 521 54544 7 paperback

53919440

For Bhikhu Parekh

Contents

Introduction: surplus violence   *page* 1

1   Muskets, terrorists   15

2   Thinking violence   30

3   Civilisation   42

4   Barbarism?   54

5   Why violence?   89

6   Uncivil wars   109

7   Ethics   128

8   Ten rules for democratising violence   165

    Further reading   210
    Index   214

Introduction: surplus violence

As a rule, dictatorships guarantee safe streets and the terror of the doorbell. In democracy the streets may be unsafe after dark, but the most likely visitor in the early hours will be the milkman.

Adam Michnik (1998)

This essay is about violence, and the pity of violence. It dwells upon its connections with democracy because unwanted physical interference with the bodies of others, such that they experience pain and mental anguish and, in the extreme case, death – violence, in a word – is the greatest enemy of democracy as we know it. Violence is anathema to its spirit and substance. This follows, almost by definition, because democracy, considered as a set of institutions and as a way of life, is a non-violent means of equally apportioning and publicly monitoring power within and among overlapping communities of people who live according to a wide variety of morals.[1] Under democratic conditions the means of decision-making are neither owned nor wielded privately. While its institutional forms are highly variable, democracy as we know it today minimally requires public respect for others who are equal but different, and such respect extends to their entitlement to organise themselves into opposition to the powers that be. Democracy requires citizens to stay alert, to open their eyes and their mouths – to understand that societies of sheep typically beget governments of wolves. It facilitates criticism of power. In principle, democracy enables everybody to act at a distance from its power centres by means of a functioning civil society that is independent of publicly accountable governmental institutions; together, elected, responsible government and the dispersal of power within civil society provide organised protection from the fear or fact of injury or loss of life.

---

[1] The pre-Greek origins, modern development and uncertain future of democracy, including its variable and disputed meanings, are analysed in detail in my *A History of Democracy*, in preparation.

Just how unique contemporary democracies are when defining and handling violence can be glimpsed by comparing them with the fascist régimes of the recent past. Ponder for a moment the Nazi euthanasia programme (1939–41), which led to the deaths, on Hitler's orders, of an estimated 100,000 German adults and children with mental disorders or incurable physical disabilities: backed by the fist of organised terrorism and mass mobilisation in the name of the nation or race, such programmes reveal how fascism was both paranoid and obsessed with unifying the body politic through the controlling, cleansing and healing effects of violence, which was often understood through 'medical' or 'surgical' metaphors.[2] Similar language is let loose in democratic countries, admittedly. It might even be said that a distinctive quality of democratic institutions is their subtle efforts to draw a veil over their own use of violence. There are also plenty of recorded cases where democratic governments hurl violence against some of their own populations. Such violence is called law and order, the protection of the public interest, or the defence of decency against 'thugs' and 'criminals', or 'counter-terrorism'. Within democracies, medical metaphors sometimes also surface, as when politicians speak of surgical strikes, sanitary cordons, mopping-up operations and fighting the 'cancer' or 'plague' of terrorism.

Mature democracies find such euphemisms embarrassing. They regard them as corrupting and contestable: on the home front, democracy is marked by a strong inner tendency to non-violence and, hence, a deep suspicion that what police and armies and men of violence do in the normal course of their duties is by definition never quite legitimate. During transitions to democracy, public suspicion of men of violence is often expressed with a sudden vengeance, like a geological upheaval: the *ancien régime* is accused of murder; searches for the

[2] See Sven Reichardt, 'Formen faschistischer Gewalt. Faschistische Kampfbünde in Italien und Deutschen nach dem Ersten Weltkrieg', *Sociologus*, 51 (2001), pp. 55–88; and 'Civil society and violence. Some conceptual reflections from an historical perspective', in John Keane (ed.), *Civil Society: Berlin Perspectives* (London and New York 2004), forthcoming.

disappeared begin; clandestine mass graves are exhumed; citizens are urged to tell their stories of suffering. Mature democracies refine and routinise these suspicions of violence and cultivate a measure of canniness: violence is not seen simply as the unlawful use of force. Ideally conceived, democracies understand themselves as systems of lawful power-sharing, whose actors are attuned to the dangers of violence – and to the mutual benefits of non-violence.

The calculation, peculiar to democracies, that the commitment to non-violence makes everyone feel safer is reinforced by the fact that many citizens and politicians – not all of them, not always a majority, take note – more or less share a peaceful outlook on the world. They tend to display a strong distaste for cruelty, a genuine interest in others' ways of life, or a simple commitment to ordinary courtesy and respect for others, wherever they live and whatever their skin colour, gender, religious or geographic background. This essay emphasises just how delicate and destructible is the *learned* quality of non-violent openness and how, paradoxically, this contingency feeds upon the fact that the daily lives of citizens in a democracy are normally cloth-bound in inherited habits and structured routines that seem banal and repetitious, but in fact, given their delicacy, should never be taken for granted.

These thoroughly contingent, existential routines of daily life are the 'raw material' of civility, as it is called throughout this essay. The members of a democracy, like all human beings, are animals of erect stature. They find it painful to remain upside down for long and therefore not only have a common understanding of up and down; they prefer uprightness. Thanks to language, they likewise have shared notions of left and right, of immobility or motion. Since they have bodies, arms and legs, they comprehend what it means to move, to squash, to kick, to be hit by something hard. Conceptions of constraint come easily to these beings: they especially dislike it when others prevent them from talking, or breathing, or when they obstruct their motion, or strike or physically hurt them. Such dispositions are in turn enmeshed within, and reinforced by, non-violent webs of more or less taken-for-granted commitments: conversations, gestures, washing bodies, patience, laughter, sexual play, cleaning, shopping for consumable items, planning journeys, tending crops and plants, worrying about income, filling out forms, paying bills, preparing food, looking after relatives, watching television, reading newspapers, telling children about the world and putting them to bed.

So the civil societies upon which today's democracies rest have a strong affinity with the will to name and to contain and to root out violence – to 'democratise' violence (as I explain in the pages that follow) wherever it appears and whatever may be its causes. This learned capacity to 'de-nature' violence, to see it as contingent, as politically removable from social and political life, is a key reason why mature democracies have an unblemished record in not waging war upon each other.[3] Their citizens are too canny for that: enjoying a measure of liberties within a civil society, they tend to see through claims of sabre-rattlers and warmongers by suspecting that the mutual deployment of organised violence would not only favour some at the expense of others, but almost certainly would drown everyone's liberties in bayous of hubris and blood. The tendency of democracies to democratise violence also explains why democracies are often good at winning wars against their anti-democratic opponents, despite the latter's military and technical superiority. 'We shall win this war', wrote a distinguished journalist as the British faced the grim prospect of fascist occupation, 'because we are still a democracy, because the eye of criticism is still kept imperious over those who might slink into slothful, unoriginal methods'.[4]

---

[3] Michael Doyle, 'Kant, liberal legacies and foreign affairs', in *Philosophy and Public Affairs*, 12, 3–4 (1983), pp. 205–35, 323–53. Compare Melvin Small and J. David Singer, 'The war-proneness of democratic regimes', in *Jerusalem Journal of International Studies*, 1, 4 (1976), pp. 50–69. The authors claim that between 1816 and 1965 58 per cent of inter-state wars were provoked by democracies – wars being defined as violent conflicts claiming at least 1,000 lives. The claim is unconvincing, if only because democracies are defined (poorly) as regimes in which just 10 per cent of the population are enfranchised.

[4] Quoted in the interview with Michael Foot, 'Old Labour', *The Independent on Sunday*, London, 20 July 2003, p. 10 (the original dates from 1940).

These antipathies of democracies toward violence are well known, but unfortunately they are not the end of the story. All democracies, as we know them today and as they have existed in the past, are forced to play noughts and crosses with the violence of others, for instance, mercenaries, dictators, armies, guerrillas and networks of terrorists equipped with various weapons of violence that they are prepared to use against democrats, wherever they show their face. Persuaded by business deals and geopolitical calculations, democratic governments – when they can get away with it – secretly succour blood-sucking despots, like Idi Amin and Joseph Mobutu, Saddam Hussein and the Shah of Iran. And faced with the violence of their opponents, democracies find themselves trapped within a conundrum: whether or when or how to develop and deploy their own means of violence in order to repel or eradicate that of others. Exactly because democracies are prone to non-violence they are unusually sensitive to its threatened or actual occurrence elsewhere. Their parties, politicians and leaders come under pressure to sail ships and fly thousands of troops to places on earth where strangers are subjected to hellish acts of cruelty. Democracies find it difficult to hide from these atrocities. If they stand aside and 'do nothing' – as every democracy did when the Indonesian military mass-murdered East Timorese citizens – then they are easily accused of double standards, and callous indifference. If, on the other hand, democracies undertake 'humanitarian intervention' – India's move into East Pakistan is an example – then they stand accused of meddling with the affairs of others, of behaving 'undemocratically' by heaping violence upon their opponents.

Especially when atrocities are hurled in their direction, democracies are prone to contradict themselves. Their structures of open power not only enable their violent opponents to work like worms through the body politic. Their openness enables the rise of parties and leaders who seek revenge, who pledge solemnly to root out violence – and in so doing are tempted to behave (here much can be learned from Herman Melville's *Moby Dick*) like the monomaniacal Captain Ahab who hunts a feared and hated object to all four corners of the earth, only to suffer crushing defeat. Fortunately – thanks to public demonstrations and communications media and judiciaries with teeth – democracies tend to place limits upon the 'nauseous self-righteousness' (Reinhold Niebuhr) of posturing leaders who tell lies, exaggerate threats, look for surrogate victims and take the side of 'good' against 'evil'. Their grandiose strategies for dealing violently with the violent come to be seen as questionable in the courts of public opinion. Their actions are media covered and not covert, and for that reason these leaders often become publicly controversial. Their behaviour breeds disquiet, and for a good reason. Many within today's mature democracies know or sense the rule first glimpsed by the ancient assemblies and democracies of Babylonia and Phoenicia and Greece: that the roads through the lands of violence are typically littered with brazen lying, hubris and corpses, all of which prove emotionally difficult for the inhabitants of democracy, who are exposed not only to embittered charges about their own double standards, or outright 'rottenness', but also to the possibility that democracy will be used to defeat democracy, for instance by invoking emergency powers that eventually transform it into some or other form of military dictatorship.

Some years ago, in *Reflections on Violence* (1996), I complained about the paucity of political reflection upon the contemporary causes, effects and ethics of violence. Violence was there understood as any uninvited but intentional or half-intentional act of physically violating the body of a person who previously had lived 'in peace'. At the time, attempts to spark discussion about the meaning or significance of violence and politics were bogged down in swamps of semantic confusion or political indifference or strong academic preferences for discussing theories of justice, communitarianism or the history of half-dead political languages. There were plenty of case studies of hot wars, cold wars, civil wars and other violent conflicts, certainly. But broad-based political reflection on the forms and causes and effects of violence – Hannah Arendt's exemplary *On Violence* and Judith

Shklar's preoccupation with cruelty were the striking exceptions[5] – seemed no longer to be of much intellectual interest.

And so *Reflections on Violence* set out to break this glum silence, initially by exposing its roots within a confused quagmire of unspoken prejudices and significant assumptions. It pointed out, for instance, that violence often so shocks our senses that it induces forgetfulness, or mumbling embarrassment or silence. Especially for the 'civilised' person, violence is not a pretty subject. It is ugly enough to make even the most cheerful thinker pessimistic, and since optimists write badly (as Valéry said) and pessimists tend not to write at all, the silence about violence of some parts of the profession of political theory was understandable. *Reflections on Violence* examined other reasons why at the time the political imagination about violence seemed frozen. It pointed out that outbreaks of violence blinker the imagination, in that they induce pragmatism – a sense that the problems at hand must be solved urgently using such means as arrest, court trial and incarceration, criminology, clinical analysis, or police or military intervention. That flat-headed pragmatism often feeds other beliefs, including the presumption that 'human nature' is prone to violence, and that that is why – inevitably – an armed body like the state should monopolise its means, without further questions.

There are signs that this latter belief (or vague impression) that violence is a 'natural' or deeply rooted element of the human condition is today on the rise. For reasons that have to do with the evanescence of post-Cold War euphoria, and especially (as explained in the pages that follow) because of the dangerous 'triangle of violence' that is now settling on the whole world, violence and threats of violence are felt by many to be an ineluctable feature of our world as it is. Violence seems to be back and here to stay, in a big and disturbing way. The first-ever global report on violence (published in 2002) tells something of the

---

[5] Hannah Arendt, *On Violence* (New York and London 1969); Judith Shklar, 'Putting cruelty first', in *Ordinary Vices* (Cambridge, MA and London 1984), pp. 7–44.

bad news: more than 1.6 million people suffer violent deaths every year. Each day, on average, over 1,400 people are murdered; roughly 35 people are killed every hour as a result of armed conflict; one quarter of the world's women have suffered sexual violence by an 'intimate partner'.[6] Such figures are grist to the mills of journalists working in the field of communications media, especially television. Indulging various motives, they help to cultivate the impression that our world is becoming ever more violent, sometimes to the point where violence is represented as 'natural' – as an eerie constant of the human condition. Proponents of violence have taken their cue and, seizing the script, have risen to the occasion: as if to prove that humans are dastardly creatures, works of violence have become works of art. The explosions, fear, injury and death are carefully staged, for a world audience. And so we are living in times when, just as night follows day, reports of violence flood in from all four corners of the earth. So too does talk of 'getting tough' with violence and calls for 'war' against its menacing forms. The old conviction, once expressed in the theory of 'democratic zones of peace', which supposed that advanced societies like the United States and Britain are no longer seriously troubled by violence, and that theories of violence are perforce losing their *raison d'être*, is on the ground, wounded and shaking.

In emphasising the *contingent* and *erasable* character of violence, this essay reminds readers that the belief that violence is 'natural' – a deep-seated predisposition in every individual, or generative of either the body politic or of the species as a whole – is both historically specific and profoundly anti-democratic. So this essay meets head-on the most sophisticated recent effort to speak of violence as a universal feature of the human condition: René Girard's *La violence et le sacré* (1972).[7] Girard sets aside the several ways in which

---

[6] *World Report on Violence and Health* (Geneva 2002); and
www.who.int/violence_injury_-prevention
[7] Translated as René Girard, *Violence and the Sacred* (London 1988), especially ch. 1; see also his contributions to René Girard *et al.*, *Violences d'aujourdhui, violence de toujours* (Lausanne 2000), pp. 13–26.

democracies democratise violence. When democracies flourish, they call into question face-value thinking about violence. The meaning of the term itself comes to be seen as contestable, as well as pliable enough to be extended onto actions that are then described and/or condemned as 'violent' – which means that they violate the norms of democratic civility. Democracies also tend to institutionalise procedures – periodic elections, police in uniform and subject to disciplinary procedures, laws against the violation of the body, chat lines, official inquiries, freedom of public assembly, press freedom, civilian control of the armed forces – for making sure not only that the violated get a fair public hearing, and fair compensation, but that those in charge of the means of violence are publicly known, publicly accountable to others – and peacefully removable from office. When they function well, democracies even enable their critics to name, and to shame, institutions – like courts of law and prisons – that inflict violence on their victims using sweeter names like 'interpretation' and 'justice'.[8] The historically unique, never-perfect bundle of non-violent power-sharing techniques that today is called democracy is written out of Girard's account of violence. He admits that violence (the term is left undefined, but seems to be synonymous with blood) does not always have an immediately felt presence in human affairs. It dons symbolic (especially religious) masks, and in its disguised form it may well appear to disappear, or to appear benign. There are times, says Girard, when violence surfaces in terrifying form, wantonly sowing the poisonous seeds of chaos and destruction. At other times, violence steps forward as a peace-maker offering the sweet fruits of justice and reconciliation. At all times, however, violence is a constant

---

[8] See the stimulating comments by Robert M. Cover, 'Violence and the word', *Yale Law Journal*, 95 (1986), pp. 1601–29, and the criticism of the 'agencies of force' of actually existing democracies in Eldridge Cleaver, *Soul on Ice* (London 1968), p. 128: 'They use force to make you do what the deciders have decided you must do . . . They punish. They have cells and prisons to lock you up in. They pass out sentences. They won't let you go when you want to. You have to stay put until they give the word. If your mother is dying, you can't go to her bedside to say goodbye or to her graveside to see her lowered into the earth.'

companion of human affairs. That is why communities can be protected from their *own* violence only by choosing surrogate victims outside themselves. Modern 'civilised' societies may appear to put an end to the practice of 'interminable revenge', but they too are based on judicial systems that offload violence onto the convicted. A common thread runs through every known procedure designed to keep violence in bounds: the thread of violence itself. 'The more men strive to curb their violent impulses', concludes Girard, 'the more these impulses seem to prosper. The very weapons used to combat violence are turned against their users. Violence is like a raging fire that feeds on the very objects intended to smother its flames.'

Violence and Democracy takes aim at this kind of reasoning, partly because it has a long pedigree in early modern political thought, and as well because today the influence of such reasoning is regaining ground. 'Wars are like deaths, which, while they can be postponed, will come when they will come and cannot be finally avoided', concludes an epic inquiry into the future of territorial states. The author seeks authority in the words of the Polish-born writer, Joseph Conrad: 'the life-history of the earth must in the last instance be a history of a really relentless warfare. Neither his fellows, nor his gods, nor his passions will leave a man alone.'[9] Along similar lines, Marx's thesis (outlined in *Das Kapital*) that 'in actual history conquest, enslavement, robbery, murder, in brief violence, notoriously play the great part' and his dictum that 'violence is the midwife of every old society pregnant with a new one' swam like a fish in early modern waters. It is exemplary of a smug conviction whose genesis is tied to the rise of the West and the birth of modern territorial states and empires: the conviction that some or other form of violence is ineluctably a feature of human affairs, that violence has a mind of its own, that violence reveals the 'real' nature of human beings and their historical strivings.

---

[9] Quoted in Philip Bobbitt, *The Shield of Achilles. War, Peace and the Course of History* (London and New York 2002), p. 819.

Gripped by this conviction, many observers (René Girard is just one among many) conclude that all political orders naturally rest upon violence, whose 'real' or 'ultimate' purpose is to contain the violent capacities of others. Other observers have gone further, either by worshipping violence or emphasising its purgative or elevating effects on human beings. Violence is seen in both functional and aesthetic terms, as a marvellous means for achieving potentially great human ends. The plain fact that violence, understood as a means, could degenerate into an ulcerous end-in-itself is of little or no concern to these observers; violence is an object of respect and hope, endlessly fascinating, an altogether positive cleansing force in the muck-filled stables of human affairs. The train of thought that supposes that violence 'like Achilles' lance, can heal the wounds that it has inflicted' (Jean-Paul Sartre), is a child of the early modern world. Its conviction that 'you can't make an omelette without breaking eggs' (Lenin); that 'political power grows out of the barrel of a gun' (Mao Tse-tung); that violence is 'as American as cherry pie' (H. Rap Brown); or that violence is needed because 'the day of salvation is near' (Osama bin Laden) was virtually absent from European political thinking five centuries ago. Prior to 1500, with the help of seminal thinkers like Augustine and Ibn Khaldun, those who reflected upon the subject typically thought in terms of 'just violence'; they insisted that although violence has a role to play in human affairs, it is merely a means that is always in need of a universal end that justifies and in turn places strict limitations upon its use.

True, those who ruminated on violence were sometimes tempted to speak loosely, for instance by describing violence as a developer of the noble virtues of heroism and endurance among youth. Yet discourses on violence were normally much more ethically rigorous than this. They were peppered with 'Thou shalt' and 'Thou shalt not'; with calls (by Muslims) for peaceful reform (*islah*) and warnings about the dangers of chaos and schism (*fitnah*); and (as in the notion of *dharamayuddha* in Hinduism and Sikhism) talk of duties towards others and strict rules governing social order and justice. Violence was said to be legitimate only when the intention to use it was declared openly by properly constituted – spiritual and temporal – authorities who could reasonably expect victory through its use; it was seen to be merely a means of last resort, an act of redress of previous violations; and violence was considered a *measured* method that should avoid humiliation, and honour and preserve the distinction between combatants and non-combatants.

The attempt of this essay to think democratically about violence – to see that it is contingent in both ontogenetic and phylogenetic terms, to regard it always as regrettable and potentially removable from political and social life – is not just an effort to revive the old tradition of 'just violence' reasoning that sought to place fences around violence. Given the technical destructiveness of today's means of violence, the imposition of practical limits and burdens of philosophical proof upon unlimited violence remains important. Yet the approach of this essay is altogether more radical. Its defence of the idea that violence can be 'democratised' – that the means and institutions of violence must always be publicly accountable and that *surplus* violence can and should be removed from the world – steers a new course between and beyond dogmatic pacifism and just war doctrines. In contrast to traditional just violence thinking, this essay does not suppose that statesmen and clerics and philosophers are entitled – at the expense of free-thinking publics – to monopolise debate about the nature and ethics of violence. *Violence and Democracy* also repudiates the crusading presumption, common to all just violence doctrines and to most versions of pacifism, that there are Universal First Principles that instruct us how to think, and how to act. This essay asks different questions and comes up with different suggestions. It does so by engaging with some of the modern 'classics' on the subject. *Violence and Democracy* reacts with and against Georges Sorel's syndicalist defence of the workers' movement in *Réflexions sur la violence* (1908) and Walter Benjamin's essay on law, justice and violence, *Zur Kritik der Gewalt* (1921). It grapples with Hannah Arendt's efforts to distinguish violence and power in *On Violence* (1969). It takes issue with

Frantz Fanon's attack on white-washing colonialism, *Les Damnés de la terre* (1961), especially its insistence that the powerless are entitled to kill their oppressors, because to do so is to kill two birds with one stone: the oppressor within and the oppressor without. The narrowly rights-based and state-centred reasoning of Michael Walzer's *Just and Unjust Wars* (1977) is questioned as well, along with the quite different treatment of violence, sacrifice and ritual in René Girard's *La violence et le sacré* (1972).

Violence and Democracy may be read as a reply to each of these works, helped along by insights provided by such disciplines as anthropology, history and psychoanalysis. In much-changed historical circumstances, it seeks to conduct a feet-on-the-ground scrutiny of the principal threats posed by violence to democratic ways of life. This essay reflects upon conceptual matters to do with the meaning of violence; tries to be sensitive to changing historical trends; and draws attention to some fundamental normative and strategic issues, including the overriding need to think democratically about the various possible remedies for violence. Such thinking requires the recognition that there is in fact no one substance (like sodium bicarbonate or plutonium 239) that is called violence. It comes in a very wide range of forms – from spitting and unwanted love bites and smacking children and street muggings to riotous assembly and political assassinations, concentration camp murders and terrorist attacks. It is more or less mediated by technical instruments, ranging from rocks and Molotov cocktails and rubber bullets to Stealth bombers, tanks and precision-guided nuclear weapons. And violence can also have many functions. From the standpoint of individuals or whole groups, it can be a form of self-defence or self-discovery or self-affirmation or self-destruction; it can be an insane act of fleeing from reality, a coldly calculated, this-worldly revenge – a means of achieving certain ends – or a mode of communication with others, even (perversely) a pleasurable form of play with the lives of others.

This essay seeks to cultivate in small ways democratic habits of mind and heart. It sets out to trigger fresh thoughts, to push inquiries in new directions, above all to ask whether and to what extent violence and its practitioners can be 'de-natured' – subordinated to democratic institutions and ways of life. In this sense, *Violence and Democracy* sets out to counter the rising feeling that our world is heading for a fall, and that democracy may not survive for much longer. While marshalling plenty of evidence that the new triangle of violence and other forms of incivility may well prove the Cassandras right – that democracy as we know it is in for a rough ride, or that it is bound to be weakened or perhaps destroyed – *Violence and Democracy* insists that that outcome is *unnecessary*. And so it encourages readers to think boldly, to think in pain: to refuse politically to set aside the animal-like pity that grips those who witness the physical violation of others.

Muskets, terrorists

Today, tragedy is collective.

Albert Camus (1946)

THE MUSKET AND THE BOMB

Shortly after the atomic bombing of Hiroshima and Nagasaki, George Orwell wrote: 'The great age of democracy and of national self-determination was the age of the musket and the rifle.' He went on to observe that the advent of the nuclear age flung humanity into a different – more depressing – order. 'Had the atomic bomb turned out to be something as cheap and easily manufactured as a bicycle or an alarm clock', Orwell continued, 'it might well have plunged us back into barbarism, but it might, on the other hand, have meant the end of national sovereignty and of the highly-centralised police state'. The mega-technology of nuclear weapons in fact had different effects. The bomb had now transformed the final Armageddon from religious prophesy into factual possibility; it had made thinkable the violent destruction of all remaining democratic states and their civilised societies. The musket and the rifle were inaccurate, yet controllable. But now, according to Orwell, the human species risked either destroying itself with its own grotesque weapons, or destroying democracy with a new form of servitude wrapped in a 'cold war' peace that was not really peace at all. 'Looking at the world as a whole', he concluded, 'the drift for many decades has been not towards anarchy but towards the reimposition of slavery . . . in a state which was at once unconquerable and in a permanent state of "cold war" with its neighbours.'[1]

---

[1] George Orwell, 'You and the Atom bomb', *Tribune*, 19 October 1945, reprinted in *Selections from Essays and Journalism: 1931–1949* (London 1981), p. 715.

Orwell's remarks were astute. They grasped the momentous global dangers posed by nuclear weapons; they pointed as well to the close relationship between violence and democracy, in particular to the general dangers posed to democratic ways of life by violence in its various forms. The half-century before Hiroshima and Nagasaki had been no paradise, as Orwell knew from bitter personal experience. The years that followed were no better, as he predicted. In matters of violence, the twentieth century proved to be the worst ever. Total war, chemical weapons, genocidal wars, firebombed cities, concentration camps, spreading plagues of private bloodletting; the whole of that century saw more than its share of planned and unplanned violence. It was – statisticians tell us – the most murderous century in recorded history. The estimated death toll of 187 million souls was the equivalent of more than one-tenth of the world's population in 1913.[2] It was a century of the break-up of empires and revolutions, and thus of the violent blurring of the boundaries between inter-state violence and violent conflicts ('civil wars') within states. It was also a century in which the burdens of war weighed ever more heavily on civilians; like defenceless pawns on a chessboard of cruelty, they became the favourite targets of military calculations. During the 1914–18 war, civilians comprised one-twentieth of the victims. During the 1939–45 war, that proportion rose to two-thirds; these days, perhaps nine-tenths of the victims of war are civilians.

Historians of this violence have begun to record tales of the courageous, who struggled to survive what Ernst Jünger famously called its storms of steel: the tunnel-builders of the ghettos, digging to outwit those who planned their genocide; the mourning women bearing white scarves, stamped with the names of their loved ones, standing in silence, in the shadows of a terrorist state; ethnically cleansed

[2] Eric Hobsbawm, 'War and peace in the 20th century', *London Review of Books*, 21 February 2002, pp. 16–18.

villagers, mourning their beloved, weeping over the destruction of their houses and farms, praying that their conquerors do not raze their crops; the Buddhist monks, dressed in crimson robes, silently witnessing cruelties inflicted on innocents by savage troops; the office employees jumping to their death from a collapsing skyscraper, holding hands. Such bright images of bravery will no doubt prove remarkable for future generations, but only because of the mountains of cruelty that cast shadows over democratic institutions and ways of life: the cruelty symbolized by the trenches of the Somme, where soil and flesh mixed to make pink-grey mud; the burning and recycling of corpses, so that they could be turned into gunpowder to make more skeletons out of future enemies; the torturer armed with prized instruments like electrodes, syringes, and the rectoscope, an instrument used to place gnawing and clawing rats inside victims; the military officers, flinging drugged or murdered bodies of young men and women out of helicopters and planes into the ocean depths below; and, as Orwell noted, the dripping flesh and swollen faces inflicted by a bomb whose flash proved brighter than the sun.

These symbols of the long century of violence now behind us have become – whether we like it or not – irrevocably part of our living history. Images of cruelty cannot easily be forgotten, which is why they need to be placed in historical perspective, as some have sought to do during the past decade by taking refuge in the consoling thesis known as the theory of democratic peace. After a terrible century of violence, its proponents say, the world has now become divided into two parts: a democratic zone of peace, an open and prosperous 'security community' comprising one-seventh of the world's population and most of its power, a community whose 'national security' calculations, military power and means of war have ceased to be instruments of politics, a patch of the earth where civil peace and parliamentary democracy is the norm; and the rest of the world, a zone of violent anarchy, hopelessly entangled in war and warlordism, famine and lawlessness, a sphere in which civility and stability are mere words because people's lives are trapped by 'coups and revolutions, civil and international wars, and internal massacres and bloody repression'.[3]

The democratic peace thesis supposes not that violence is withering away, but that it is an external problem, a threat emanating from *outside* otherwise peaceful democratic institutions and ways of life. The thesis is unconvincing. For citizens who today live in the so-called democratic zone of peace, the world is not so neatly subdivided into peaceful and violent zones. The old rule that mature democracies do not fight each other certainly applies, but that does not mean that democracies can forget about violence, or consider it a marginal phenomenon. The truth is that various trends are conniving to unsettle the comfortable image of a democratic peace. Most of them, including the tightening links between the two worlds forged by global arms production (currently valued at around US $40 billion per annum) and the violence-ridden drugs trades, are obvious. So too are the tensions aroused by the military supremacy of the United States, and the enclaves of violent lawlessness – dangerous areas like the Strasbourg district of Neuhof, the Los Angeles suburb of South Central or ravaged cities like Ahmadabad in Gujurat – within nearly every urban area of the developed democratic world. It could even be said, paradoxically, that life within the democratic zone of peace feels *more* violent than elsewhere in the world, mainly because within the democratic countries images and stories of violence move ever 'closer' to citizens who otherwise live in peace. Violence feels omnipresent. Insurance companies remind potential clients of the need for risk calculations and safety requirements. Policing authorities advertise the dangers to citizens. The flourishing private security business markets its wares. Campaigns to publicise violence and to mobilise the criminal process (against rapists and child molesters, for instance) compound this feeling that the world is

---

[3] Max Singer and Aaron Wildavsky, *The Real World Order: Zones of Peace/Zones of Turmoil* (Chatham, NJ 1993), ch. 1.

taking a violent turn. So too does the development of a global system of communications, parts of which know that violence – horror movies, blood sports, horrific murders – attracts audiences, and so is driven by market instincts that follow the editorial rule that 'if it bleeds, it leads'.

The last factor is one important reason why the democratic peace thesis is implausible.[4] Thanks in part to the growth of communicative abundance and high-pressure media coverage, the rooms of the world feel increasingly stuffed with violence. According to some observers, Tanaka Akihiko, Giuseppe Sacco and Umberto Eco for instance, communications media are helping us see that we are drifting, despite all illusions of 'progress' and 'peace' and 'security', in the direction of a self-contradictory, multilayered 'new middle ages' marked neither by the spiritual unity of Christendom nor the secular unity of empire. This emerging neo-medieval order, they claim, is a world in which the political significance of territorial boundaries declines. The range of claimed authorities and conflicting types of legitimation multiply. Positively speaking, it is a world in which there is a marked growth, on a global scale, of supranational law which takes precedence over the domestic laws of states without being rooted in popular sovereignty; in which there is a return, in both political and everyday discourse, of the notion of a 'world society'; and in which – reminiscent of the doctrine of *ius gentium intra se* defended by Francisco Suárez, Francisco de Vitoria and other Spanish theologians and teachers of law – there is a strengthening sense among powerful states of the *droit de regard* over the domestic affairs of other states, of the duty to intervene wherever human rights are violated. But, Sacco and Eco argue, the new medieval order is not without its troubles and dangers. Negatively speaking, it is a world defined by the spread of plagues of private violence and 'permanent civil war' sanctioned by decentralised powers – new warlords, pirates, gunrunners, gangsters,

---

[4] Jeffrey Goldstein (ed.), *Why We Watch: The Attractions of Violent Entertainment* (New York 1998).

sects – which the modern state was supposed to crush, but which it has manifestly failed to do.[5]

THE TRIANGLE OF VIOLENCE

The claim that our world is slipping back or sliding forwards into a new and violent form of mediaevalism is a healthy corrective to the illusions of the democratic peace hypothesis. The weaknesses of both can be set aside by concentrating on a different, more precise account of the novelty of our situation. Quite aside from the ongoing tendency of democracies and their civil societies to produce troubling amounts of violence at home – rapes, muggings, gang-land crimes, bizarre Columbine High School-style murders[6] – there is also mounting evidence that actually existing democracies, despite the end of the Cold War, are today falling under the shadow of a new and highly unstable *triangle of violence.*[7]

One side of the triangle is the instability caused by nuclear-tipped states in the post-Cold War world system of geopolitics. This system is currently dominated by the United States, which can and does act as a vigilante military power, ultimately backed by threats of nuclear force. As a dominant power, it is engaged in several regions without being tied permanently to any of them, but its manoeuvres are complicated by the fact that it is presently forced to coexist and interact peacefully with four power blocks, three of whom are nuclear powers: Europe and Japan, and China and Russia. The geometry of this

---

[5] See Umberto Eco, 'Living in the new Middle Ages', in *Faith in Fakes. Essays* (London, 1986), pp. 73–85. The twentieth-century version of the medievalisation of violence 'without Giotto, Dante, or the inspiration of Christ' is traceable to Guiglielmo Ferrero, *Peace and War* (London 1933), p. 96 (translation amended). It is developed in new directions in Tanaka Akihiko, *The New Middle Ages. The World System in the 21st Century* (Tokyo 2002), esp. ch. 7.

[6] There is a vast literature on such forms of violence, which are analysed in more detail below. See Robert Jackall's thought-provoking study of disorder in New York, *Wild Cowboys: Urban Marauders and the Forces of Order* (Cambridge, MA 1997) and my *Reflections on Violence* (London and New York 1996), especially pp. 113–22.

[7] The following section draws upon my *Whatever Happened to Democracy?* (London 2002).

arrangement clearly differs from the extended freeze imposed by the Cold War, when (according to Raymond Aron's famous formula) most parts of the world lived in accordance with the rule, 'peace impossible, war unlikely'. With the collapse of bipolar confrontation, this rule has changed. There is no evidence of the dawn of a post-nuclear age, and the freedom from the fear of nuclear accident or attack that that would bring. Nowadays, peace has become a bit less impossible and war a bit more likely, principally because a form of unpredictable nuclear anarchy has settled on the whole world.[8]

It may be, as some observers claim, that nuclear weapons have so reduced the need for mass mobilisation of troops that they sustain a permanent 'civilianisation' of daily life in some Western states.[9] Insofar as these nuclear weapons have also reduced the likelihood of war among the dominant powers, it may also be true that the probability of a nuclear apocalypse, in which the earth and its peoples are blown sky-high, has been permanently reduced.[10] The deep trends are nevertheless uncertain, and arguably those living within

---

[8] See the concluding interview in Pierre Hassner, *La violence et la paix: De la bombe atomique au nettoyage ethnique* (Paris 1995), especially p. 383: 'In the past, the doctrine of deterrence matched the civil character of our societies: an invisible hand, or abstract mechanism, took charge of our security, and we did not have to bother our heads with it. But today the nuclear issue can no longer be considered in isolation, it is inextricably mixed up with everything else.' A more activist perspective is provided by Helen Caldicott, *The New Nuclear Danger* (New York 2002).

[9] Paul Hirst, *War and Power in the 21st Century. The State, Military Conflict and the International System* (Oxford 2001), p. 39.

[10] A classic reflection on the problem is Hans Morgenthau's *Politics Among Nations: The Struggle for Power and Peace* (New York 1954). Following the nuclear attack on Japan, he claimed that the avoidance of a nuclear World War III required the structural transformation of the anarchic territorial state system into a world state. He saw that requirement as necessary, but as impossible to satisfy. No world state – except one that was imposed in the aftermath of World War III – could be built unless it was built upon a sense of world community nurtured by shared moral and political values. Morgenthau concluded that such a world polity was unlikely, since no such community of values was available, either in the present or in the foreseeable future. Some observers, including the American 'realist' scholar Kenneth Waltz, have turned Hans Morgenthau's conclusions upside down, to argue that the gradual spread of nuclear weaponry is more to be welcomed than feared, principally because the rising dangers of accident or attack will spawn the growth of global self-restraint in all matters nuclear. See Jonathan Schell, 'The folly of arms control', *Foreign Affairs*, 79, 5 (September/October 2000), pp. 29–30.

democracies, or those who aspire after a democratic way of life, need
to be on guard. For various reasons, perpetual peace is a very long
way off in the future. The key political powers are currently preoccu-
pied with seeing through a 'revolution in military affairs',[11] in which
armed force will be geared increasingly to electronic intelligence gathering, computerised communications networks, protective screens,
and highly destructive, precision-guided or 'smart' weapons capable of
use anywhere on the globe. It is highly doubtful whether such weapons
can eliminate 'frictions' (as von Clausewitz called them) from battles.
There are doubts too about whether the claimed level of precision can
be affordably and reliably achieved, or whether civilians uninterested
in military heroism will be prepared to witness, in silent gratitude,
the violent elimination of others by remotely piloted vehicles, nano-
weapons and sophisticated information systems. Major wars using
these and more old-fashioned weapons remain a long-term possibility, including even the use of nuclear-tipped weapons in conflicts that
originate in local wars and disputes.

Whether nuclear conflict can be avoided is unclear; alternative
scenarios are equally likely. Actually existing democracies are now
embedded within a risk-producing system in which the possibility
of a damaging theft or spillage of nuclear materials, or nuclear reac-
tor meltdown or the open use of nuclear weapons is chronic. A taste
of things to come is governments' talk of radiological weapons and
dirty bombs, the private trafficking of 'orphaned' nuclear materials
and the routine dropping of depleted uranium shells on the victims
of war. Meanwhile, nuclear weapons sprout like the dragon's teeth of
Cadmus. The arsenals of the United States and the Russian Federation
each contain somewhere around 7,000 nuclear warheads.[12] Despite

---

[11] The policy trends are analysed in Michael O'Hanlon, *Technological Change and the Future of Warfare* (Washington 2000); E. A. Cohen, 'A revolution in warfare', *Foreign Affairs* (March–April 1996), pp. 37–54; and in J. Arquilla and D. Ronfeldt (eds.), *In Athena's Camp: Preparing for Conflict in the Information Age* (Santa Monica 1997).

[12] *The Times*, London, 10 *February* 2001, p. 16.

the 1972 Anti-Ballistic Missile Treaty, nuclear capacity, as can be seen in the arms races between Pakistan and India, and between Israel and the Arab states, is spreading, despite any prior agreements about the rules of nuclear confrontation and despite the fact (revealed in the so-called National Missile Defense system planned by the Bush administration) that the issue of nuclear weapons is now deeply implicated in the so-called 'modernisation' of weapons systems. American officials, aware that their old Cold War rival is no longer so, meanwhile like to speak of a 'generic' threat, a bundle of potential dangers that might well arise at any moment, somewhere else in the world. Hence the investment, since the early 1980s, of some $60 billion in the project of developing a National Missile Defense programme that takes aim at 'rogue' powers equipped with nuclear weapons. One trouble with this roguish project is that there are potentially large numbers of other rogues; the US State Department currently lists forty-four governments endowed with nuclear weapons' capacity, which helps explain why the world's governing institutions are already plagued by rivalries between new-comer nuclear governments. The world's first nuclear confrontation unrelated to the Cold War – five tests conducted by India in May 1998, followed by seven tests by Pakistan – has been reinforced by a long sequence of new and equally threatening developments: North Korea's ongoing efforts to build weapons; worries about the undetectable 'basement proliferation' of gas-centrifuge and laser-enrichment methods of producing nuclear weapons material; continuing doubts about Russia's ability to keep safe its nuclear weapons and materials (despite American contributions of $2.3 billion per annum under the Nunn–Lugar legislation); American interest in developing 'low-yield' nuclear weapons that could be used against hardened or deep underground targets; and American assurances that it will not object to China's plans to expand its nuclear arsenals – plans which would in effect lead to the end of the current worldwide moratorium on nuclear testing, as codified in the Comprehensive Test Ban Treaty. The worst fears of Orwell are beginning to materialise: nuclear armaments appear to be breeding nuclear armaments. Talk of 'throw-weight gaps', 'windows of vulnerability' and 'missile gaps' admittedly no longer echoes through the corridors of power. Yet ominous signs are everywhere. New revelations of past and present administrative carelessness and 'normal' nuclear accidents are streaming into public circulation. Compensation claims are finding their way into the world's courts. The sequence of developments actually runs longer and deeper than this, and is by definition (like the future) uncertain. But one conclusion is unavoidable: all democracies are now potentially threatened by a world system that produces a rabble of self-interested nuclear powers that are sharply opposed to the aim of either reducing or abolishing outright nuclear weapons.

UNCIVIL WAR

And so to the second side of the triangle of violence: democracies are today also threatened by the violence unleashed in uncivil wars. These comprise armed conflicts that rip apart political institutions, poison the institutions of civil society and fling their combatants into self-preoccupation with survival.[13] Examples of this second form of violence are to be found in abundance, and include two decades of fighting in the Sudan, fuelled by constant imports of arms that reach the hands of state and non-state actors, who struggle to use these arms in highly complex ways to kill and maim others in order to preserve or acquire land, cattle, wealth and power. The conflict has resulted in the death of at least 2 million people and another 4 million are refugees in their own country – internally displaced people, in the jargon of the INGO world.[14]

---

[13] Uncivil wars are analysed in my *Reflections on Violence*, pp. 131ff. General remarks about such forms of conflict are scattered throughout Gérard Prunier, *The Rwanda Crisis: History of a Genocide* (New York 1995) and Fergal Keane, *Season of Blood: A Rwandan Journey* (New York 1995), especially pp. 1–40, 161–98.

[14] See Francis Deng, *War of Visions* (Washington, DC 1995); Abdelwahab El-Affendi, *For a State of Peace. Conflict and the Future of Democracy in Sudan* (London 2002); and the report by the International Crisis Group, *God, Oil and Country. Changing the Logic of War in Sudan* (Brussels 2002).

Uncivil war zones of the Sudanese kind are marked by terrible suffering. Those who are caught up in their maelstroms of violence suffer a shrinking of existential horizons caused by unimaginable cruelties. Armies, militias and rag-tag criminal gangs rape, pillage and murder to the point where virtually all remaining islands of civility are wrecked, beyond repair. The flames of violence typically are fuelled by global flows of arms, money and men, who take advantage of the fact that local political institutions are crumbling and competitor power groups are jostling for territory and resources. Whole populations are consequently dragged down into dark holes of violence. The results can hardly be described or analysed as 'civil war', a term that has always supposed, under modern conditions, that combatants were locked into a violent but disciplined struggle for control over the key resources of territorial state power. Civil wars are carefully planned and executed struggles to seize or to preserve the means of state power by using rational-calculating violent methods. They are considered civil because civilians participate in the struggles for state power; and they are considered to be wars because violence is used as a tactical means by all parties.

The problem with the concept of civil war (as we shall see in more detail later in this essay) is its inability to grasp the ways in which struggles for political power can and do easily become a euphemism for the most terrible experiences of anarchic destruction and death. The Sudan, Sierra Leone, Kashmir, the ill-named Democratic Republic of the Congo are just a few of the many conflicts in which combatants' violent struggle makes a terrible descent into hell – towards a place where the means and acts of violence assume a life of their own. Within uncivil war zones, violence becomes a grisly end in itself. People get killed and wounded ultimately for no other reason except that they *can* be killed and wounded. It is as if the violent can only affirm their identity through violence projected onto others. The violent need enemies who appear to threaten them with extinction, and who therefore must be persecuted, tortured, mutilated, annihilated. In uncivil war zones, violence has a profound functional advantage. Rivalries, jealousies, quarrels within the community of the violent are projected outwards, onto others, in life-affirming acts of desperate cruelty against 'surrogate victims'.[15] All sober restrictions governing the ground rules of war are swept aside.

The enemy is demonised as all-powerful, as all-threatening, as all-violent. The rituals of violence against them are thus repeated endlessly, shamelessly, without limit. Acts of violence become gratuitous. The killers' faces look blank. Sometimes they smile. Their words are cynical, or spill out as clichéd accounts of their private or group fantasies. Alibis flourish, certainly. Yet the laws of engagement are quite transparent: murder and counter-murder innocents, sever the hands and genitals of the enemy, cut out their tongues or stuff their mouths with stones, destroy graveyards, rape women, poison food, torch crops, make sure the victims' blood flows like water. Guarantee that there are no innocent bystanders. Punish waverers – like the moderate Hutu leader, Agathe Uwilingiyimana, who was murdered by her fellow Hutus for her moderation, her half-naked body left dumped on a terrace, a beer bottle shoved up her vagina. Everybody on the side of the violent must be baptised in blood, made into an accomplice of dastardly crimes. Ensure that everybody witnesses rape, torture, murder. Make sure that they are defiled, that they do not forget what they have seen or done. Trouble democrats and others with painful questions: what bestial instincts drive Bosnian Serb torturers to amuse themselves by forcing their Muslim victims to bite off the testicles of other Muslims? What class of unreason prompts a Rwandan priest to set fire to his own church where terrified citizens have sought sanctuary? Why did Serbian bulldozer drivers dig mass graves *before* the murder of their victims began? What manner of people are we who accept such degradation in our midst? And when all is said and done, be prepared, as Slobodan Milošević did before the Hague Tribunal, to

---

[15] René Girard, *Violence and the Sacred* (London 1988), pp. 4–6, 8–10, 269–73; cf. the fine study of the uncivil war in the Lebanon by Samir Khalaf, 'The scares and scars of war', in *Cultural Resistance. Global and Local Encounters in the Middle East* (London 2001), especially pp. 201–33.

boast to journalists and judges that the butchers are actually heroes, that the victims are fictions or that they deserved what they got – that this was no crime against humanity.

APOCALYPTIC TERRORISM

Every nook and cranny of the democratic world is today threatened by a third form of violence: apocalyptic global terrorism. Terroristic violence of this kind arguably dates from the early 1980s. Of course, the phenomenon of terrorism – the word itself dates from the revolutionary *terrorisme* of the period from March 1793 to July 1794 in France – is much older.[16] Its so-called 'classical' forms include operations that use (or threaten to use) violence to instil fear into others for the purpose of achieving defined political goals. While states can certainly be terrorist, in the sense that they can use assassins and other violent undercover agents to govern through their subjects' fear of violent death, conventional terrorism of the non-state variety is typically the work of fighters who are neither uniformed soldiers nor organised in elaborate hierarchical command structures. They are trained in the arts of handling explosives and light weaponry, usually within urban areas. Unlike guerrillas, such as the Kenyan Mau Mau and the Algerian FLN and today's Revolutionary Armed Forces of Colombia (FARC), conventional terrorists do not seek to occupy their enemy's territory. Even though they too use lightning attacks and swift retreats, terrorists have neither the numerical strength nor the military capacity nor the will physically to defeat their opponents. Like rats in a sewer, they operate in small and practically autonomous units within the more or less invisible channels of the local civil society, in order to wear down and demoralise their governmental enemy, whom they suppose – ultimately, despite everything – to be capable of negotiation, concession and retreat. New means of communication, such as mobile phones and the Internet, definitely enable terrorists to widen and multiply their contacts into all-channel networks, all the while keeping

[16] See Walter Laqueur, *The Age of Terrorism* (London 1987).

their activities invisible or 'private' in order – paradoxically – to win over public support for their case. Propaganda of the violent deed – planting bombs in the consciousness of the people – is among their specialties. So too is the struggle for victory by means of fear induced by measured acts of violence that have socially and politically disruptive effects.

The cruel but *measured* deployment of violence – not indiscriminate killing and maiming on a large scale – was always and still remains a critical feature of classical terrorism, including its fascist variants. The fascist action squads that formed after World War I typically comprised demobilised men in their twenties and thirties who vented their frustrations on domestic targets – communists, Catholics, socialists, trade unionists, Jews – through 'punitive expeditions' geared to curing the body politic of disorder and disease.[17] Latter-day acts of violence by Basque and Irish and Colombian gunmen, hijackers and bombers similarly mean business and want publicity, but the cruelty and panic they inflict is also restrained, even when (as the Red Army Faction thought) the task was to unmask the fascist character of the state and to create a parallel army of the people. Like the old proponents of *squadrismo*, these acts of violence do not aim to kill lots of people, which is why terrorism of the apocalyptic kind is a new departure. It is true that strongly 'classical' elements of terrorism were evident in the suicide attacks on American and French military facilities in Beirut in the early 1980s, the Aum Shinrikyō's attack on the Tokyo Metro, the bombing in early 1995 of the Federal Building in Oklahoma City, the simultaneous attacks on the American embassies in Dar es-Salaam and Nairobi in August 1998, and the assaults on the Pentagon and the World Trade Center in September 2001. Each of these attacks aimed at a fundamental

---

[17] Note Mussolini's view of squad violence as a controlled medical experiment: 'The expeditions must always have the character of a just retaliation and a legitimate reprisal. We do not make violence into a school, a system or, worse still, an aesthetic. Violence must be generous, chivalric and surgical' (quoted in Margherita G. Sarfatti, *Dux* (Milan 1926), p. 250).

change of the political order; and each unleashed violence in urban settings without however attempting to occupy its territory. Yet each attack represented a rupture with the tactics of conventional terrorism. Apocalyptic terrorists thought of themselves as engaged in total war against an enemy that was unworthy of negotiation and incapable of compromise. The enemy was seen as both morally null and void and good for nothing but annihilation. Hence unlimited violence, bloodcurdling in its technical simplicity and witnessed by millions, is justified. The aim of apocalyptic terrorism is to take advantage of the vulnerability of complex systems, to choose targets – key symbols of American power, for instance – and then to come out of hiding to kill indiscriminately on a massive scale. Not just embassies or airports or nightclubs or hotels, but whole cities should be razed. The point is neither to win over public support nor to negotiate political deals. A deathly zero-sum game has to be played. Anonymity should be preserved.[18] Responsibility need not be claimed. Like a God, the terrorist should be everywhere and nowhere. The terror must be neither directly graspable nor manageable: it should function as noise whizzing through the heads of its potential victims. The name of the game is militant defeatism. The minds and bodies of the enemy should be shaken to their core. They should (to use prison language) be buried alive, tortured in their isolation, compelled to doubt themselves into oblivion. Meaning itself should be destroyed. The rottenness of the present-day world should be exposed. Nothing but catastrophe should result.

[18] See the remarks of Jürgen Habermas in Giovanna Borradori, *Philosophy in a Time of Terror. Dialogues with Jürgen Habermas and Jacques Derrida* (Chicago and London 2003), p. 29: 'partisans fight on familiar territory with professed political objectives in order to conquer power. This is what distinguishes them from terrorists who are scattered around the globe and networked in the fashion of secret services . . . The terrorism we associate for the time being with the name "al-Qaeda" makes the identification of the opponent and any realistic assessment of the danger impossible. This intangibility is what lends terrorism a new quality.'

Thinking violence

The problems of violence still remain most obscure

Georges Sorel (1906)

ON VIOLENCE

Can democracies survive this triangle of violence? Can they do anything to attenuate, even eliminate, its globally destructive consequences? Possible replies to such questions initially require greater
clarity about the troubled and troubling term 'violence'. What exactly
is the meaning of this much-used, much-abused term?

Like all concepts in the human sciences, categories like violence are as dangerous as they are necessary. They can be fatal for the
imagination, in that they lull their users into a false sense of certainty
about the world, seducing them into thinking that they 'know' it like
the backs of their hands; on the other hand, without such categories,
thinking is swamped, sometimes drowned, by the world's otherwise
unintelligible tides and waves and storms of events, people and things.
One way of escaping this dilemma, which undoubtedly grips political
thinking about violence, is to build a measure of indeterminacy into
the category of violence by defining it abstractly as an 'ideal-type' –
understanding it as an arbitrarily chosen, yet clearly defined term
that seeks to redescribe the world in order to attune our senses to
its complex political realities, marking them off as 'significant', as
'problematic' and therefore as worthy of our attention.

The task of clearly defining violence is complicated by the fact
that since the middle of the eighteenth century the term itself has
undergone a definite 'democratisation', by which I mean three things.
The scope of application of the term 'violence' has been broadened;
its meaning has come to be seen as heavily context-dependent and,
hence, as variable in time and space; in consequence of which the term

'violence' and its negative connotations are now notoriously contested in such fields as criminal law, journalism, public policy and everyday life. It is vital to take note of this democratisation process, if only to offset the bad habit of some historians, who use the term imprecisely and anachronistically. In the sixteenth and seventeenth centuries life was much more dangerous than now, Muchembled writes, because violence constituted 'the common thread of human relations and of the sociability characteristic of various groups of the population'.[1] Sweeping statements of this kind lose track of the historicity of their key term. Consider for a moment the striking contrast between Darnton's gripping account of the lynching, burning and torture of cats in pre-1789 France, Germany and England, and current controversies about 'cruelty to animals'. The contrast reminds us that acts that were once considered as unproblematic, as carnavalesque, as by no means violent but even a matter of fun, come to be regarded, at a later moment and in a different context, as strangely cruel, even repulsive curiosities.[2] The same lesson – that the concept of violence has no

[1] Robert Muchembled, *La violence au village: sociabilité et comportements populaires en Artois du Xve au XVIIe siècle* (Turnhout 1989), p. 9.

[2] These reflections on violence and democratisation necessarily prompt questions about whether or not it is justified to speak of violence by *humans* against the living creatures of the biosphere. Reasons of space prevent proper treatment of the subject, although as far as I can see there are no good reasons in principle why the concept of violence being developed here should be confined to human affairs. The growing public sensitivity to 'cruelty to animals' in democratic countries is probably symptomatic of the long-term historical shift that is taking place in favour of extending the term 'violence' into fields of life previously ruled by other descriptors. Normatively speaking, non-violent campaigns and laws against single-minded, cold-blooded violence against nature are on balance to be welcomed, if only because they problematise the ugly callousness of vivisection practices that extend back into the nineteenth century (see Frances Power Cobbe, *The Modern Rack: Papers on Vivisection* (London 1889) and Albert Leffingwell, *The Vivisection Controversy: Essays and Criticisms* (London 1908)). Proud of its achievements and potentials, vivisectionism came dressed in the uniform of hubris, and not surprisingly the claim of the animal experimenters that science and industry required freedom from inspection, ethical judgement and legal controls helped prepare the ground, historically speaking, for respectable and often well-intentioned doctors performing hideous experiments upon helpless human beings (see Alexander Mitscherlich and Fred Mielke, *Doctors of Infamy: The Story of the Nazi Medical Crimes* (New York 1949)).

straightforwardly universal meaning – can be learned by pondering the riots that erupted from early modern European religious festivals and popular preaching, in which crowd members regularly practised rites of violence against those whom they considered diabolic filth without however calling their rituals acts of violence, exactly because they came clothed in symbols drawn from the Bible, the liturgy and folk traditions.[3] A similar rule applied to medieval Europe's customs of ritualised combat or 'deep play' – dangerous and bone-breaking games, like football, bridge-fighting and bull running, that were again *not* seen as remedial acts of violence because they were typically tied to the agricultural cycle and self-consciously expressed as a community's self-understanding as a tightly bonded *communitas*.[4]

Those who use the concept of violence must be aware of these spatial and temporal anomalies. Such anomalies help to explain why the term itself has undergone a measure of democratisation. Face-value thinking about the term 'violence' is in decline. There is growing awareness of its ideal-typical – contestable, alterable – character. This process of conceptual democratisation is arguably part of a much wider – politically embattled – historical shift in favour of the democratisation of violence in the real world. Whereas once upon a time cruelty was excused through euphemisms or talk of honour, those who are cruel towards others now find themselves called violent. This denaturalisation of acts that are harmful to others, the tendency to name them as 'violent' and so to disrupt their taken-for-granted quality, is evident in the remarkable extension of the term from the 'core' domains of the military and police and institutions of criminal law – the so-called repressive apparatuses of government – into other spaces of life and classes of action, as has happened during

---

[3] Natalie Z. Davis, 'The rites of violence', in her *Society and Culture in Early Modern France: Eight Essays* (Stanford 1975), pp. 152–87.
[4] Clifford Geertz, 'Deep play: notes on a Balinese cockfight', in his *The Interpretation of Culture: Selected Essays* (New York 1973), pp. 412–53; and Julius R. Ruff, *Violence in Early Modern Europe* (Cambridge and New York 2001), ch. 5.

the past several decades with the emergence of talk of 'domestic violence', stalking, 'road raging' and 'bullying' of children.[5]

Such trends are to be welcomed, even if they unavoidably complicate efforts to think more deeply about the relationship between violence and democracy. So how can such efforts best proceed? Are there rules for thinking prudently about violence? Certainly, complications should be seen as no stranger to reflections on violence. Given the potency of the term – its capacity to throw light on the strengths and vulnerabilities of democratic institutions and ways of life – it should be handled with care and modesty, even with a sense of irony. And especially in the face of attempts to dismiss it as a uselessly muddled category, as Robert Paul Wolff tried to do from a philosophically anarchist perspective,[6] there is a strong *prima facie* reason for holding to its narrowest possible core meaning, untainted by loose metaphorical allusions (as when a standard or treaty is said to be 'violated' or somebody suffers a 'violent convulsion', or shakes 'violently', or hears their speech acts called 'violent' because they are passionate or immoderate). Other rules for thinking about violence are worth observing. While efforts to define violence should acknowledge the importance and power of intentional action, they should not be tied too closely to any one particular motivation. Definitions of violence that draw upon references, say, to 'Man's sinfulness' or to 'aggressive instincts' should be rejected, for the plain truth (as the following pages show) is that people can be violent for a bewildering variety of reasons. Violence should also not be thought of as the opposite of legality, as merely the 'unlawful' exercise of physical force (as Sidney Hook once put it) 'the illegal employment of methods of physical coercion for

[5] Robert Darnton, *The Great Cat Massacre and Other Episodes in French Cultural History* (London 1984), ch. 2; Wini Breines and Linda Gordon, 'The new scholarship on family violence', *Signs: Journal of Women in Culture and Society*, 8, 3 (Spring 1983), pp. 490–553; and Liz Margolies and E. Leeder, 'Violence at the door: treatment of lesbian batterers', *Violence against Women*, 1 (1995), pp. 139–57.
[6] Robert Paul Wolff, 'On violence', *Journal of Philosophy*, 66 (October 1969), pp. 601–16.

personal or group ends'.[7] Finally, the term violence should not be weighed down by elitist presumptions, such as the modern bourgeois conviction that 'violence against things' is somehow equivalent to 'violence against people', as if 'property' equals 'people', as if entering a military base by cutting through its reinforced steel fence and occupying its runway is the same as dropping bombs on living people from flying machines 10,000 metres up in the air.

Throughout this essay, the concept of violence has been used as carefully – as ironically – as possible. Every effort has been made to preserve its old-fashioned connotations, themselves traceable to the earliest (late medieval) English usages of the term (from the Latin *violentia*: *vis* (force)) and *latus* (the past participle of 'to carry') to describe 'the exercise of physical force' against someone who is thereby 'interrupted or disturbed' or 'interfered with rudely or roughly' or 'desecrated, dishonoured, profaned, or defiled'. It is important to preserve this older and more precise meaning of violence, and not just because of its continuing pertinence in a world full of potential and actual cruelty. Attempts (such as Johan Galtung's) to craft 'an extended definition of violence', to stretch its meaning to include anything – from maiming human bodies and government discrimination against minorities to debt burdens and sexist language – that impedes human self-realisation effectively makes a nonsense of the concept. The term violence comes to resemble an injustice detector. It measures everything that stands in the way of 'peace'. Violence is stretched to encompass the personal, the institutional and the cultural and is then linked to a questionable ontological account of 'the satisfaction of human needs' – 'survival needs', 'well-being needs', 'identity, meaning needs', 'freedom needs' – that makes violence indistinguishable from

---

[7] Quoted in K. W. Grundy and M. A. Weinstein, *The Ideologies of Violence* (Columbus, OH 1974), p. 12. Compare the retort of Herbert Marcuse against legalist definitions of violence (*New York Times Magazine*, 27 October 1968, p. 90): 'Thanks to a kind of political linguistics, we never use the word violence to describe the actions of the police, we never use the word violence to describe the actions of the Special Forces in Vietnam. But the word is readily applied to the actions of students who defend themselves from the police, burn cars or chop down trees.'

experiences like 'harm', 'misery', 'unhappiness', 'alienation', 'cultural discrimination' and 'repression'. To say that 'violence is present when human beings are being influenced so that their actual somatic and mental realizations are below their potential realizations',[8] is paradoxically to wreck the concept. It makes it virtually synonymous with all human failures to live happily, like angels, unburdened by the curse of politics, within a universe of 'symbiotic, equitable relations among diverse partners' held together by 'cooperation, friendliness and love'.

Violence needs to be defined more soberly, with less normative flourish. It is better understood as the more or less intended, direct but unwanted physical interference by groups and/or individuals with the bodies of others, who are consequently made to suffer a series of effects ranging from shock, speechlessness, mental torment, nightmares, bruises, scratches, swellings, or headaches through to broken bones, heart attacks, loss of body parts, or death. As we shall see, violence can take many forms, some of them highly paradoxical. Extreme cases of enforced self-violation, such as suicide or euthanasia or dirty protests that symbolically reduce the body to shit, urine and menstrual blood, all fall within this category.[9] So do acts that entail the physical restraint of others, against their will, as when someone who is acting violently is handcuffed and pinned to the floor under a boot, or someone is knocked out so as to prevent them from rushing into a blazing building, purportedly to rescue others. In each case, despite these paradoxes, acts of violence always have an *intentional* component. Gandhi's well-known distinction between the non-violence (*ahimsā*) of the surgeon wielding a scalpel and the selfish malevolence of the thief and sadist accurately grasps the intentional quality of violence. Violent acts are consciously intended or half-intended acts of

[8] Johan Galtung, 'Violence, peace and peace research', *Journal of Peace Research*, 6 (1969), p. 168; see also his 'Cultural violence', *Journal of Peace Research*, 27, 3 (1990), pp. 291–305.
[9] See Begoña Aretxaga, 'Dirty protest: symbolic overdetermination and gender in Northern Ireland ethnic violence', in Catherine Besteman (ed.), *Violence. A Reader* (Houndsmills and New York 2002), pp. 169–92.

interference with the bodies of others; their limit or borderline cases, as judges know well, are injuries caused to others' bodies by reckless-ness (wilful or otherwise) or institutional settings marked by bureau-cratic violence, in which nobody seems directly responsible for the act of violating the bodies of single individuals or those of whole groups.

So even when it comes dressed in velvet, violence is a relational act in which the victim of violence is regarded, involuntarily, not as a subject whose 'otherness' is recognised and respected, but rather as a mere object potentially worthy of bodily harm, or even annihi-lation. It is worth reiterating that violence is always 'embodied'. It is *palpable*. Violence directly touches the body of its victim, even when (as in the deliberate poisoning or gassing or irradiating or besieging of others) it takes time to make its mark. The embodied quality of violence helps us to understand why the blocking off of a highway by chanting demonstrators who lie down on the pavement is not an act of violence. The 'gentle removal' of their bodies by big-fisted police wielding truncheons, rubber bullets and pepper spray is. Such sayings as 'He laid violent hands on her' or 'He was in a violent temper' remind us that violence is unwanted physical interference with a subject – as when (to take a more clear-cut case) a woman or child or man has their thighs forced apart by a man who molests their bodies by stuffing their genitals with a revoltingly alien organ.

It is worth remembering as well that acts of violence are not always face-to-face, hand-to-hand conflicts. In our times, people kill and are killed by proxy. Violence seems increasingly to be mediated by large-scale institutions, like armies equipped with state-of-the-art surveillance and monitoring and killing equipment. These institu-tions of violence have the effect of blurring the intentions and camou-flaging the culpable negligence and responsibility of the violent. Those who inflict physical pain and suffering upon others do so not because they are thugs and sadists (although they may be this), but because they are trained in the habits and skills of behaving in accordance with the logic and imperatives of the institutional system in which they are operating. Violence tends to become 'anonymous'. Harm earns the status of a profession. But it remains violence, nonetheless. The victims are still physically or mentally assaulted by actors who act: they programme software, press buttons, tap keyboards, fill out forms, make decisions around tables, load weapons, grease engines and fly aircraft, and they do so with at least some awareness that what they are doing may well, however directly or indirectly, have effects that are regarded by others as violent. This trend towards 'institutional violence' certainly includes all the forms of industrialised killing of the past century.[10] It also encompasses the cases analysed by scholars such as Michel Foucault, in which the bodies of subjects are deliberately confined, against their will but in the name of their 'improvement', in houses of discipline and punishment in which, so to say, violence is redeployed from public sites of punishment – 'privatised', sanitised, and camouflaged within the walls of a prison, hospital or asylum, sometimes with a smile.[11]

To emphasise the unwanted character of violence implies that violence is one – extreme – form of the denial of a subject's freedom to act in and upon the world. However that subjectivity and freedom are defined – narrowly 'liberal' or 'property-centred' or 'European' ways of life are not presumed in this discussion – violence obstructs subjects' bodily motion. It *silences* them as well. Violence has been interpreted as a form of communication, and it is true that it always comes wrapped within a matrix of specialised language rules and speech acts.[12] Yet those who are violated always slip beneath the surface of their own speech. They drown in the awful noise of violence.[13] They then suffer their own silence, if only for a fleeting

[10] See Jean Claude Pressac and Robert-Jan Van Pelt, 'The machinery of mass murder at Auschwitz' and Andrzej Strzelecki, 'The plunder of victims and their corpses', in Yisrael Gutman and Michael Berenbaum, *Anatomy of the Auschwitz Death Camp* (Bloomington 1994), pp. 183–245, 246–66; and Omer Bartov, *Murder in Our Midst: The Holocaust, Industrial Killing, and Representation* (New York 1995).

[11] Michel Foucault, *Discipline and Punish* (London 1977).

[12] Birinder Pal Singh, *Violence as Political Discourse* (Shimla 2002), p. 32.

[13] 'Noise. That's the first word that comes into my mind when I think of the last ten years', writes David Grossman of the Israeli–Palestinian conflict in *Death as a Way of Life. Israel Ten Years After Oslo* (New York 2003), p. vii. 'So much noise.

moment, before they scream. Sometimes their muteness is forever. Violence is world-destroying. It cuts the tongue, and the pain that is felt is partly due to this dissection of speech from the body. Kafka's account (in *The Penal Colony*) of the clever machine that kills its victims by forcible redescription accurately grasps this point: just as that device equipped with inkjets inscribes the name of the crime over the victim's body, even as it bleeds to death, so those who are violent rob their victims of their bodily and linguistic integrity. Violence is theft. The world of the violated is narrowed to the space of the inexpressible pain and suffering that is inflicted; the world of the violators is correspondingly enlarged, so that for at least a moment, extracting all power from their victims, they rule absolutely.[14] That vast power discrepancy shows why violence is incompatible with the civil society and political democracy rules of complex liberty, solidarity and equality of citizens. When individual citizens are violated, they experience interference with their bodies, which may consequently suffer damage, physically, linguistically and psychically. Note that violence affects the bodies of *individuals*. While various collective identities of a democracy are damaged or annihilated when its constituent members are violated – violence can destroy the mutual interdependence of the living, the dead, even the unborn – violence only has this effect because ultimately it bears down on and threatens embodied individuals, who are treated as mere objects, as bodies deemed worthy of a kick and a punch, or a knife, a bullet or a bomb.

Those individuals who experience violence against them find in effect that they are treated, as Aristotle put it, as 'a solitary advanced piece in a game of draughts', or (as he says elsewhere) like a wild animal 'meant to be hunted'.[15] Aristotle's formulation of course supposed

Gunshots and shouts, incendiary words and mournful laments, and explosions and demonstrations, and heaps of clichés and special broadcasts from the scenes of terrorist attacks, and calls for revenge and the throb of helicopters above and the screeching sirens of ambulances and the frantic rings of the telephone after each incident.'

[14] Elaine Scarry, *The Body in Pain: The Making and Unmaking of the World* (New York 1985).

[15] Aristotle, *Politics*, bk. 1, ch. 2, 1253a, and bk. 7, ch. 2, 1324b.

the inevitability of violence within both the pre-political realm of the *oikos* and the extra-political 'barbarian' world beyond the *polis*. 'The world would be a curious place', he remarked, 'if it did not include some elements meant to be free, as well as some that are meant to be subject to control; and if that is its nature any attempt to establish control should be confined to the elements meant for control, and not extended to all.'[16] This Aristotelean distinction between the (violence-ridden) realm of necessity and the (pacified) realm of freedom needs to be abandoned.[17] And yet Aristotle's basic insight that violence instrumentalises potentially speaking and interacting subjects remains compelling. Rephrased in language that he would not have properly understood: a democratic order protected and supported by publicly accountable state institutions implies the existence of speaking and peacefully interacting subjects, whereas the (at least temporary) effect of violence is to render them mute objects – even to herd them into death's cave.

The search for definitions may be fraught, but at the very least it shows that the ambiguous term 'violence', like all concepts within the human sciences, is *idealtypisch*, which is to say that it selectively highlights certain aspects of reality, which nowhere exist in the pure form suggested by the concept. So long as it continues to be used, the concept of violence (*Gewalt, himsā, violenza, nasilje, bou ryoku, ūnf*) will for that reason of selectivity – and the complicated ethical issues it raises – forever remain controversial, especially under democratic conditions. Smart and street-wise questions will always be asked: is a bank robber's accomplice who wants the robber to beat him up in order to throw the police off the scent an object of violence? Did the drunk driver who ran into a cyclist commit an act of violence? What about the elderly shopper knocked to the pavement by a careless group

---

[16] Ibid., bk. 7, ch. 2, 1324b; cf. bk. 7, ch. 14, 1333a–4a.
[17] John Keane, *Public Life and Late Capitalism* (Cambridge 1984); 'Structural transformations of the public sphere', in Margaret Scammell and Holli Semetko (eds.), *The Media, Journalism and Democracy* (Aldershot and Burlington, VT 2000), pp. 53–74; and *On Communicative Abundance* (London 1999).

of head-phoned youths horsing around? Or the British soldier who forcibly entered the dwellings of a Muslim, with sniffer dogs on the leash?

Such questions are to be welcomed, and not only in courts of law, essentially because a razor-sharp sense of complexity helps alert democracies to the contingent character of violence in its various forms. Democracies thrive on (and are in turn troubled by) the 'denaturing' of violence, understandably so when it is considered that the 'purest' forms of violence are undoubtedly those that result in involuntary death. Death is potentially the ultimate consequence of an act of violence. Of course, for each individual, death is inescapably a terminus and a reference point on the map of life. It marks out the intersection of the finite and the infinite. Death can serve as the point from which individuals evaluate their lives unencumbered by the pressures of the world. They are able to reflect upon what they have or have not achieved; what they have become; and what might be in store for them. In this sense, death is at the same time birth, for it is precisely in death that life reaches its apogee. There are of course lots of different ways of dying. Lucky are those who can die among friends or relatives, in dignity, photographed or filmed with a look of indefinable authority on their brave faces. Unlucky are those – there have been several hundred millions during the past century alone – who are robbed of an 'individual death' (Rainer Maria Rilke) by an act of violence. Their deaths are forced, and anonymous. It is as if they die twice; their own deaths die a sudden death, stealing from them the possibility of taking stock of their lives, past, present and future. There are lots of different ways in which the violent can kill, but there is only one result: you are dead, you are no more, you are no longer to be found anywhere. For someone, somewhere, you may become a statistic. And, if you are lucky, your photograph and treasured belongings will be held in perpetuity by relatives, friends, colleagues or lovers. But the truth is that those who suffer violent death have been pushed over the edge. Death is their unwanted centre of gravity. It marks the end of their fall. They are no longer on the streets. They are no longer on the food ration lists, not in the water and bread queues, no longer in their beds, kitchens or in the arms of their loved ones. They are just a blood-stained body covered in ants and flies. They are a shallow grave dug in a park or a corpse in a sports stadium, perhaps a twisted heap in the desert, or a motionless hulk on a stone slab – end of story.

Civilisation

Civility [from *civil*] . . . Freedom from barbarity; the state of being civilised . . . Politeness; complaisance; elegance of Behaviour . . . Rule of decency; practice of politeness . . .

Samuel Johnson (1786)

REDISCOVERING CIVIL SOCIETY

Like all terms in our language, violence has a relational quality. It obviously takes on its meanings and assumes significance for us insofar as it is enmeshed within a wider web of other terms and concepts that stand in relationships of similarity and difference. The old contrast between violence and a 'civil' or 'civilised' society is a case in point. Seen against the backdrop of a long century of organised cruelty and the new triangle of violence in which our world is now living, it is little wonder that there has been, in recent years, a remarkable renaissance of interest in the idea of civil society – even expressed hopes for the formation of a global civil society.[1] Orwell did not foresee this innovation, and it is interesting to speculate whether his well-known pessimism about the future might have been tempered by the normative ideal of a civil society, to which his political writings are certainly close. Carefully interpreted, the concept of civil society has a close affinity with the issues of violence and democracy. This is so for at least four assorted reasons: the old-fashioned, still-living connotative links between the word civil ('polite, obliging, not rude', 'not military') and the ideal of non-violence; the global flourishing of the concept of civil society during recent decades within

[1] The following discussion presupposes some familiarity with my *Global Civil Society?* (Cambridge and New York 2003); *Democracy and Civil Society. On the Predicaments of European Socialism, the Prospects for Democracy, and the Problem of Controlling Social and Political Power* (London and New York 1998); *Civil Society and the State. New European Perspectives* (London and New York 1998); and *Civil Society: Old Images, New Visions* (London and Stanford 1998).

democratic movements opposed to government by violence; the fact that in modern times every recorded example of durable democratic institutions and ways of life has rested upon a solid foundation of civil society; and the uncomfortable empirical fact that every known civil society has been plagued by tendencies towards cruelty that openly contradict its democratic potential, especially its normative vision of a social order structured by values like openness, equality, difference and non-violent solidarity.

The tight links between the themes of violence and civil society and democracy are not always spotted. Consider the surprising silence about violence within Ernest Gellner's *Conditions of Liberty: Civil Society and its Rivals* (1994). Gellner presents a good summary case for the fundamental contemporary relevance of the civil society perspective in the social and political sciences. 'Civil Society' (the phrase is capitalised throughout by him), 'is that set of diverse non-governmental institutions which is strong enough to counterbalance the state and, while not preventing the state from fulfilling its role of keeper of the peace and arbitrator between major interests, can nevertheless prevent it from dominating and atomizing the rest of society.'[2] Gellner has an unfortunate tendency to conflate different forms of civil society and to speak of civil society in economistic terms. His thesis that Muslim societies are incapable of developing civil society institutions is deeply flawed, sometimes to the point where the whole book reads like a nineteenth-century Orientalist tract. Yet Gellner's account of civil society makes the clear and powerful point that the contemporary popularity of the term is traceable to the fact that, wherever it appears, civil society, ideal-typically conceived, is a site of complexity, choice and dynamism, and that it is therefore the enemy of all forms of political despotism.

Gellner emphasises that the opposition of civil society to political despotism was especially strong under the crisis-ridden,

---

[2] All quotations are from Ernest Gellner, *Conditions of Liberty. Civil Society and its Rivals* (London 1994).

twentieth-century totalitarian regimes of the Soviet type, or what he calls 'Caesaro-Papism-Mammonism'. The main feature of these regimes was a 'near-total fusion of the political, ideological and economic hierarchies'. Soviet totalitarianism was driven by the avowed aim of creating a new socialist man and woman emancipated from the evils of capitalism: possessive individualism, commodity fetishism, and subservience based upon waged labour. It manifestly failed to achieve any of these aims, Gellner argues, partly because it cultivated only cynical, conformist subjects. *Homo sovieticus* was skilled at double-talk, yet the sad fact is that these 'individualists-without-opportunity' were incapable of effective enterprise, not least because they were imprisoned in a world 'where it was barely possible – or literally not possible at all – to found a philatelic club without political supervision'.

Then came the *annus mirabilis* 1989. The largely non-violent revolutions that erupted in the central-eastern half of Europe in the autumn of that year put paid to this system. Not only did these 'velvet' revolutions represent a practical victory for the forces of the emerging civil society over the totalitarian regimes of the Brezhnevite or Titoist type; they also vindicated the intellectual shift of emphasis towards the category of civil society. But why did the downtrodden and humiliated – some of them in some countries, at least – find themselves attracted to the utopia of civil society? Why did they come bitterly to resent its absence, to feel its lack as 'an aching void'? Gellner couches his answers primarily in terms of a theory of the irreversible transition from agricultural to industrial orders. Living in complex, market-driven industrial orders, we have come to accept civil society as 'second-nature'. So we are the fruit of what we must desire and endorse. Strivings for civil society have become encoded within our historical traditions. Civil society has become part of our make-up. We actually like it, and therefore have no desire to live under any form of state despotism or tradition-bound communitarianism. 'Civil Society . . . seems linked to our historical destiny', he writes. 'A return to stagnant traditional agrarian society is not possible; so, industrialism being our manifest destiny, we are thereby also committed to its social corollaries.'

It may be objected that Gellner is too strongly tempted to talk in such abstractions as 'we' and that he pays too little attention to the uneven spatial and temporal distribution of the civil society traditions in which he claims we are steeped. These weighty objections can be skipped, in order to concentrate upon Gellner's closely related, 'structuralist' argument that a civil society is a necessary condition of liberty. Gellner reiterates the familiar point that civil society is not a stifling segmentary community ridden with cousins and rituals and other forms of ascribed identity. Civil society 'is based on the separation of the polity from economic and social life' and 'the absence of domination of social life by the power-wielders'. It is exactly this 'spatial' independence of civil society, its ability to act at a distance from political rulers, that enables the subjects of civil society to become confident, self-transforming citizens. Not only does the sheer complexity and diversity of patterns of life within civil society militate against essentialist notions of the human condition ('the inhabitant of Civil Society is radically distinct from members of other kinds of society. He is not *man-as-such* [sic]', writes Gellner). Among the additional charms of civil society is that its multiplicity of activities and standards of excellence fosters the illusion of equality of opportunity. Hence, it cultivates, and thrives upon, the struggle for self-improvement. 'Civil Society . . . allows quite a lot of people to believe themselves to be at the top of the ladder, because there are so many independent ladders, and each person can think that the ladder on which he [sic] is well placed is the one that really matters.'

INCIVILITY

Gellner's positive characterisation of civil society as a realm of freedom correctly highlights its basic value as a condition of democracy. Where there is no civil society there cannot be citizens with capacities to choose their identities, entitlements and duties within a publicly accountable, political-legal framework. His characterisation of civil society is nonetheless myopic, indeed symptomatic of a virtually universal habit among its recent friends to idealise its peaceful promotion of citizens' freedom. There is much talk of a 'global associational revolution', of civil society as 'that domain in which people voluntarily associate to express themselves', as the sphere supportive of core values like 'minimising violence, maximising economic well-being, realising social and political justice, and upholding environmental quality'.[3] Various negative tendencies of civil society – ranging from confusions about the limits of party competition and the dissembling role of communications media to chronic unemployment and sexual discrimination within and outside households – are overlooked. There is also a striking omission from Gellner's account – and most other contemporary accounts – of the problem of *incivility*, the extreme case of which can be called an *uncivil society*, a type of social order torn apart by extreme forms of violence.

Further reflection upon this problem is essential, even if the terms 'incivility' and 'uncivil society' are strange-sounding, maladroit, at worst malapropisms, at best anachronisms, or so it seems. English-language dictionaries tell us that the root word 'uncivility' is now virtually obsolete. The sixteenth-century adjective 'uncivil', we are told, refers to behaviour which is 'contrary to civil well-being', or 'barbarous', 'unrefined', 'indecorous', improper', 'unmannerly' and 'impolite'. It was in this sense that country folk spoke of 'bad and uncivill Husbandry' (1632) or Shakespeare instructed (in *Two Gentlemen of Verona* (1591)) one of his characters to command: 'Ruffian: let goe that rude uncivill touch.' During the eighteenth century, this strange-sounding talk of 'uncivility' became the subject of philosophical and literary analysis – during precisely the same period when discourses on 'civil society' (*societas civilis, koinōnia politiké, société*

---

[3] These quotations are drawn from several leading sources of 'civil society purism', as discussed in my *Global Civil Society?*, especially pp. 57ff.

civile, bürgerliche Gesellschaft, Civill Society, società civile) were flourishing, and when the traditional meaning of this old concept as a synonym for peaceful, well-ordered political association experienced a lengthy process of 'disordering' and 'subdivision', such that civil society and the state, traditionally linked by the relational concept of *societas civilis*, came to be seen as *different* entities.

The old philosophic concern with uncivility is evident in the travel writings of the Anglo-Irish author Jonathan Swift, himself a protagonist of the old-fashioned but commonplace eighteenth-century meaning of civil society as a politically well-regulated community devoid of violence. Swift's preoccupation with violence stands in stark contrast to the odd silence about violence in recent accounts of civil society. His concern is powerfully evident in the records of his frequent journeys through the Irish countryside, during which he often observed that the bulk of its inhabitants was 'uncivil' compared with the refined islands of English-speaking civility of his compradore friends and acquaintances living in town and country mansions. Swift's travel reports conjure up the society of unsafe journeys of the medieval period, when setting out meant making a will (as in the departure of Anne Vercos in Paul Louis Claudel's *L'Annonce faite à Marie*), and travelling itself meant crossing the paths of wild animals, vagabonds and bandits.

Swift's presumption that the English oligarchy was a model civil nation is reflected in his descriptions of the summers spent away from his native Dublin, usually in the company of a rural gentry or clergy living in sanctuaries of Anglican refinement and comfort. 'I hate Dublin, and love the Retirement here, and the Civility of my Hosts', he wrote to his friend Thomas Sheridan from the estate of Sir Arthur and Lady Acheson, at Market-hill, County Armagh in the summer of 1728. Swift liked to think of his times as caught up in a momentous struggle between premodern barbarity and modern civility. The struggle unfolded spatially, resembling a hostile geographic division of territory, in which the traveller who moved from the zone of civility across into the realm of incivility had the unusual experience of going back in time by rushing forward through space. 'You will find what a quick change I made in seven days from London', he told Alexander Pope after returning to the comfort of his residence in his native Dublin. He described moving 'through many nations and languages unknown to the civilised world. And I have often reflected in how few hours, with a swift horse or a strong gale, a man may come among a people as unknown to him as the Antipodes.' Contact with the uncivilised in an Ireland where 'Politeness is as much a Stranger as Cleanlyness' was both fascinating and repulsive. Swift's description of the then village of Kilkenny was typical of his view of Ireland as a land largely filled with bestial, dung-throwing Yahoos:

> a bare face of nature, without houses or plantations; filthy cabins, miserable, tattered, half-starved creatures, scarce in human shape; one insolent ignorant oppressive squire to be found in twenty miles riding; a parish church to be found only in a summer-day's journey, in comparison of which, an English farmer's barn is a cathedral; a bog of fifteen miles round; every meadow a slough, and every hill a mixture of rock, heath, and marsh; and every male and female, from the farmer, inclusive to the day-labourer, infallibly a thief, and consequently a beggar, which in this island are terms convertible.[4]

Swift's observations about 'uncivility' echoed the much older principle of 'civility' elaborated in sixteenth-century Italian courts and seventeenth-century Parisian salons. This principle supposed that the everyday interactions of men may, in such matters as commerce

---

[4] The quotations are respectively from letters written by Jonathan Swift to the Reverend Thomas Sheridan (Market-hill, 2 August 1728); to Alexander Pope (Dublin, August 1726); to Miss Esther Vanhomrigh (7 August 1722); and to Dean John Brandreth (30 June 1732), in *The Correspondence of Jonathan Swift*, ed. Harold Williams, 5 vols. (Oxford, 1962–72), vol. III, p. 296; ibid., p. 158; vol. II, p. 433; and vol. IV, p. 34. Joseph McMinnis, *Jonathan's Travels. Swift and Ireland* (Belfast and New York 1994) is a good account of Swift's life from a traveller's viewpoint.

and love, not only be freed from the threat of violence – from incivility – but also become a source of human pleasure. Men are not naturally violent. They can learn to shake hands. Their aggression may be overcome by *artificial* conventions, such as 'refined' speech, 'polite' manners, 'effeminate' styles of dress (wigs with long curls, jewels, ribbons, sinously high-heeled pumps), all of which serve to distance individuals from uncivil habits variously dubbed 'rustic', 'crude', 'rude' or 'unpolished'. During this period, the French verb *civiliser* was used to name this process. *Civiliser* is 'to bring to civility, to make manners mild and civil' under 'good government' and 'good laws'.[5] Mirabeau's *L'Ami des hommes ou Traité de la population* (1756), the first French text to use the new-fangled word *civilisation*, added that those who enjoyed a reputation for civility were considered exemplars of 'confraternity' or *sociabilité*; they were 'polished' men whose hearts had been softened, deflected from the temptations of taking violent revenge against others.

Within this literature, there was by no means general agreement that resistance to incivility was a good thing. The cultivation of civility as an antidote to incivility bred controversy. There were, for example, abundant complaints about the hypocrisy of civility, in particular because of the role it played in masking the conniving egoism and violence of men with a reputation for refined manners. Mahatma Gandhi's famous remark that the idea of British civilisation would be a good one stands towards the end of a long line of complaints of this sort, of which Novalis's complaint about the 'wild civilised barbarism' of Europe, Diderot's comments on the 'insulting politeness' of those on high, and Jean-Jacques Rousseau's sarcastic attack on Hobbes and modern civil societies are among the most famous. 'I open the books on Right and on ethics; I listen to the professors

---

[5] See Edmond Huguet, *Dictionnaire de la langue française du seizième siècle* (Paris 1925), vol. II, p. 302; and also the various entries around 'Zivilisation' in *Deutsches Wörterbuch von Jacob Grimm und Wilhelm Grimm* (Leipzig 1956), vol. XV, pp. 1723–38.

and jurists; and, my mind full of their seductive doctrines, I admire the peace and justice established by the civil order', wrote Rousseau, who in the same breath insisted that polite or 'polished' civility is not a virtue, but rather a form of artifice that serves to adorn villainy. Civility is polite barbarism. 'I bless the wisdom of our political institutions', continued Rousseau, 'and, knowing myself a citizen, cease to lament I am a man. Thoroughly instructed as to my duties and my happiness, I close the book, step out of the lecture room, and look around me.' Just as blood is more visible on white gloves, so civility makes horror appear more terrible. 'I see wretched nations groaning beneath a yoke of iron', concluded Rousseau. 'I see mankind ground down by a handful of oppressors. I see a famished mob, worn down by sufferings and famine, while the rich drink the blood and tears of their victims at their ease. I see on every side the strong armed with the terrible powers of the Law against the weak.'[6]

Not only were there attacks on the double standards of civility. There were attempts – well illustrated by the later Jonathan Swift's questioning of English civility in defence of Irish independence – to turn the tables on the powerful by emphasising that their civility was the ally of cruel arrogance, that it had the unintended effect of producing and reproducing incivility among the powerless, the key implication being that the powerful must somehow change their ways and let the 'uncivilised' find their own path to civility. The vigorous eighteenth-century discussion of cannibalism is revealing of this shift. There were of course those who straightforwardly condemned the practice as a form of 'inhuman, hellish Brutality' (Defoe) that fell far short of the superior European standards of 'civilisation'; and there were other observers (Voltaire's *Candide* [1759] counts as an example) who reacted to talk of cannibalism with coyness and witty *sangfroid*. But striking in retrospect is the way in which the whole subject of

<hr/>

[6] Jean-Jacques Rousseau, 'Fragments of an essay on the state of war' (written *circa* 1752), in *A Lasting Peace through the Federation of Europe and the State of War* (London 1917), pp. 124–5. (The original is reprinted in C. E. Vaughan (ed.), *Political Writings of J. J. Rousseau*, vol. I, pp. 293–307.)

anthropophagy during this period is used by the protagonists of civility to appeal to Europeans to open their eyes, to see with different eyes, to recognise (as Georg Forster famously summarised the point after travelling with Captain Cook around the world) that the cannibalism practised by the Maori peoples was nothing compared with the barbarism of Spanish 'civilisers' who regularly throw Indian babies to the dogs.[7] From that type of sentiment it was only a short step to the biting satirical recommendation of Jonathan Swift's *A Modest Proposal for Preventing the Children of Poor People from Being a Burden to their Parents or the Country* (1729): that the incivility built into the European civilising process presented new opportunities for the powerful, that incivility should be commercially exploited by harvesting the bodies of infants as food for the rich.

Swift's attack on double standards, his tongue-in-cheek call for greater public honesty about barbarism in the heartlands of the 'civilised' world, caused a stir, in part no doubt because it exploited the ongoing fears of violence that lurked within the early modern concern with civility. Incivility was the ghost that haunted civil society. In this respect, *civilisation* was normally valued as a long-term project charged with discharging and sublimating violence; incivility was the permanent – beatable – enemy of civil society. To speak of 'civilisation' during this period is to refer to an incomplete historical process, in which civility, a static term, was both the aim and outcome of the transformation of 'uncivil' into 'civil' behaviour. From this thesis it was merely a short step away from the thought that the civilising process was a march through stages of gradually increasing perfection. During the eighteenth century, the word civilisation connotes both a fundamental process of history and the end result of that

---

[7] The boomerang effects of European civility upon Europe itself are examined in Claude Rawson, 'Savages noble and ignoble: natives, cannibals, third parties, and others in South Pacific narratives by Gulliver, Bougainville, and Diderot, with notes on the *Encyclopédie* and on Voltaire', *Eighteenth-Century Life*, 18 (November 1994), pp. 168–97. Some nineteenth-century developments are examined in Catherine Hall, *Civilising Subjects. Metropole and Colony in the English Imagination, 1830–1867* (Cambridge 2002).

process, in which the distinction between the advances of present-day civilisation and the actual or hypothetical primitive primordial state (called variously 'nature', 'barbarism, 'rudeness' or 'savagery') becomes ever clearer. The privileged classes of Europe represent themselves as treading a path stretching from primitive barbarism through the present half-civilised condition of humanity towards perfection through education and refinement.

The journey towards civilisation was seen to be a slow but steady elimination of violence from human affairs, as Adam Ferguson, influenced by lectures delivered by Adam Smith in 1752, emphasised when first using the word civilisation in English. Ferguson describes the process of civilisation as progress from rudeness to refinement, in which the contemporary 'civil society' is understood as a 'polished' and 'refined' form of society with 'regular government and political subordination'. Ferguson emphasised that 'the epithets of *civilised* or of *polished*' properly refer to 'modern nations' marked by the discretionary use of violence, and that these nations stand in contrast to 'barbarous or rude' peoples. In barbarous nations, Ferguson insisted, 'quarrelling had no rules but the immediate dictates of passion, which ended in words of reproach, in violence, and blows'. Tides of violence flooded the field of government as well. 'When they took arms in the divisions of faction, the prevailing party supported itself by expelling their opponents, by proscriptions, and bloodshed. The usurper endeavoured to maintain his station by the most violent and prompt executions. He was opposed, in his turn, by conspiracies and assassinations, in which the most respectable citizens were ready to use the dagger.' Barbarous nations were equally rude in the conduct of war. 'Cities were razed, or inslaved; the captive sold, mutilated, or condemned to die.' By contrast, Ferguson noted, civilised or polished nations had 'gone some way in extruding crudely violent scenes' from the stage of contemporary life. 'We have improved on the laws of war, and on the lenitives which have been devised to soften its rigours', he wrote. 'We have mingled politeness with the use of the sword; we

have learned to make war under the stipulations of treaties and cartels, and trust to the faith of an enemy whose ruin we meditate.'
Civilised societies are guided by the principle of 'employing of force,
only for the obtaining of justice, and for the preservation of national
rights'.[8]

---

[8] Adam Ferguson, *An Essay on the History of Civil Society* (Edinburgh 1767), especially
pt. I, sect. 4 ('Of the principles of war and dissension'), pp. 29–37, pt. 2 ('Of the history
of rude nations'), pp. 112–64; and pt. 3, sect. 6 ('Of civil liberty'), pp. 236–56.

Barbarism?

> It is neither easy nor agreeable to dredge this abyss of viciousness, and
> yet . . . it must be done, because what could be perpetrated yesterday
> could be attempted again tomorrow, could overwhelm us and our
> children. One is tempted to turn away with a grimace and close one's
> mind: this is a temptation one must resist.
>
> Primo Levi (1988)

STATE VIOLENCE

Among the weaknesses of Ferguson's type of eighteenth-century interpretation of the problem of violence and civil society is its more or
less secret commitment to an evolutionary or teleological understanding of history as a process of transformation from 'rude' societies to
'civilised' societies. Although Ferguson worried about the possible
relapse into barbarism,[1] his overall approach presumed that modern
times are superior to earlier eras of rudeness, exactly because – the
point is important for contemporary democracies – violence is potentially removable from significant areas of social and political life. The
presumed evolutionary spiral is explicit in the works of Scottish colleagues of Ferguson – such as James Dunbar's *Essays on the History
of Mankind in Rude and Cultivated Ages* (1780) and John Logan's
Elements of the Philosophy of History (1781) – who both treat of violence as the antithesis of civil society and assume, optimistically, that
violence is on the wane in modern civil societies.

In its time, this presumptuous optimism helped to kill off old
perceptions about the eternal cycles of violence in human affairs.[2] Its

---

[1] Adam Ferguson, *An Essay on the History of Civil Society* (Edinburgh 1767), pt. 6,
sects. 3–4 ('Of the corruption incident to polished nations'), pp. 382–401.

[2] An example is the poem by Ihean de Mehune cited in George Puttenham, *The
Arte of English Poesie* (London 1589), pp. 173–4: 'Peace makes plenty, plenty makes
pride,/ Pride breeds quarrel, and quarrel brings warre:/ Warre brings spoile, and spoile
povertie,/ Povertie pacience, and pacience peace:/ So peace brings warre and warre
brings peace.'

optimism today remains of interest and consequence, since precisely the same premise is invisibly at work in latter-day 'purist' accounts of civil society, Gellner's included.[3] The premise is arguably rendered both questionable and undesirable, not only by the terrible crimes of state violence committed during the past century, but also by the dangerous triangle of violence of our times. Evolutionary optimism is invalidated by three other basic trends: the chronic persistence of violence within all extant civil societies; the (not unrelated) permanent possibility that civil societies can and do *regress* into *uncivil* societies; and the related, but opposite trend, for the first time on any scale, of a new *civility politics* that aims to publicise and eradicate such disparate phenomena as murder and rape, genocide and nuclear war, the violence of discipinary institutions, cruelty to animals, child abuse and capital punishment. For the purpose of refining present-day understandings of civil society and probing more deeply into the subject of violence and democracy, let us examine these complicating trends and counter-trends in more detail.

Within the human sciences of the past generation, Norbert Elias did more than anybody to stimulate awareness of the dialectics – the strengths and weaknesses – of modern civil societies. His account of the so-called 'civilising process' remains of vital importance to any effort to think in fresh ways about democracy and violence. Comparable in aim and scope to the older work of Rondelet, Tocqueville and others, his key work, *Über den Prozess der Zivilisation* (1939),[4] traces the transformation in western Europe of the warlike, knightly order of late medieval society into a state-building court society whose threshold of shame and embarrassment about violence was qualitatively higher. From the sixteenth century onwards, particularly in the ruling circles of the *courteoisie*, Elias shows, social standards of conduct

---

[3] John Keane, *Global Civil Society?* (Cambridge and New York 2003).

[4] See C. Haroche, 'La civilité et la politesse – des objets négligés de la sociologie politique', *Cahiers internationaux de sociologie*, 94 (1993), pp. 97–120. The key work of Norbert Elias referred to here is *Über den Prozess der Zivilisation. Soziogenetische und psychogenetische Untersuchungen*, 2 vols. (Basel 1939).

and sentiment began to change drastically. Codes of conduct became stricter, more differentiated and all-embracing, but also more temperate. Within this 'habitus' of the *courteoisie*, spontaneous behaviour was repressed. Excesses of self-castigation and self-indulgence were banished. Restraint was internalised. Social life underwent pacification. Men who had once eaten from the same dish, or drunk from the same cup, or spat or relieved themselves in each other's presence came to be separated by a new wall of restraint and embarrassment at the bodily functions of others. They learned to shake hands and to keep calm under duress. Physical impulses (such as farting, defaecating, urinating, nudity itself) were checked by self-imposed prohibitions that followed new rules of privacy. Prudery came to surround wedding ceremonies, prostitution and discussions of sexual matters. Language became more delicate. Even death, particularly violent death, became an embarrassment to the living. To express pleasure in violence, torturing and mutilating one's opponents in battle, for instance, came to be regarded as rudeness. So too did the harbouring of grudges and the angry desire for revenge. Elias shows that this transformation was closely related to the construction of territorial states – particularly to the application of stricter controls of the warrior classes and the 'courtisation' of the nobles. Later, highly unevenly, the civilised manners of the *courteoisie* percolated 'downwards' into the ranks of the urban bourgeoisie and (though heavily contested) the peasant and working classes. The whole process found its expression in a new term launched by Erasmus of Rotterdam – the term 'civility' – which later gave rise to the verb 'to civilise'. Soon there was a family of terms – civil, civilised, civility, civilisation, civism – that were used in many other countries as symbols of the new struggle to refine and polish manners.

Subsequent historical research suggests that Elias's general thesis is quite plausible, that this period in western Europe indeed saw a considerable reduction of violence both within the ranks of the dominant classes and within everyday social relations more generally.[5] Elias handles the implications of this finding with some subtlety. It is true that his work contains traces of the eighteenth-century progressivist view of civility. Symptomatic is his general neglect of the ways in which the civilising process redeployed, sanitised and camouflaged disciplinary and other violence without necessarily diminishing it.[6] The nineteenth-century reduction of capital offences and the abolition of public hangings in 1868 in England, for example, can hardly be attributed to the growing practical triumph of liberal civility.[7] There were many who found themselves ashamed of public displays of violence, certainly. But prosecutions and capital convictions had risen so dramatically in the early nineteenth century that by the 1830s more than 90 per cent of death sentences were not carried out lest the English landscape be clogged with gibbets, and not primarily because of mounting sympathy among 'the civilised' classes for the condemned. Similarly, the privatisation of hangings, their removal from the public eye, beginning with the abolition in England of the Tyburn procession in 1783 to the dismantling of scaffolds inside prison walls in 1868, had little to do with a principled commitment to civility. The transfer of executions indoors, the hiding away of violence from public eyes, was often seen by its advocates as a means of dampening public attacks on the whole dirty business of capital punishment. One consequence was that hanging arguably became more cruel, since the abolition of public displays of violence meant that felons were from here on denied the active sympathy formerly extended to them by onlookers. Those whose hourglasses had been turned for the last time were now left to face death alone, in the hope – pious evangelicals calculated – that their sinful souls would repent.

---

[5] Examples include Julius R. Ruff, *Violence in Early Modern Europe 1500–1800* (Cambridge and New York 2001); and Eric A. Johnson and Eric H. Monkkonen (eds.), *The Civilisation of Crime: Violence in Town and Country since the Middle Ages* (Urbana 1996).

[6] Michel Foucault, *Discipline and Punish. The Birth of the Prison* (London 1977).

[7] V. A. C. Gatrell, *The Hanging Tree. Execution and the English People, 1770–1868* (Oxford 1994).

Despite such oversights, Elias consistently points out that the western European civilising process was and remains historically contingent. It is a fragile historical episode linking the medieval and contemporary modern European worlds. His reasoning is again quite even-handed. Elias always considered that the modern civilising process has brought definite gains. By creating violence-free islands of social life, men and women have in effect learned to shake hands. Yet – the point is not fully elaborated[8] – he also notes that there were other paths to other forms of 'civility' elsewhere on the earth, which explains why Elias criticizes the tendency to use terms like 'civilisation' and 'civil society' normatively, as if they were synonymous with the triumphs and achievements of modern Europe or 'the West' in the wider world. He comments:

> In 1798, as Napoleon sets off for Egypt, he shouts to his troops: 'Soldiers, you are undertaking a conquest with incalculable consequences for civilisation.' Unlike the situation when the concept was formed, nations from here on consider the process of civilisation as completed within their own societies; they see themselves as bearers of an existing or finished civilisation to others, as standard-bearers of civilisation in foreign lands. Of the whole preceding process of civilisation nothing remains in their consciousness except a vague residue. Its impact is understood simply as an expression of their own higher gifts; the fact that, and the question of how, during the course of many centuries, their own civilised behaviour has been formed is of no interest.[9]

Elias convincingly warns that amnesia about the socio-genesis of specifically European standards of civility can have (as it did in

---

[8] Hartmut Kaelble, *Europäer über Europa: die Entstehung des europäischen Selbstverständnisses im 19. und 20. Jahrhundert* (Frankfurt am Main and New York 2001).
[9] Elias, *Über den prozess der Zivilisation*, vol. I, p. 63; and 'Zivilisation', in B. Schäfers (ed.), *Grundbegriffe der Soziologie*, 3rd edn (Opladen 1992), pp. 382–7. On the more general problem of the transferability of his theory of the civilising process see Stephen Mennell, *Norbert Elias: An Introduction* (Oxford 1992), pp. 232–3.

Napoleon's case) pompous and violent consequences. Civilisation is not only taken for granted. It becomes synonymous with a superiority complex that potentially regards others as inferiors, as indeed happened within the tiny courtly-aristocratic upper class of Europeans who tried to lord over the rest of the world and considered themselves as bearers of true 'civilisation'. They were a social enclave intensely proud of their achievements – Elias argues – despite clear evidence that the originally European mode of civilisation suffered from self-paralysis.

His emphasis upon the *self-destructive* qualities of the European civilising process is particularly important food for fresh thought about violence and democracy. According to Elias, modern civil societies are chronically threatened by an *exogenous* source of incivility. His reasoning can be summarised briefly: the modern civilising process, he points out, is directly related to the formation and growth of political classes – the French monarchy, the framers of the American constitution, the twentieth-century champions of decolonisation – that in their own way and using various means sought to disarm competitor power groups, and to monopolise the means of violence over a given territory and its inhabitants. The creation of the modern state – an impersonal, abstract entity that stands above and is distinct from both the government of the day and the governed – was both a precondition and effect of the civilising process. State-builders developed standing professional armies to deal with armed banditry, homicide and assaults, rape and riot. They codified criminal laws: the German Lands' *Constitutio Criminalis Carolina* (1532), France's Criminal Ordinance of Villers-Cotterêts (1539), and Philip II's Criminal Ordinance for the Spanish Netherlands (1570) are examples. State-builders also sought to regulate their subjects' lives through a multitude of rules and ordinances governing such matters as dress and sporting codes, gender relations, the incarceration of violent household members, tavern closure hours, duelling, smuggling and other forms of organised crime. In each case, the job of the sovereign and indivisible state apparatus was to put an end to social violence. Nasty, dirty, uncivil habits were to be outlawed. The state was to wield a monopoly of armed force over a population that would then enjoy freedom from everyday violence precisely because it comes to regard the state's monopoly of violence as legal – as a legitimate monopoly of violence.

Elias is aware that such concentrations of violence were heavily contested through various forms of 'collective bargaining by riot'.[10] And while he is aware that in democratic countries violence is normally controlled and managed by elected governments, backed up by the military and police as their administrative organs, he is convinced that, like so many other human inventions, well-armed territorial state institutions have had highly equivocal effects. According to Elias, whose position on this point is close to the 'realist' school of international relations, state-building resembles the invention of fire. Just as the taming of fire favoured 'civilised' progress in the cooking of food as well as the barbarian burning down of huts and houses, so the political invention of armed territorial states is an utterly ambiguous innovation. States are positively dangerous instruments of pacification. They ensure (as Orwell said in 'Rudyard Kipling') that 'men can only be highly civilized while other men, inevitably less civilized, are there to guard them'.[11] On the one hand, within their given territories, states are peace-enforcing and peace-keeping agencies. The peace enjoyed by political subjects assumes the form of state-controlled and legalised violence, which releases individuals and groups from the hellish reality (in Hobbes's famous words) of 'continuall feare, and danger of violent death'. The exercise of violence consequently becomes, at least in principle, predictable and – Hobbes disapproved of this – democratically controllable. On the other hand – here is the rub – the modern process of state-secured pacification is not extended to the relationships among states. Despite inter-state negotiations,

---

[10] E. P. Thompson, 'The moral economy of the English crowd in the eighteenth century', *Past and Present*, 50 (1971), pp. 77–136.

[11] George Orwell, 'Rudyard Kipling', *Collected Essays and Journalism: 1940–1943* (London 1981), p. 581.

diplomacy and peace agreements, all states continue to be caught up in a *bellum omnium contra omnes*. According to Elias, the modern state is too civil by half. 'As in every system of balances with mounting competition and without a central monopoly, the powerful states forming the primary axes of tensions within the system force each other in an incessant spiral to extend and strengthen their power position.'[12] The implication is that war, whose essence is violence, sparing the use of which under battle conditions is imbecility, constantly threatens particular states' monopoly of the means of violence (in that they can be defeated militarily by their enemies abroad or by civilian unrest at home). War in turn threatens the non-violent, civil conditions enjoyed by the subjects of states. Elias's point is that when the power to deploy the means of violence is placed in the hands of a few, and for the benefit of certain small groups, it can be used to make war on other states and their populations. War and rumours of war are omnipresent conditions of the civilising process.

Monopolists of the means of violence can turn life-threatening weapons against their own subject populations. Rousseau's remark that 'the whole life of kings, or of those on whom they shuffle off their duties, is devoted solely to two objects: to extend their rule beyond their frontiers and to make it more absolute within them'[13] applies to the whole of the modern period of territorial state-building. While early empires and tributary regimes normally attempted to ensure the obedience of their subjects and to extract from them as much surplus as possible, they frequently lacked the resources for permanently pulverising the societies they attempted to control. They consequently resorted often to the paradoxical strategy of allowing local communities and whole regions to administer themselves, in return for which the political authorities obliged them to supply produce or *corvée* labour, on pain of punishment. The modern territorial state, by

[12] Elias, *Uber den Prozess der Zivilisation*, vol. II, p. 435.
[13] Jean-Jacques Rousseau, 'A lasting peace through the Federation of Europe (1756)', in *A Lasting Peace through the Federation of Europe and the State of War* (London 1917), p. 95.

contrast, functions as a *permanent* and potentially *total* instrument of exploitation with concentrated armed force at its centre. It operates in this way because at an earlier point in its history it managed to disarm autonomous feudal lords, communal militias, mercenaries, pirates and duelling aristocrats. The modern state is therefore potentially more terrible in its effects than pre-modern political systems. Its monopoly of the means of violence, as Hobbes remarked, places its subjects permanently under a cloud of terrible violence.

The historical record shows that Elias is right to observe that state violence can and does destroy civility, leaving in its wake social relations riddled with incivility: cruelty, insecurity, aggravated conflict, old scores to be settled tomorrow, or the day after.[14] The period after 1500 saw a dramatic growth in the size of armies. There were, not surprisingly, many recorded cases of expansionist centralised states undercutting the ability of actors to organise themselves into non-violent, intermediary associations. From the time of the first assaults by *guastatori* ('devastators') upon the crops, vines and olive groves of communities during the Italian Renaissance through to the random attacks upon peasants by marauding soldiers during the Thirty Years War and the attempted annihilation of religious groupings like the Huguenots by the French monarchy in the sixteenth and seventeenth centuries, state-builders often gutted their societies and robbed their populations of the capacity for peaceful self-organisation. The whole bloody business is famously summarised in Jacques Callot's *Miseries and Misfortunes of War* (1633): a series of eighteen engravings that illustrate the brutalities of battle, the looting and atrocities by soldiers, the banditry and brigandage of the free booters who followed in the footsteps of armies, and the cruel punishments meted out to offenders.

Elias himself illustrates this state production of barbarism in a chilling account of the Freikorps' revenges in the Baltic area after the

---

[14] Charles Tilly, 'War making and state making as organized crime', in Catherine Besteman, *Violence. A Reader* (Houndsmills and New York 2002), pp. 35–60.

1919 Treaty of Versailles. Pressured by the peace treaty, the Berlin government ordered the withdrawal of German troops out of the Baltic region. Many resentful Freikorps refused. They stayed and carried on fighting, not against the Red Army, which had already retreated, but against reorganised Estonian and Latvian troops backed by British warships. The barbarism that ensued is illustrated by Elias by means of a citation from the diary of a Freikorps officer:

> We fired into surprised crowds, and raged and shot and struck and hunted. We drove the Latvians across the fields like rabbits and set fire to every house and blasted every bridge to dust and cut every telegraph pole. We threw the corpses into the wells and threw in hand grenades. We killed whoever we captured, we burned whatever would burn. We saw red, we no longer had any human feelings in our hearts. Wherever we had camped, the ground groaned under our destruction. Where we had stormed, where formerly houses had stood, there now lay rubble, ashes, and glimmering beams, like abscesses in the bare fields. A huge trail of smoke marked our paths. We had ignited a huge pile of wood, which burned more than dead matter. On it burned our hopes, our desires, the bourgeois tablets, the laws and values of the civilised world, everything that we had dragged along with us as moth-eaten rubbish, the values and faith in the things and ideas of the time that had abandoned us. We pulled back, boasting, exhilarated, loaded with booty.[15]

Such details of the slide into barbarism are frightening. They were the prelude to something that had never happened before – the chillingly more efficient, well-organised extermination of millions in the name of 'race hygiene'. They anticipated thousands of recorded twentieth-century instances where the wielders of state violence

---

[15] Norbert Elias, 'Violence and civilisation. The state monopoly of physical violence and its infringement', in John Keane (ed.), *Civil Society and the State. New European Perspectives* (London and New York 1988), pp. 196–7 (my translation).

devoured not only democracy, but all remnants of civility, along with their subjects. What began as illegal punitive expeditions into a civil society perceived as diseased and in need of amputation ended up (in the case of totalitarianism) as 'medicalised killing': mass murder in the form of state-organised sterilisation and euthanasia programmes and the use of ovens and gas chambers, lethal injections and concentration camps, all for the purpose of ridding the polity of so-called 'human ballast' (Ballastexistenzen).[16] Future moralists, political historians and philosophers will no doubt debate whether organised state murder was worse than random terrorist killings on a global scale. Whatever they decide, hopefully they will not let posterity forget the most bizarre cases of extreme violence by (would-be) officials of the modern state: the systematic rape of women by soldiers, often with terrified local men forced at gunpoint to look on; the ritual mutilation of victims, such as cutting off their noses, breasts, ears or penises; and the practice of forcing members of a family group at knife- or gunpoint to kill each other (slowly) in turn, or even to force parents to maim or kill or hack their children to pieces, and to cook and eat the prepared dish prior to their own execution.[17]

These cases of violence are profoundly antithetical to civil society and democracy. They are grotesque reversals of Claude Lévi-Strauss's dictum that 'primitive' cultures are anthropophagic (they 'devour' their adversaries) while modern civilisations are anthropoemic (they segregate, evict, marginalise or 'vomit' their adversaries). Yet – this is their most disturbing feature – these cases do not represent a lapse into 'traditionalism' or 'tribalism'. It is a big mistake to suppose that such grotesque violence is somehow 'beneath' and 'below' otherwise modern and civilised and democratic standards. The fact is

[16] Robert Jay Lifton, 'Medicalised killing in Auschwitz', Psychoanalytic Reflections on the Holocaust: Selected Essays, ed. S. A. Luel and P. Marcus (New York 1984), especially pp. 14–19.
[17] All of these practices are documented in K. B. Wilson, 'Cults of violence and counter violence in Mozambique', Journal of Southern African Studies, 18, 3 (September 1992), pp. 527–82.

that they are quintessentially modern, and not only because of their implication in the struggle for territorially bound state power. They are illustrations of the thoroughly modern, rational-calculating use of violence as a technique of terrorising and demoralising whole populations, of preventing them from engaging in organised or thought-out resistance. An extreme version of this cunning use of exemplary violence to cow and control the state's subjects is symbolised by the Central African Republic regime operated by Jean-Bedel Bokassa, himself renowned for doing by day what civilised human beings fear by night: ordering on one occasion the murder of fellow ministers, politicians, officials and army officers; personally murdering several dozen children who were disappeared after protesting against school uniforms; and using the structures of armed state power to practise cannibalistic rites, in the process (according to the rumours) filling his Kologa Palace fridges with human corpses stuffed with rice in preparation for eating.[18]

BARBARISM

It is tempting, in the face of such cruelty, to draw the pessimistic conclusion that democratic institutions and civil societies have about as much chance of long-term survival as a snow-flake in hell. Surely they cannot escape either today's triangle of violence or the violent grip of the armed sovereign state, within whose shadows each newborn child is today expected to do within a few years what is virtually impossible: to acquire a civilised sense of shame and self-control which it took European populations many centuries to develop, and then only imperfectly?

Zygmunt Bauman's sophisticated *Modernity and the Holocaust* (1993) reinforces this pessimistic line of questioning.[19] Previous

[18] See Brian Titley, *Dark Age. The Political Odyssey of Emperor Bokassa* (Quebec City 1997).

[19] Zygmunt Bauman, *Modernity and the Holocaust* (Oxford 1993), especially pp. 12–18, 27–30, 107–11.

accounts of the modern European civilising process, Elias included, are charged with ignoring its perversely self-destructive dynamics. The modern civilising process, typically understood as the slow but steady inculcation of shared norms such as the abhorrence of murder, the disinclination to violent assault, moral responsibility for one's actions in the world and the fear of a guilty conscience, not only results (Bauman agrees with Elias) in dangerous concentrations of violent means in state hands. It is also a process of divesting the patterns of ownership and deployment of violent means from moral calculus. Hence, it carries within it the seeds of calculated cruelty on a mass scale. The civilising process logically leads to the kind of amoral attitude displayed by Dr Servatius in his summary defence of Adolf Eichmann in Jerusalem: figures like Eichmann, Servatius remarked, are decorated for acts if they triumph over their enemies, whereas they go to the gallows in disgrace if they are defeated.

Bauman argues that zones of civility in everyday life are possible only because somewhere in the wings physical violence is stored up, set aside for rainy days – in institutional places and in quantities that effectively place it beyond the control of ordinary citizens. Everyday codes of conduct thus mellow in a cage of powerlessness. Civility is possible only because the subjects of state power are constantly threatened with violence in case they are violent – with violence they themselves cannot match or reasonably expect to repulse. The pacification of everyday life renders most people defenceless; they potentially become the playthings of sinister managers of coercion, whose own barbarism is a form of quest for civilisation. When the Nazis tested gas chambers on disabled Germans, this was not atavism, or an aberration from normality, or a surfacing of innate aggressive drives and instincts. Under modern conditions, the urge to exterminate others functions as a form of civilising violence. It is a way forward, a more modern method of improving the health and purity of the political and social order.

In effect, Bauman's thesis is the mirror image of the late-eighteenth-century view of the civilising process as an upward spiral into civility. Civilisation, far from 'lapsing' into barbarism, progresses by tumbling headlong towards it. Civility and barbarity are not contradictory opposites. They lie side by side on a down-spiralling continuum of violence. When Elias himself describes the murder of the Jews as 'a throwback to the barbarism and savagery of earlier ages', or as 'one of the deepest'[20] modern regressions to barbarism, his words are misleading. According to Bauman, civility and barbarism are negative dialectical twins. There is no dividing line between civilised norms and uncivil abnormality. The quest to 'civilise' others is at the heart of fascist barbarism. And so the word civilisation should be a synonym for the constant potential, under modern conditions, of political power perfecting itself into the bureaucratic planning and execution of genocide. 'Holocaust-style phenomena must be recognized as legitimate outcomes of [the] civilising tendency, and its constant potential.'

Seen from the standpoint of democratic politics, Bauman is surely right to insist that totalitarianism is no mere accident on the superhighway of modern progress. His thesis also helpfully points to one of the most disturbing enigmas that political thinking about democracy and violence must face: that there are indeed times and places when civilised manners can and do peacefully cohabit with mass murder. Twentieth-century totalitarianism was full of examples. Stalin was a doting father to his little daughter 'Setanka'. His close ally, Nikolai Yezhov, the dwarflike alcoholic who managed (and liked to lend a personal hand to) the NKVD's terror during the mid-1930s, also enjoyed a reputation as a tender daddy who spoiled his daughter with presents and games. At the Great Gatsby-style party in late April 1935 in Moscow, hosted by the first American Ambassador to the Soviet Union, William C. Bullitt, the entire Soviet elite, bar Stalin himself, reportedly socialised with smiling faces and cigarettes and drinks in hand, knowing that the guests included both henchmen

---

[20] Norbert Elias, *The Germans: Power Struggles and the Development of Habitus in the Nineteenth and Twentieth Centuries* (Cambridge 1996), pp. 302, 308.

and victims, many of whom were both. Fascism also specialised in these fine arts of melding civility and barbarity. The atmosphere was reportedly friendly and relaxed at Wannsee, where in January 1942 Müller, Heydrich, Eichmann and their Nazi colleagues sipped champagne and smoked cigars after a hard day's work of detailing how to organize the *Endlösung*. In Paris, the French Gestapo liked to throw lavish parties for collaborationists and German officials. The suave gatherings often culminated in drunken visits to basement cells, where prisoners would be tortured before the guests' blood-shot eyes. The hand of civilised barbarism outlived the military defeat of Nazism. Those attending the civilised trials of war criminals at Nuremberg were shocked to find a city whose ruins were literally carpeted with tens of thousands of corpses, whose rotting flesh made local water dangerously undrinkable – exactly because it was water trickling from a morgue created by Allied bombers.

The key point made by Bauman, that civility is prone to barbarism, is salutary. Yet his conclusion that modern civility is merely the ally of barbarity has its costs, one of which is his dogmatic existentialism. The postulates of 'mutual assistance, solidarity, reciprocal respect etc.', qualities to which Bauman pays lip service (since they are antithetical to totalitarianism) and which are normally considered among the organising principles of any functioning civil society, are brushed aside conceptually as mere phantoms. Civil society, a democratic category that Bauman needs in order to get beyond modernity by overcoming its de-civilising potential, is defined out of existence. The consequence, formally speaking, is that Bauman's account assumes a strange resemblance to the Marxian reduction of civil society to bourgeois domination and violence. Not surprisingly, Bauman's conclusions slip into political pessimism. Civil society and democracy become just two old-fashioned – modern – words. All that is left is the vain struggle by individuals against barbarism – a forlorn quest for a vaguely defined authenticity.[21]

---

[21] See my remarks on Bauman's critique of ethics in *Global Civil Society?*, pp. 199–200.

OVERKILL

The proposition that modern civility equals barbarity has another weakness. It obscures the point that the modern civilising process contains several potentially productive – if highly dangerous – contradictions. The most obvious is the frightening development of techniques of total war and universal violence that threaten overkill: the capacity to overwhelm *all* political institutions and to reduce to zero their power of securing their subjects' lives against the ravages of violence. The problem of overkill needs to be built in to democratic thinking and politics, and not just because it is a fishbone in the throat of irresponsible political power. The process of overkill is an *ultimate* problem because it has the potential to eliminate politics by killing many millions of the earth's species, perhaps even to exterminate *homo sapiens* itself.

All weapons of violence tend towards overkill, of course. From the beginning, the weapons invented and used by humans – the rock, spear, javelin, dart, arrow – bestowed a form of power to produce effects out of all proportion to the means employed. That power transformed hominids into humans by enabling them to become the first sizeable creatures on earth to effect change by committing acts of violence at a distance – and so surviving and exploiting even the largest land animals. Humans became what they threw. The arts of manipulating fire and the later means of killing at a distance – the crossbow, the trebuchet, Greek fire – greatly added to the stock of human powers to be violent. The invention of gunpowder, by the Chinese, at the end of the first millennium BCE, proved to be especially important. It facilitated the rise of the so-called gunpowder empires, such as those of the Ottomans, Russians and Mughals.[22] European powers embraced gunpowder as if it were a new love; they wielded its charms and cruelties against various enemies, especially in the New World,

---

[22] An excellent short survey of the history of weaponry is to be found in Alfred W. Crosby, *Throwing Fire: Projectile Technology Through History* (Cambridge and New York 2002).

where (as Montaigne put it) 'the lightning flashes of our cannons, the thundering of our harquebuses'[23] had both propaganda purposes and killing effects.

The harnessing of gunpowder for more destructive ends – for the development of weapons with a potentially global reach – brought human beings into contact, for the first time, with the possibility of *total war*. Mechanised total war is an invention of the late eighteenth century, but it only reached perfection – and the height of self-contradiction – during the long twentieth century of violence that is now behind us. In the era of triangular violence, it is most definitely still with us. Born on the high seas in all-devouring confrontations, in which the aim is skilfully to destroy one's opponents and their equipment completely, total war, according to Admiral Friedrich Ruge, aimed 'at destroying the honour, the identity, the very soul of the enemy'. During the 1930s, Lieutenant-General von Metsch agreed: 'In total war, everything is a front!'[24]

It evidently never occurred to von Metsch to consider whether war, or at least certain types of war, would still be possible in a world flooded with weapons with a universal reach. Here is the question that escaped him: are there weapons which, if used by their respective combatants, would necessarily catapult us, say, from the early nineteenth-century world of Colonel Shrapnel testing his deadly new fragmenting shell on the wildlife of Foulness Island, into a world in which weapons of war potentially render (certain forms of) war obsolete, simply because human beings could no longer survive their devastating effects?

The history of the development of modern weapons systems was from the outset pregnant with this possibility that violence so begets violence that it threatens the utility of violence. Michael Howard's

---

[23] Michel de Montaigne, *The Complete Essays* (London 1987), p. 1030.
[24] Cited in Paul Virilio, *Speed and Politics. An Essay on Dromology* (New York 1986), p. 75. See also Jan Patočka's classic essay, 'Wars of the twentieth century and the twentieth century as war', in *Heretical Essays in the Philosophy of History* (Chicago and La Salle 1996), pp. 119–37.

study of the growth of weapons of violence in Europe pinpoints a number of episodes in which the invention of a new weapon paralysed the ability of the combatants to fight a war effectively.[25] One example: in 1346, in the battle at Crécy, Edward III introduced longbow archers against enemy cavalry. These longbows, which shot five or six arrows in the same period of time that an old-fashioned crossbow took to shoot just one of its darts, devastated opponents; according to reliable estimates, more than 1,500 of them were killed for about 100 English casualties. Thereupon, cavalry commanders everywhere become convinced that their 'men-at-arms' must don heavier plate armour. The net effect of that move (as the French discovered to their cost at Poitiers in 1356 and Agincourt in 1415) was to render cavalrymen on both sides useless when dismounted, and incapable of speedy or clear-sighted manoeuvres when mounted.

The same self-contradictory logic of obsolescence within 'modern' weapons, whose propensity to devastate and to kill grows exponentially, precisely because that is their purpose, first became publicly evident in the early years of the twentieth century. Long before Hitler's rise to power, for instance, the Reichswehr command had formulated a strategy for taking advantage of the latest weapons of war by drawing up detailed plans for the defence of Germany against a possible French invasion.[26] It recommended that in such circumstances Germany and the Germans would have to be treated like a subject African colony. Every bridge, road and telephone line would have to be destroyed; mustard gas bombs would need to be dropped on German citizens to hinder the French advance; and it would be necessary to wage semi-permanent guerrilla operations without regard for the distinction between civilians and armies.

The bizarre logic of total war evident in the German generals' insistence that Germany might have to be destroyed in order to save

---

[25] Michael Howard, *War in European History* (London, Oxford and New York 1976), pp. 11–12.

[26] See W. Deist (ed.), *The German Military in the Age of Total War* (Leamington Spa 1985), p. 123.

it may be said to have reached its apogee – we return to Orwell – with the invention and deployment of nuclear weaponry, the destructive potential of which is symbolised by the dripping flesh, swollen faces and molten and confused bodies left behind on the scorched earth of Hiroshima by the bomber plane Enola Gay, following its swoop over the city one summer's morning early in August 1945. Since that day, the principle of annihilation, which recognizes no 'class principle' (Khrushchev), has bedevilled the whole world. The human species has had to contend not only with its own individual mortality but with the possibility of the collective death of humanity. In the era of triangular violence, the number of nuclear-tipped states continues to grow, and there is no end to talk of the 'benefits' and 'necessary evil' of nuclear weaponry – despite growing evidence (of the kind produced by the British testing of nuclear weapons in Australia[27]) that their development and use has *hideous* ecological and human effects.

Nervous arguments for and against nuclear weapons are sometimes combined in assessments of the post-Cold War world, for instance in the rather confused proposals for 'minimal nuclear pluralism' developed by Singer and Wildavsky.[28] They yearn for a tripolar world in which, ideally, the United States, China and a combined European Nuclear Force (comprising the weaponry of Britain, France and the former Soviet Republics) together exercise strict oligopolistic control over the development and deployment of nuclear arsenals for the ultimate purposes of expanding the democratic zone of peace and creating a safer 'non-nuclear world'. Nuclear weapons are not especially dangerous, and they are for the time being a necessity, they say. The 'natural' condition of nuclear weapons is to be unused. Besides, there are clearly definable defensive benefits accruing to

---

[27] See my 'Maralinga's afterlife', *The Sunday Age*, Melbourne, 11 May 2003, pp. 1–3.
[28] Max Singer and Aaron Wildavsky, *The Real World Order. Zones of Peace/Zones of Turmoil* (Chatham, NJ 1993), pp. 60–76.

nuclear-tipped states, since their potential non-nuclear enemies are forced to think twice about the probable consequences of military engagement. The cost to the big powers of developing effective shields against would-be nuclear competitors is not especially prohibitive, and in any case, they add, the negative consequences of using nuclear weapons in battle have been exaggerated by their critics. 'While fallout would cause many deaths outside the zone of combat if large numbers of weapons were exploded near the ground', they claim, 'the numbers would not be large compared to the number of people otherwise dying of diseases and accidents and would not substantially change people's life expectancy in any country not in the war itself.'

Given these bold considerations, it is surprising that Singer and Wildavsky ultimately remain unconvinced of their own confident claims. Their confusion in fact expresses the nuclear overkill problem they want otherwise to wish away. They admit that even though the maintenance of nuclear forces is expensive, cost considerations and arms-control agreements are proving incapable of preventing states of all description from acquiring the technical capability of building nuclear weapons. Besides, the two basic forms of missile defence systems, the space-based brilliant pebbles method of filling the heavens with orbiting satellites trained to collide with airborne ballistic missiles, or the 'brilliant eyes' method of using ground-based interceptors, have their technical limitations. Such systems also remain vulnerable to the clandestine delivery of weapons of mass destruction ('suitcase bombs') by means of ships, or as airfreight. Moreover – the honest reasoning of Singer and Wildavsky becomes powerful from here on – the more countries that have nuclear weapons, the more probable it is that some nuclear weapons will be used by 'desperate, irresponsible, or crazy' governments, or escape from governmental control and fall into the hands of groups that might either have an accident with them or actually use them. Then there is the ultimate risky fact about the bomb: 'Nuclear weapons have the possibility of getting out of control. Countries can produce thousands of them. They can be made very large. Through unimaginable circumstances, there can be wars in which many thousands of them are used and hundreds of millions of people are killed. Even though this is extremely unlikely, the possibility is inherent in the nature of nuclear weapons.'

DAMOCLES AND DEMOCRACY

Singer and Wildavsky's reasoning clearly illustrates the self-contradiction within the 'realist' logic governing the interaction of heavily armed territorial states hell-bent on constantly 'modernising' their armaments. This self-contradictory capacity for overkill within modern weapons systems strikes down von Clausewitz's dictum that victory in modern warfare goes to the side that can will itself to survive and to persuade its adversary to surrender. That dictum falls foul of the problem of overkill, which in turn – in accordance with the paradox of Damocles[29] – encourages experiments with various counter-strategies that aim to regulate and resist state-produced violence.

The paradox of Damocles teaches political thinkers to ponder the powerlessness that sometimes results from the (threatened) use of violence. According to the well-known story, in the court of Dionysius, the terrible tyrant ruler of Syracuse during the fourth century BCE, there was a sycophantic courtier named Damocles. Even though Dionysius heaped cruelty onto all his subjects, who hated him in return, Damocles praised the ruler's greatness. He agreed with all his opinions, and laughed at everything the despot found funny. Damocles had only one regret; he wished to become a ruler just like the violent Dionysius. The tyrant was no fool, and easily spotting the crude flattery of his simpleton subject, he decided to teach Damocles a lesson by commanding him to dress in royal garments and a gold crown, and to preside as ruler at a magnificent banquet held in his honour. Damocles was overjoyed. But his mood swung suddenly when he

---

[29] John Keane, 'Fear and Democracy', in Kenton Worcester *et al.* (eds.), *Violence and Politics: Globalization's Paradox* (New York and London), pp. 226–43.

discovered, hanging by a single hair immediately above his throne, a huge sharpened sword aimed directly at the centre of his skull. Damocles cried out in horror. He begged to be seated with the rest of the guests, but Dionysius at first refused. Before hurrying off the throne, greatly relieved, his foolish courtier had to be taught a fundamental lesson about violence: since those who rule by the sword potentially die by the sword, those who govern, or have designs on government, are sometimes best advised to seek means other than violence through which to command the allegiance of their subjects.

The story of the flight of Damocles from the hot seat of violence reminds us that the history of modern state-building is more paradoxical and self-contradictory than scholars such as Elias and Bauman have supposed. It provides one clue as to why the development of an international system of empires and territorial states struggling to monopolise the means of violence has everywhere been a history of more or less sustained resistance, organised from above and below, to the potentially destructive effects of the violence inherent in this system. Hobbesian 'realism' should not be allowed to have the last word on the subject of state violence: the mosaic of overlapping and often contradictory tendencies that we loosely call modernity includes imaginative attempts to invent and to deploy new *nonviolent* methods of publicly checking and regulating the institutions of violence. These prophylactics, outlined in the following pages, are examples of what this essay has already called the *democratisation of violence*: they are techniques for ensuring that the institutions of violence – police forces, armies, secret intelligence bodies – neither engage in overkill nor become permanently 'owned' by any particular power group, including the government of the day. This modern struggle to demonstrate that the institutions of violence are *contingent* by turning them into disembodied or 'empty' spaces of power that can be restrained or made to change course or be reshaped by others, citizens included, can be understood as an attempt to resolve the paradox of Damocles. The effort to minimise or eradicate the threats of violence confronting civil society from the outside has deep and multiple historical roots. They cannot be traced here, but worth examining in more detail are *three* types of pacification strategy, each of which is vital to democracy and its future.

PHILADELPHIA

One such pacification strategy is represented by the various constitutional experiments that aim to counter the so-called Westphalian model of inter-state power. According to this model, whole regions and ultimately the globe itself must perforce be divided territorially among sovereign states enjoying a monopoly of the means of violence. Each state is left free to enter into irenic agreements with others, or to make war on those states it declares to be an enemy. For a succession of relatively neglected political analysts, stretching from Pufendorf and Althusius through to Paine, Calhoun, von Seydel and Jean Monnet, this model of inter-state power has never deserved to be hegemonic. Some of them have pointed to constitutional alternatives, including the old Swiss Confederation that survived from the later medieval period until 1789, the United Provinces of the Netherlands that lasted from 1579 to 1795, and the German Bund between the years 1815 and 1866. Each of these regimes, it is worth noting, was guided by the broad aim of developing a type of supra-state government founded upon a *foedus* or treaty among states, whose rulers and ruled would see a distinct advantage: the practical transcendence of a system of sovereign states prone constantly to war and rumours of war.

The Philadelphian model, born of the American colonists' struggle against the British and implemented as the United States of America between the establishment of the Union (1781–89) and the Civil War (1861–65), is an example of this alternative trend. It is important to the subject of democracy and violence, and not only because the United States is now the most powerful democracy on earth. The whole point of the Philadelphia experiment was to constitutionalise the means of violence in such a way that the unaccountable quality of state violence and the bellicose anarchy among states typical of the Westphalian model are overcome.[30] The core structures of the Philadelphian model, described by James Madison as a 'compound republic', combined forms of popular (male) sovereignty exercised as citizens' rights within civil society, including the right to a free press and (twisting Hobbes's maxim that covenants without the sword are nothing) the right to bear arms, codified in the Second Amendment: 'A well-regulated Militia, being necessary to the security of a free State, the right of the people to keep and bear Arms, shall not be infringed.'[31] The principles of the Philadelphian model also included the formal equality of the member states of the union, as well as a balance and division of power within the two-tiered system of state institutions, including its policing procedures and war-making powers (symbolised, for instance, by the subdivision of powers of war-making, military command and foreign affairs between the President and a two-chamber Congress divided along federal lines). To reinforce this architecture of checked-and-balanced armed power, the model also provided for citizens' militia as a means of restraining the central government from waging unpopular foreign wars. In each of these innovations, the Philadelphia model was driven by an overall desire to avoid the emergence of another Europe, the essence of whose systems of government was seen to be political hierarchy, self-destructive power politics and constant wars among states.

Some features of this Philadelphia experiment, especially the will to overcome the old Westphalian model through the

---

[30] See Gerald Stourzh, *Alexander Hamilton and the Idea of Republican Government* (Stanford, CA 1970); Daniel H. Deudney, 'The Philadelphian system: sovereignty, arms control, and balance of power in the American states-union, circa 1787–1861', *International Organization*, 49, 2 (Spring 1995), pp. 191–228; and my account of Thomas Paine's advocacy of federalism in the new American republic in *Tom Paine: A Political Life* (New York and London 1995), ch. 7.

[31] Among the best recent discussions of the origins of the Americans' right to retain violent weapons are Joyce Lee Malcolm, *To Keep and Bear Arms: the Origins of an Anglo-American Right* (Cambridge, MA 1994); Stephen P. Halbrook, *That Every Man Be Armed: The Evolution of a Constitutional Right* (Albuquerque 1984); and, on the republican genealogy of the right to bear arms, Lois G. Schwoerer, *'No Standing Armies!' The Antiarmy Ideology in Seventeenth Century England* (Baltimore 1974).

constitutional apportioning of power over the means of violence, have found their way into such twentieth-century constitutional experiments as the League of Nations the United Nations and the still-unfinished project of the European Union. They have developed in tandem with efforts to criminalise certain forms of state violence.[32] The International Military Tribunals at Nuremberg and Tokyo and, most recently, the tribunals for ex-Yugoslavia, Rwanda and Sierra Leone, are examples of path-breaking efforts to democratise state violence: to define and to prosecute war crimes, crimes against humanity, and genocide. In each case, the firm presumption is against the rule, outlined in Thucydides' *History of the Peloponnesian War*, that the strong are entitled to do whatever they have the power to do, while the weak must accept what they have to accept. These constitutional experiments suppose that armed territorial states and their men of power are capable of becoming cold-blooded monsters.

It is true that these constitutional efforts to apply due process of law have suffered numerous flaws and bitter controversies.[33] They have been accused of being 'kangaroo courts' or 'lynching parties' or even 'show trials' dispensing 'victors' justice' retroactively ('The victor will always be the judge, and the vanquished the accused', complained Göring[34]). They have been accused of the opposite weakness: that they extend the rule of law to defendants who are unworthy of such respect, or the time and money and tedium involved. That is a fair point: they do indeed reject the old view that bastards should be court-martialled and shot next morning, or castrated (the view of both Franklin Roosevelt and Winston Churchill) or flung into concentration camps. The tribunals have as well been ensnared in disputes about how to define unambiguously war crimes (such as rape and genocide) and their appropriate means of punishment. Some observers

---

[32] Further details of the development of a global political/legal system of 'cosmocracy' are found in my *Global Civil Society?*

[33] Gary T. Bass, *Stay the Hand of Vengeance. The Politics of War Crimes Tribunals* (Princeton and Oxford 2000).

[34] G. M. Gilbert, *Nuremberg Diary* (New York 1947), p. 4.

have even complained (understandably) that tribunals cannot address the fact that violent crimes against humanity are worse than that: that they resemble 'a sin against the Spirit'.[35] And, until recently, tribunals have been hampered by the fact that they have operated against the backdrop of the ongoing failure of 'the international community' to establish a permanent international criminal court, where trials that would otherwise be impossible for political reasons elsewhere can in fact be held.

Notwithstanding these various weaknesses and disputes, the tribunals that date from the botched trials of German war criminals and Young Turk perpetrators of Armenian genocide in the early twentieth century are beginning to have effect. They have begun to unpick the key assumption of Westphalian jurisprudence, that international law ought to reflect the will of sovereign territorial states, whose self-centred nature compels them to defend and to respect their international commitments only in so far as their territorial power and 'vital interests' (Henry Kissinger) are honoured. The war crimes tribunals of the past hundred years have directly challenged this precept: they revive and amend and radicalise the old Christian doctrine of 'just war', with its imperatives of discrimination and proportionality, and its converse principle, 'just cause', according to which violence may be used to punish the guilty party in war in the name of a universal duty of solidarity with the Christian or human communities. In assuming responsibility for dispensing punishment where punishment is due, these tribunals recognise the perils of taking an eye for an eye. Out of respect for the victims, and in the name of civility, they reject the old maxim that justice should be done even if the world perishes (*fiat justitia et pereat mundus*). They expound the inverse maxim: that

---

[35] Gérard Prunier, *The Rwanda Crisis: History of a Genocide* (New York 1997), p. 355. See also Martha Minow, *Between Vengeance and Forgiveness: Facing History after Genocide and Mass Violence* (Boston 1998) and the remarks of Hannah Arendt to Karl Jaspers (17 August 1946), in their *Correspondence, 1926–1969* (New York 1992), p. 54: 'It may be essential to hang Göring, but it is totally inadequate. That is, this guilt, in contrast to all criminal guilt, oversteps and shatters any and all legal systems. That is the reason why the Nazis in Nuremberg are so smug.'

justice should be done lest the world should perish (*fiat justitia ne pereat mundus*).[36]

Torture

The twentieth-century rethinking of the Westphalian model has concentrated not only on constitutionalising and reducing the quantity and types of violence within the world of inter-state relations. Driven by the democratic maxim that states are bellicose the more that they exercise power violently over their subjects at home, international constitutional efforts have also concentrated on the domestic 'pacification' of states. The Council of Europe, founded in 1949 with three key objectives – pluralist democracy, commitment to the rule of law and the protection of human rights – is something of a prototype of this strategy, since for the first time anywhere in the world it sought, in the following year, to codify these objectives in the European Convention of Human Rights, and to provide mechanisms for enforcing them effectively.

Observance of these objectives is considered the key condition of a state's membership of the Council of Europe. Unlike most supranational organisations, admission to it is not automatic. Applicant states must first accept both its Statute (which embodies the three objectives) and scrutiny of their laws and practices to establish whether in fact the objectives are being fulfilled. Yet the Council's role in defending individuals' rights, regardless of their formal citizenship status, goes well beyond scrutinising individual states' laws and practices at the time of entry. Membership also entails a continuous obligation to observe these rights, which the Council seeks to ensure by means of specific enforcement procedures, including the prospect of a member state, after the exhaustion of domestic remedies, being taken to the quasi-judicial European Commission and the European Court of Human Rights in Strasburg. Among the unusual features of the enforcement process is that violations of human rights, such

---

[36] See the 1994 Report to the United Nations of the International Criminal Tribunal for the former Yugoslavia in *ICTY Yearbook 1994* (New York 1994), p. 87.

as freedom from torture, are deemed to extend to potential or actual incidents outside a state's territory (as in cases of deportation or extradition of an individual to a country where he or she is at risk of state violence).

The Council's enforcement process additionally tries to address the fact that even when a state is deemed to have violated a basic human right, its policing and justice system may carry on as before, displaying its old bad ways. The Council does so through such mechanisms as the Torture Committee, which has the specific mandate of examining, by means of inspection visits, the treatment of individuals deprived of their rights with a view, where necessary, to protecting them from inhuman or degrading treatment or punishment. The Committee works on the democratic assumption that state violence against its subjects flourishes when hidden from the public eye. Its overall strategy is therefore describable as the de-concealment or democratisation of violence. Although the Committee must give prior notification of a visit to a particular country, that state is obliged to permit its visits unannounced to any place within the state's jurisdiction, including prisons, military barracks, asylum centres, hospitals for the mentally ill and children's homes. The Committee tries to counter the state's propensity to hide its violence through the element of surprise, which is reflected in the limited time-scales (usually two weeks) of its announced but unscheduled visits. It further relies on the tactics of interviewing allegedly violated individuals in private and requesting from local civil society groups additional relevant information. After each visit, the Committee is required to produce a report, whose publication depends either upon the request of the state party – which is becoming the norm – or upon the unilateral decision of the Committee to embarrass that state by making the report publicly available.

CIVILITY POLITICS

Efforts to democratise the means of governmental violence are not exclusively concentrated within the spheres of government. They also arise *from below*, from within the overlapping civil societies that make up the global civil society that is emerging. These non-governmental public initiatives aim to problematise the arbitrary use of violence – and to place stricter limits upon its use by armed governmental institutions.

Whether these initiatives succeed, or to what degree they succeed, is not at issue here. The important point is that since the birth of the anti-slavery movement at the end of the eighteenth century – a movement that fed publicly upon the deep tensions within the prevailing language of 'natural law' that was used to justify slavery[37] – the world has begun to witness the growth, for the first time on any scale, of what might be called a *civility politics*, that is, organized citizens' initiatives that seek to ensure that nobody 'owns' or arbitrarily uses the means of state violence against civil societies at home and/or abroad. Those (like Elias and Bauman) who ignore this new politics of civility are usually attached, sometimes without recognising it, to an image of the modern territorial state first sketched by Hobbes. That image was revived last century in Carl Schmitt's fascist interpretation of the modern state as 'the mortal God', as the first artificial product of the modern technological world, as a humanly invented mechanism of command that leads the struggle, if necessary by means of violence, against all domestic and foreign competitor powers, actual or potential.[38]

This view of the state as a mortal God is becoming unrealistic. Recent citizens' efforts to publicise and to denounce the use of rape as a weapon of war, to call for the abolition of landmines and for squeezes upon the arms trade, to argue the illegality of nuclear weapons in such bodies as the International Court of Justice, even to block the detonation of these weapons by direct action, serve as a reminder that 'peace' is now of concern not only to statesmen,

[37] Robert M. Cover, *Justice Accused. Antislavery and the Judicial Process* (New Haven and London 1975).

[38] Carl Schmitt, *Der Leviathan in der Staatslehre des Thomas Hobbes* (Hamburg 1938).

generals and diplomats, it is also the preoccupation of citizen-civilians as well.

Exemplary of this trend is the growth of peace movements, which have their spiritual and organisational roots in two older currents of the modern pacifist tradition: 'separational' pacifism, whose proponents, though accepting the magistrate's sword as a necessary evil in the world, rejected participation in civil government by their own members; and the 'integrational' pacifism evident in the civil initiatives of groups like the Quakers, who rejected not government but its use of injurious force.[39] The onset of total war, and the advent of nuclear and biochemical weapons during the last century, have arguably hot-housed the growth of peace initiatives, a vocal example of which was the swelling peace movement in Britain during the first half of the 1980s.[40] Judged by its number of activists, supporters and sympathisers, that movement was more popular than its predecessors in the 1950s and 1960s – the early Campaign for Nuclear Disarmament and anti-Vietnam War protests – and it arguably represented, for its time, the largest single social movement of modern European history.

The movement was marked by two striking characteristics; they should be noted, if only because any public effort to counter the triangle of violence will probably have to come to terms with their legacy. First, the peace movement managed to bring the subject of nuclear weapons out from under a shroud of official secrecy and scientific-technical expertise into the field of active public discussion, much of it based at the level of the small group. In opposition to the bellicose nationalism and nuclear weapons policy of the Thatcher government, this peace movement invented autonomous public spheres of debate, action and disobedience. In respect of its anti-statism, it can be seen in retrospect to have constituted an important contribution to the

[39] Peter Brock, *Pacifism in Europe to 1914* (London 1972) and Martin Ceadel, *The Origins of War Prevention. The British Peace Movement and International Relations 1730–1854* (Oxford 1996).

[40] The following is a brief summary of John Keane, 'Civil society and the peace movement in Britain', *Thesis Eleven*, 8 (1984), pp. 5–22.

unending, long-term struggle for renewing and enriching old British traditions: parliamentary democracy, independent public criticism and suspicion of overextended power. The movement was marked, second, by a great diversity of goals and methods. Its remarkable pluralism was expressed in its highly decentralised and diverse patterns of social support; in its thousands of campaign groups, service-oriented organizations and lateral groups drawing upon particular constituencies; and in its reliance upon a bewildering variety of concrete objectives and actions, which ranged from street-petitioning, pressuring local parliamentary representatives, organising nuclear-free zones, to such forms of direct action as 'die-ins', the refusal to handle and transport nuclear waste, silent vigils and the civilian encirclement of nuclear bases.

Given the plurality of its concrete strategies and patterns of social support, this peace movement, like all contemporary social movements, cannot easily be analysed and summarised in general propositions. The movement's preoccupation with the phased deployment of cruise missiles on British and continental European soil was nevertheless a key unifying factor in its civility politics. It was not by chance that nuclear weapons systems became the most visible symbols of what were opposed unconditionally. For within the movement these missiles were widely viewed as the most advanced expression of a strategic doctrine that developed during the 1950s, and that later became conventional wisdom among nuclear strategists, research technicians, industrial producers and political elites: the doctrine of counterforce.

In its various forms, this doctrine asserted that technical precision and the controlled and limited use of force could be introduced into the fighting of nuclear battles. It replaced, or at least supplemented, the view, of the late 1940s and early 1950s, that the threat of mutual assured destruction (MAD) would deter enemies and ensure the reign of universal peace – that safety, as Winston Churchill put it, was to be the child of terror, survival the twin brother of annihilation. By early 1980, when the numbers of activists and sympathisers within the peace movement began rapidly to swell, this old doctrine of MAD had given way to a new and undoubtedly more dangerous official policy – counterforce – whose newly miniaturised and more precise arsenals were packaged in the language of 'Air–Land Battle', 'flexible response', 'surgical strikes' and (in the Soviet version) 'defence through war-fighting'. In the course of four decades, in other words, research and development and strategic deployment of weapons had moved from H-bombs and ABMs, through multiple warheads and MIRVs (multiple independently targeted warheads) to 'first strike' and 'flexible' weapons such as neutron bombs, SS2Os, and cruise and Pershing missile systems.

This development of 'tactical weapons' was seen by most within the movement to have lowered the threshold separating nuclear from conventional arms. The doctrine of counterforce supposed, contrary to von Clausewitz, that war, even nuclear war, could be free of 'friction', and therefore restricted and winnable. It was this so-called 'modernisation' of nuclear weapons policy that the movement sensed to be perilous. The process of 'deterrence' was seen widely to be unstable, leading to preparations for a type of war that would be qualitatively different, and certainly worse, than the old European wars of Napoleon or Frederick II. The claim (defended in the early 1980s by Atlanticists) that the policy of deterrence had 'kept the peace since '45' was therefore rejected as an apology for what E. P. Thompson, the movement's most famous publicist, called exterminist tendencies. Détente was seen as synonymous with the steady increase of more 'advanced' and ever more dangerous and decadent weapons, whose level of sophistication and hyper-complexity rendered them vulnerable to mechanical and 'human' failures. The famous 1958 warning of Bertrand Russell that some unforeseen circumstance might spark off a worldwide catastrophe was widely felt. The movement saw détente as equivalent to an incumbent Prime Minister who vowed publicly to press the button when pushed into a corner. It associated the word détente with a tottering-on-the-brink pattern of pseudo-negotiation and struggle for 'advantage' and 'superiority' between the superpowers, in which (as the failed Geneva INF and START talks indicated) negotiations and arms control agreements were at best momentary pauses within a wider process of arms proliferation and military posturing. Under pressure from détente, many within the movement believed, existence was beginning to degenerate into the state of nature described by Hobbes. There developed a sense that the constant rearmament associated with the 'modernisation' of nuclear (and chemical and biological) weapons was an endless struggle for power that could only ever end in death organised on a mass scale.

This was one key reason why civil society networks in Britain began in this period to rouse themselves. Large sections of the population began to lose trust in the official image of 'deterrence', which they criticised and resisted as a codeword for rearmament, as a new ideology of state power. Détente, the supposed easing of tensions among states and citizens, had the effect of producing a generalised anxiety about the visible increase in the scope and power of the nuclear state and its new and improved weapons – like ground-launched cruise missiles that must be fired from civilian areas, or Trident submarines 2,500 times more destructive than one Hiroshima bomb. Such public anxiety was evident, for instance, in the widespread belief at the time that nuclear war was probable within the next decade. It was also apparent in the panicky outrage produced by the government's 'civil defence' circulars, which emphasised the need for the state to control the sick, starving and dying survivors of a nuclear attack through commissioners with dictatorial powers, armed police, special courts and internment camps. The whole process of anxiety production was summed up in the mixture of laughter and fear catalysed by the 1980 Home Office pamphlet *Protect and Survive* – a pamphlet which brought the subject of nuclear war into the heart of civil society by instructing every household, in 'humane' and surgically precise language, how to survive a nuclear war by taking down its curtains, stocking up on batteries and mechanical clocks, crouching under tables and stairways, and tuning in to the BBC, to be told what to do next.

Through such experiences, various groups and institutions within the civil society caught a glimpse of themselves as passive hostages in a wider struggle among nuclear states. Détente began to have another unintended effect – the perceived destruction of civil society – in that it promised either a permanent smouldering war or total destruction. Détente symbolically dissolved the distinction between the 'experience of the front' (the words of the distinguished Czech philosopher, Jan Patočka) and the safe hinterland normally associated with wars before the twentieth century. Memories of saturation bombing and fire-bombing of whole cities and civilian populations returned. The apocalypse of the front, in which troops struggle to endure a night of absurdity and horrible death in order to secure for others 'back home' a life of peace, became generalised. The frightening image of the front acquired a significance for the *whole* of civil society.

By giving public form and direction to this generalised anxiety, the British peace movement generated deep support within all strata of civil society, as well as within governmental institutions. But the cultivation of repulsion for the menacing possibility of total war was not its only achievement. As its vigorous campaigns for nuclear-free zones demonstrated at the time, the movement heightened the common sense of civil society that its hard-won democratic freedoms were at stake. The half-baked nuclear peace, the 'cold war' of which Orwell had written, the game in which the antagonists mobilise in order to demobilise their opponents, was felt widely to accelerate the militarisation of society and to promote the growth of the dictatorial elements deeply ingrained within the parliamentary state. So the movement helped important parts of civil society to conclude that there had been a violation of the 'contract' between civil society and the state – an old theme in British political culture, according to which individual citizens intuitively grant their loyalty to the state in return for its guarantee of their personal freedom and security. The conclusion that this contract had been violated explains why the reaction of the peace movement and civil society against nuclear weapons was not (as was claimed at the time by Cornelius Castoriadis and others) a 'zoological' defence of mere life, the slave-like expression of the inability to fight (and to die) for freedom. The peace movement was not merely a fearful reaction against the possibility of death by nuclear battle. It was also a *civilising* resistance to intrusive and violent forms of state power that were capable of extinguishing the plurality of independent and peaceful associations that are the stuff of which civil society (ideally) consists.

Why violence?

> The exercise of violence cannot be avoided when conflicting interests are at stake.
>
> Sigmund Freud (1932)

THE ROOTS OF INCIVILITY

The contributions of constitutional initiatives and civilian peace efforts to the vast project of democratising the means of governmental violence are important. In the age of triangulated violence, they warn against defeatism by forcing us to rethink the old objection that democracy always degenerates into violence. One of the first versions of that celebrated dogma appeared in the eighth book of Plato's *Republic*, where democracy is described not as the government of the people but of the poor against the rich. The guiding principle of democracy is said to be liberty, which is quickly transformed into licence due to democrats' lack of public and private restraint. Such licentiousness of the people is reinforced by their indulgence of superfluous needs and immodest desires, their lack of respect for law and their general tendency to question authority, so that the old condescend to the young, parents fear their children, 'the master fears and flatters his scholars and the scholars despise their masters and tutors'. Polybius repeated this later famous line of attack:

> For the people, having grown accustomed to feed at the expense of others and to depend for their livelihood on the property of others, as soon as they find a leader who is enterprising but is excluded from the honours of office by his penury, institute the rule of violence; and now uniting their forces massacre, banish, and plunder, until they degenerate again into perfect savages and find once more a master and monarch.[1]

---

[1] Plato, *The Republic*, 8, sect. 563a, in B. Jowett (ed.), *The Dialogues of Plato* (New York 1897); Polybius, *The General History of Polybius* (London 1756), bk. 6, sect. 9.

This spiteful view of democracy as synonymous with violent struggles for power, repeated in Reinhart Koselleck's influential critique of eighteenth-century intellectuals' loss of concern over the dangers of civil war and their love affair with democratic 'Revolution',[2] is contradicted both by democratic efforts to constitutionalise political power and by the involvement of citizens in anti-violence and peace movements. Civilian peace initiatives in particular may be seen as part of an older social tradition that dates back to the nineteenth-century campaigns against the trafficking of women, slaves and children. This many-sided civility politics specialises in repairing the torn fabric of civil societies. Not only does it target the violence of governmental institutions, it also seeks to name and root out the violence *within* actually existing civil societies. This civility politics today encompasses such diverse themes as campaigns against homicide and the rape and stalking of women; road rage and violence projected onto children; racial abuse and bullying in schools; cruelty to animals; and the more or less concealed violence that infects disciplinary institutions like prisons, asylums and hospitals.

Among the ironic effects of these social campaigns is to heighten the perception of many citizens that civil societies as we know and experience them are in fact riddled with pockets of violence, some of them dangerous – and that they are in urgent need of more and better surveillance and policing, as well as new forms of legal regulation, social policy or outright repression. In practice, this sense that violence is omnipresent is reinforced by many other factors, ranging from the risk and safety requirements of insurance companies to government 'law and order' campaigns and citizens' willingness to use their mobile phones to report violence to the authorities. Their combined long-term effect is to highlight to the members of civil society their own propensities to violence – and to flag the need to do something

[2] Reinhart Koselleck, *Kritik und Krise. Eine Studie zur Pathogenese der bürgerlichen Welt* (Munich 1959).

about them. These forces not only ensure that statistical 'facts' about violence are always and necessarily 'fictitious' (a point well noted by criminologists). These forces also cast doubt upon the claim of Elias and others that 'civilised' societies forget their historical origins, that they take for granted their own civility, as if it were 'natural'.

This last point can be toughened, for all known forms of civil society are plagued by *endogenous* sources of incivility. On empirical grounds alone, it is imperative to reject simple-minded, 'purist' accounts of civil society as havens of sub-tropical calm. True, civil societies as we know them generate *socialising* conflicts. Antagonisms and cooperation tend to form a durable helix, in that through their disagreements civilians learn that social life consists in reciprocal concessions. Civilians rub along together by learning more about each other; they cotton on to the arts of mutual adjustment and of harmonising expectations.[3] Yet despite these socialising trends, incivility is also chronically produced by all known civil societies. Incivility is one of their limits and, hence, a permanent thorn in the side of the goal of creating a fully 'civilised' civil society. 'Gradually violence on the part of the existing powers will diminish and obedience to the laws will increase', predicted Kant when reflecting on the advantages of republican government and civil society: 'There will arise in the body politic perhaps more charity and less strife in legal disputes, more reliability in keeping one's word, and so on, partly due to love of honour, partly out of well-understood self-interest.'[4] The presumed or implied positively teleological relationship between civil societies and violence in this formulation is unwarranted. Civil societies, contrary to Kant, are not necessarily synonymous with the drift

[3] R. J. Rummel, *Understanding Conflict and War* (Beverly Hills and London 1981), vol. V, p. 32.
[4] Immanuel Kant, 'Welchen Ertrag wird der Fortschritt zum besseren dem Menschengeschiecht abwerfen?' (1798), in *Der Streit der Facultäten in drey Abschnitten*, in *Schriften zur Anthropologie, Geschichtsphilosophie, Politik und Pädagogik* (Darmstadt 1975), pt. 2, sect. 2, p. 365.

towards 'perpetual peace'. Highly developed civil societies can and do contain violent tendencies. Sometimes these 'uncivil' propensities accumulate and combine, through feed-back and feed-forward loops, to the point where a civil society can or does commit something like sociocide. It then degenerates into an *uncivil society*, a more or less legally framed ensemble of social institutions that are dominated by 'uncivil' forms of interaction, ranging from everyday rudeness tinged with veiled threats of bodily harm to others, through to 'post-civilised barbarity',[5] ugly forms of systematically organised violence that rip the guts out of all remaining civil society institutions.

This inner contradiction within the workings of civil society – that it tends to produce its own antithesis – has been poorly analysed. It has been obscured by the originally eighteenth-century theory of the upward spiral towards civilisation and, more recently, by the strange silence about violence within purist accounts of civil society. A key question has been ignored: what exactly is the source of this troubling contradiction?

The most common explanation of incivility resorts to ontological considerations. 'We see even in well-governed states, where there are laws and punishments appointed for offenders', wrote Hobbes, 'particular men travel not without their sword by their sides for their defences; neither sleep they without shutting not only their doors against fellow subjects, but also their trunks and coffers for fear of domestics'. Incivility is here treated as a primeval energy:

> the condition of Man . . . is a condition of Warre of every one
> against every one; in which case every one is governed by his own
> Reason; and there is nothing he can make use of, that may not be
> a help unto him, in preserving his life against his enemyes; It

---

[5] Claus Offe, 'Moderne "Barbarei": Der Naturzustand im Kleinformat', in Max Miller and Hans-Georg Soeffner (eds.), *Modernität und Barbarei. Soziologische Zeitdiagnose am Ende des 20. Jahrhunderts* (Frankfurt 1996); and Stephen Mennel, 'Decivilising processes. Theoretical significance and some limits of research', *International Sociology* (1990), pp. 205–23.

followeth that in such a condition, every man has a Right to every thing; even to one anothers body.[6]

Three-and-a-half centuries later, Hobbes's reasoning still enjoys a reputation. Partly this is because we have not yet shaken off the old bourgeois fascination with neo-Hobbesian themes – Peter Gay's compelling study has shown just how strong was this fascination during the past century[7] – and partly because the view of human nature as violent has a certain intuitive appeal, especially when 'the facts' seem to speak for themselves. What else but dastardly human nature is behind such evil acts as government soldiers who chop off their victims' ears or genitals, and force them at gunpoint to chew them, before suffering execution? Surely the willingness of soldiers to force mothers at gunpoint to shoot their own terrified children through the head before an assembled crowd, only then to shoot the killers and the crowd itself, proves that we have an inborn need to be violent? What else explains the perversely sadistic pleasure of the torturer who places a rat inside his victim, so beginning the slow process of death by cruel humiliation? Or the cold-blooded character of men who are prepared to kill thousands of innocent civilians using bolt-cutters and mobile phones to turn civilian aircraft into cruise missiles?

There can be no doubt – as traditions of psychoanalysis have emphasised – that in order to understand such acts of violence it is vital to have an understanding of the character structure or personality formation of the individual perpetrator, who, although he or she often acts in concert with a wider group of perpetrators, is at some point caught in the act of violence alone with the victim, pushed along by inner instincts and thoughts. Armies or gangs alone do not kill, not even when violence is administered by war machines that

---

[6] Thomas Hobbes, 'Preface to the Reader', *Philosophical Rudiments concerning Government and Society* (London 1651) and *Leviathan, or The Matter, Forme, and Power of a Common-Wealth Ecclesiastical and Civill* (London 1651), pt. 1, ch. 14.

[7] Peter Gay, *The Cultivation of Hatred. The Bourgeois Experience, Victoria to Freud* (London 1994).

physically or visually distance the violent from the violated. And yet when seeking to understand why individuals are violent it is clear that a distinction needs to be drawn between two different types of micro-level or 'human nature' explanations. Stretching from St Augustine to Freud, each seeks to trace the causes of violence to human nature itself.

There are first of all those ahistorical 'hard' ontologies that suppose that Man is essentially wicked (as in Machiavelli's claim that all men at all times are 'ungrateful, changeable, simulators and dissimulators, runaways in danger, eager for gain'[8]). Such ontologies have difficulty side-stepping institutionally based explanations that help to account for why and how individuals and, indeed, whole societies, are from time to time pacific, sometimes for extended periods. Then, secondly, there are those 'softer' ontologies that admit that although 'human nature' tends to be perverted, or even naturally bloodthirsty, it can, under certain institutional circumstances, be diverted or harnessed into pacific ways. William James's proposal that the world would become a safer place if its youth were drafted into mining coal, manning ships, building skyscrapers, washing dishes and laundering clothes, is an example of this 'soft' form of ontology. So too is the eighteenth-century (but originally premodern) formulation that civil societies are handcuffed (as Mirabeau put it) to a tragic 'natural cycle from barbarism to decadence by way of civilisation and wealth'.[9]

The trouble with 'human nature' approaches to violence is not only that they tend to paralyse policy innovations by implying, ultimately, that little or nothing can be done to stem the floods of violence that periodically sweep away the protective walls of civility that maintain peace among citizens, but it is also difficult to substantiate them in either theoretical or empirical/interpretative terms. In

[8] Niccolò Machiavelli, *The Prince*, in *Machiavelli. The Chief Works and Others*, trans. Alan Gilbert, 3 vols (Durham, NC 1965), vol. I, p. 62.
[9] William James, 'The moral equivalent of war', in *Memories and Studies* (New York 1912), pp. 262–72, 290; Honoré-Gabriel Riqueti, Comte de Mirabeau, *L'Ami des hommes ou Traité de la population* (Paris 1756), p. 176.

both their 'hard' and 'soft' forms, attempts to explain violence with sole reference to the meanness of 'human nature' are forced to admit of the explanatory importance of socio-institutional factors. Broadly speaking, two different types of explanations are available.[10] One of them (already examined in the discussion of the legacy of the work of Elias and Bauman) points to the *exogenous* factors – the world's system of armed territorial government – that stir up violence and produce the implosion and breakdown of civil societies. The other type of explanation insists that violence on a limited or extended scale derives primarily from the historically specific organising principles of civil society itself. Here another important distinction should be drawn: between *capitalism-centred* explanations and more comprehensive *civil society-centred* explanations of why these societies tend to generate from within themselves various types of threatening violence.

The most influential example of the former is Marx's emphasis on the conflict potential of the wage-labour/capital relationship. The modern bourgeois era, Marx pointed out, is unique because it effects a separation of government from social forms of stratification. It sub-divides the human species for the first time into social classes; divorces individuals' legal status from their socio-economic role within civil society (*bürgerliche Gesellschaft*); and sunders each individual into private egoist and public-spirited citizen. By contrast, feudal society had a directly 'political' character. The main elements of civil life (property, the household, forms of labour) assumed the form of landlordism, estates and corporations. The individual members of feudal society enjoyed no 'private sphere'; their fate was bound up inextricably with the network of interlocking 'public' organisations to which they belonged. The 'throwing off of the political yoke' is a distinguishing mark of modern bourgeois orders, according to Marx. Civil society, the realm of private needs and interests, waged labour

---

[10] Compare the differently formulated account of these types of explanation in Kenneth N. Waltz, *Man, the State and War: A Theoretical Analysis* (New York, 1959).

and private right, is emancipated from political control; it becomes the basis and presupposition of the modern state.

Civil society is represented by Marx – correctly – as a contingent historical phenomenon, and not as a naturally given state of affairs. Modern, state-guaranteed civil societies do not conform to eternal laws of nature, and they certainly do not arise from their members' propensity for 'society'. They are historically determinate entities, characterised by particular forms and relations of production, class divisions and struggles, and protected for a time by 'corresponding' political-legal mechanisms. Not only are bourgeois civil societies products of modern times. Their life expectancy is limited, inasmuch as they give birth to the proletariat, the class with radical chains, the class in civil society that is not of civil society, the potentially universal class that signals the dissolution of all classes, if need be through violence. Although he was not alone in this conviction, Marx was right to pinpoint the wage-labour/capital relationship as a potential point of violent antagonism within modern civil societies. The Marxian theses on civil society are nevertheless riddled with problems,[11] among which are Marx's mistaken assumption that lumpen-proletarian and proletarian mugging and murder would give way to the organised militancy of the working class, and especially his poor grasp of both the violence-producing and shock-absorbing potential of *non-market* institutions within civil society.

In well-established civil societies, there is a comparatively limited scope for the display of strong feelings, of strong antipathies towards people, let alone heated anger, wild hatred or the urge to belt someone over the head. Wherever stress- or humiliation-induced tensions develop, they tend to be absorbed or sublimated into the social structures, and civility prevails, or so Elias argues. 'Most human societies', he writes, 'as far as one can see, develop some counter-measures

---

[11] See my *Democracy and Civil Society. On the Predicaments of European Socialism, the Prospects for Democracy, and the Problem of Controlling Social and Political Power* (London and New York 1988 [1998]), pp. 57–64, 215–28.

against stress-tensions they themselves generate. In the case of societies at a relatively late level of civilisation, that is with relatively stable, even and temperate restraints all round and with strong sublimatory demands, one can usually observe a considerable variety of leisure activities with that function, of which sport is one.'[12] If that is so, then a fundamental question remains unanswered: why is it that the rules of taken-for-granted niceness do not always apply in actually existing civil societies? Why are their members unable to live comfortably on Pleasant Street, in Friendly Town, in the County of Civility, in the Country of Charitable Works? Why do the 'shock-absorbing' institutions of civil societies tend to be overburdened, such that they generate from within their own structures patterns of violence that contradict the freedom, solidarity and civility that otherwise makes them so attractive?

A distinctive feature of civil societies is that they provide various – contestable – answers to these questions, and it is on balance a good thing that they do so. By cultivating the sense that violence has *social* roots, and that it is therefore *contingent* and *removable*, explanatory controversies about violence keep civil societies on their toes. Perhaps that is why boredom has often been cited as the key cause of incivility. According to this interpretation, the bored are well-fed victims of the bland homogeneity produced by civil societies, particularly in the field of consumption. The consumer society – note the unconvincing stereotype – produces two kinds of people, the bores and the bored. The latter may still go through the motions of civility, but stuck in their boredom they begin to feel constricted and to crave variety and release. They are constantly on the lookout for the strange, the exotic, the dangerous. Not surprisingly, they take their revenge by committing acts of 'anomic' violence that are rarely experienced as loss, or as a lapse into nothingness. The hard fact, say the

[12] Norbert Elias, 'Introduction', in Norbert Elias and Eric Dunning, *Quest for Excitement. Sport and Leisure in the Civilising Process* (Oxford and Cambridge, MA 1993), p. 41.

analysts of boredom, is that violence is experienced as pleasure, as fulfilment, as a form of excitement that tickles the fancy of not only the violated – expressed in masochistic pleasure – but also the violent and the witnesses of acts of violence. Individuals who are violent, alone with their victims, sometimes treat their actions as entertainment, as in the case (described by Arthur Miller) of the young misfit 'stuck with his boredom, stuck inside it, stuck to it, until for two or three minutes he "lives"; he goes on a raid around the corner and feels the thrill of risking his skin or his life as he smashes a bottle filled with gasoline on some other kid's head. It is life . . . standing around with nothing coming up is as close to dying as you can get.'[13]

Boredom theories of violence are interesting, but given their symptomatic quality – they ignore the dynamics of both psyches and social institutions – they turn out to be rather more provocative than persuasive. Explanations that trace violence to the openness and pluralism that are characteristic of civil societies get closer to the mark. In effect, the argument is that these societies' nurturing of a plurality of forms of life that are themselves experienced as contingent is at the root of their tendency to violence. Various – potentially conflicting – examples are cited. According to some observers, the well-recognised fact that they enable groups to organise for the pursuit of wealth and power has made their capitalist economies and political institutions not only restlessly dynamic at home, but also prone to expansion on a global scale, one consequence of which has been the widespread exporting of violence to tribes, regions, nations and whole civilisations considered 'rude' or 'savage'. Modern civil societies have indeed provided handsome opportunities for certain power groups tempted by dreams of expansionism. This has ensured in turn

---

[13] Arthur Miller, *The Misfits* (London 1961), p. 51; cf. his 'The bored and the Violent', in Shalom Endleman (ed.), *Violence in the Streets* (London 1969), pp. 270–9. A different version of the boredom theory is suggested in Hannah Arendt's *The Origins of Totalitarianism* (Cleveland 1958), p. 82, where late nineteenth-century Parisian high society developed a fascination with 'underworlds', the bizarre, the dangerous.

that the whole modern history of colonisation and bullying of the 'uncivilised' has been riddled with violence, to the point where it may be said, with a touch of bitter irony, that the current world-wide appeal of civil society is the bastard child of the violence of metropolitan civility.

The legal or informal freedom to associate in complex ways afforded the members of any civil society evidently also makes them prone – despite generous reserves of civility – to violence at home. It is not simply that civil societies provide convenient hideouts and stalking grounds for psychopaths, who take advantage of civility in order better to maim it. Nor is it just because of the increasing availability and cheapness of weapons of violence within actually existing civil societies. These societies no doubt facilitate the free flow of cheap arms – German-made Brocock ME38 air pistols, Uzi submachineguns from Israel, US Mac 10 machine pistols – although the degree to which they do so remains uncertain, which is why half-hysterical media claims about 'gun crime' and the need for 'gun control' should be tempered with sober reflection on both the multiple roots and forms of violence, together with the ways in which the resort to arms are symptomatic of the deeper tendency of civil societies to disorientate and discriminate against their members.

Civil societies, ideal-typically conceived, are complex and dynamic webs of social institutions in which the opacity of the social ensemble – citizens' inability to conceive of and to grasp the horizons of social life – combined with the chronic uncertainty of key aspects of life (employment and investment patterns, who will govern after the next elections, the contingent identity of one's self and one's household) makes their members prone to stress, anxiety, humiliation and revenge. All modern civil societies are more or less caught in the grip of what Heinrich von Kleist called the 'fragile constitution of the world' (*die gebrechliche Einrichtung der Welt*). Such fragility increases the probability that the customary moral sanctions and restraints upon the resort to violence can be rejected or avoided by some of their members. Especially when combined with social discrimination, say in the form of racial prejudice and joblessness, this amoral anxiety and frustration – the perception of being 'diss'd' – adds to the ranks of the losers.

Losing against others is a chronic problem within civil societies. They no doubt encourage their members to perform successfully – and to believe in the chances of successful performance. Choices that are never hard to make, excellent health, an undamageable body, illimitable energies, unshakeable self-confidence, fabulous unbroken luck, fully realisable ambitions, inexhaustible sexual vitality and continuous erotic gratification – which members of actually existing civil societies in their right minds would ever pass up acceptance of these gifts if they were offered them, with no strings attached? The question is of course self-answering, but the reply veils a troubling difficulty. It is the *impossibility* of every mortal member of a civil society getting their way and realising their dreams that can and does breed loathing, or something much worse. Hannah Arendt has pointed out that if we examine the historical cases in which the *engagés* were transformed into *enragés*, then hypocrisy much more than injustice has been the driving force.[14] Profound hatred for 'bourgeois' society and its double-standards is certainly evident in the writings of those authors – Pareto, Sorel, Céline, Fanon – who glorify violence for violence's sake. The same burning desire to tear the mask of hypocrisy from civil society is common among those who tear into its structures with knives and guns and bombs. Their response is not 'irrational' since the failure of civil societies to live up to their own standards of openness, freedom and justice for all – their inability to prevent the humiliation of some of their members – makes them vulnerable to those who become hell-bent on revealing hypocrisy's conceits. That is probably one reason why – shamefully – the homicide rate among black Americans is seven times higher than for whites; why nearly two-thirds of persons arrested for murder and violent robbery are black; why half

---

[14] Hannah Arendt, *On Violence* (New York and London), pp. 65–6.

the population of US gaols is black; and why one black man in five is incarcerated – even though black people represent only around 12 per cent of the overall population.

The creation and *humiliation* of losers should worry the friends of civil society because there is plenty of psychoanalytic evidence that in certain circumstances humiliation encourages violent responses, sometimes directed by the downtrodden against themselves.[15] Consider one randomly chosen case: that of Charles Starkweather (about whose crimes the movie *Badlands* was made). Starkweather grew up in poverty and family neglect in small-town Nebraska, where in early 1958 he killed and mutilated eleven people in a week-long shooting spree. Bow-legged, of unprepossessing physical appearance and red hair, he was known locally as 'garbage man'. His autobiography, written just before his execution, explains that well before the murders he committed he had felt himself to be garbage, a loser. His self had long ago died – an experience so intolerable that as a man he preferred his own and others' physical death to the humiliation he had experienced as 'life'.[16]

The dynamics linked to cases like Starkweather's are often bizarre, and tragic. Broken object relations with parents during early childhood, especially the experience of neglectful mothers, or fathers who are absent, sometimes produces a condition far worse than emotional sadness: it results in the failure of subjects to mentalise their own selves or the mental selves of those around them. Those who fail

---

[15] The literature is vast, and contested. A sample of the best includes James Gilligan, *Preventing Violence* (London 2000); Adam Jukes, 'Violence, helplessness, vulnerability and male sexuality', *Free Associations*, 4:1, 29 (1993), pp. 25–43 and Rosine Perelberg (ed.), *Psychoanalytic Understanding of Violence and Suicide* (London 1999). Note that humiliation can slake a thirst for violence within whole societies, as in the nationalistic 'militarism of the little people' that developed in Germany during the late nineteenth century. See Thomas Rohrkrämer, *Der Militarismus der 'kleinen Leute'. Die Kriegervereine im deutschen Kaiserreich 1871–1914* (Munich 1990).

[16] James M. Reinhardt, *The Murderous Trail of Charles Starkweather* (Springfield, IL 1960), pp. 49–50: 'The people I murdered had murdered me. They murdered me slow like. I was better to them. I killed them in a hurry.'

to mentalise themselves and their surrounding world feel as if they are nothing, and that nothingness makes them prone to project their own chaos forcibly upon others, or back on to their own selves. They suffer from the profound fear of losing everything. Violence is a desperate effort to shore up their weak or absent selves, either through self-harm ('if I kill myself then I won't have to think about what I think') or through the violation of others ('if I kill you I won't have to think about what you think'). The violence may be deluded, but that very delusion, paradoxically, provides a safe refuge against the battering that has been taken by the self. Like oxygen, violence momentarily breathes life back into a self that has suffered asphyxiation, choked on whatever remained of a self that barely resembled a self in the first place.

The practical upshot of these assorted violence-producing dynamics within actually existing civil societies is to create archipelagos of incivility within their midst: a murder here, a rape or battering there. Then serial murders, even pockets of violence in whole geographic areas that have strongly 'medieval' qualities. Just as in the Middle Ages men always carried arms, never lightly ventured beyond the towns, and feared that the forests were full of frightening foes, so the white middle-class inhabitants of cities such as New Orleans – where each year there are around 250 murders, 200 reported rapes, 1,500 armed robberies and over 2,000 assaults – choose never to go to New Orleans East; they try to avoid taking public transport alone after midnight (or earlier, if they are women); and they are wary of setting foot after dark in certain quarters of districts like Bywater and Faubourg St John.

VIOLENCE AS ENTERTAINMENT

But there is another, less obvious reason why the fragile openness of civil societies contributes to their violent feel: their dependence upon networked systems of public and private communication. These media ensure that images of violence are circulated more or less freely and instantly to large numbers of people. That freedom of communication within civil societies in turn ensures that violence against others can and is often turned into entertainment, that is, made the object of popular fascination, thrill and pleasure. Cruel forms of group pleasure in being violent – like Serbian soldiers swilling *šljivovica* and singing their way through scores of daily murders in Bosnia – is nowadays common (if still puzzling) news. More common and puzzling still is the fascination and pleasure experienced by millions of people when confronted by violence in the form of entertainment. Contrary to the claims of some contemporary campaigners against violence in the media, the packaging and marketing of violence as entertainment is an old phenomenon traceable to the middle of the eighteenth century. Pay-TV sexual murders, violent video games, vomit-provoking splatter films, and musicians who cavort with death, safety pins jammed through their bloodied noses, rapping about guns and murder, midnight ramblers, psycho-killers and sympathy for the devil, are by now fairly ancient themes of modern popular culture. The tradition of entertaining violence stretches back through films such as *Night of the Living Dead* and *Psycho* to magazine ghost stories, horrid melodramas, newspaper sensationalism and the Gothic literature and Graveyard poets of the Enlightenment. There is admittedly insufficient historical research on these public representations of violence, yet it is clear that in modern times sensations and scandals generated by violence are older than the trial of O. J. Simpson and the Washington Sniper. The scaffold, for example, was a dominant emotive symbol in early nineteenth-century England. The totemic image of the 'hanged man' pervaded popular culture, for instance appearing on tarot cards and in dream books, and in Punch and Judy shows. The tanned skin of the executed was used to bind books about his or her crimes; and death masks of hanged criminals attracted big crowds at Madame Tussaud's. A parallel transformation of violence into entertainment, this time involving the violated female corpse, surfaced in Weimar Germany, whose civil society, consumed by fear of inside and outside threats, was riveted by Jack the Ripper's deeds in Wedekind's Lulu plays, Otto Dix's paintings of disembowelled prostitutes and Alfred Döblin's sexualisation of the murder of Rosa Luxemburg.[17]

With the advent of mass circulation and niche-marketed, electronic media operating on a global scale, the age span, size and spatial reach of audiences potentially interested in violent entertainment grows exponentially. The point is reached where the spectators of violence virtually anywhere in the world can be titillated by hair-raising gore so explicit that it seems unsurpassable in terms of technical perfection and verisimilitude. Why so many millions – gasping and shuddering involuntarily, cold sweat on their brows, upstanding hairs on the nape of their necks – are fascinated by the violent things they might otherwise be expected to run screaming from is an enigma. It lends credence to the originally Freudian thesis of the uncanny (*das Unheimliche*), according to which death, for which there is no known cure and which is the inevitable destiny of all individuals, is (in civilised societies) 'kept from sight . . . withheld from others'. That rendering of death as a stranger boomerangs back on the individual. It heightens his or her sense that death, the ultimate consequence of violence, is 'uncomfortable, uneasy, gloomy, dismal . . . ghastly'.[18] Freud supposed, misleadingly, that the experience of the uncanny, the primitive fear of the dead that inhabits the strange realm between the living and the dead, was a *universal* human experience. He did not see that the uncanny can and does assume different *historical* forms, so that for instance in premodern systems definitions of the

---

[17] See the account, which is based upon source materials from newspapers, criminal archives and popular ballads, by V. A. C. Gatrell, *The Hanging Tree. Execution and the English People, 1770–1868* (Oxford 1994). The nineteenth-century development of unbridled newspaper sensationalism of acts of violence – the insistence on the hot currency of the news, claims for the unique ferocity of murders, the reportage of gruesome details – is traced in Thomas Boyle, *Black Swine in the Sewers of Hampstead: Beneath the Surface of Victorian Sensationalism* (New York 1989). The Weimar fetish of violence against women is documented in Maria Tatar, *Lustmord. Sexual Murder in Weimar Germany* (Princeton 1995).

[18] Sigmund Freud, 'The uncanny' (1919), in *The Standard Edition of the Complete Psychological Works*, ed. James Strachey (London 1955), vol. XVII, pp. 219–52. Among the interesting recent discussions of death and the uncanny are Walter Kendrick, *The Thrill of Fear: 250 Years of Scary Entertainment* (New York 1991).

uncanny tended to he monopolised and strictly defined by core institutions such as religious authorities, warrior classes and local communities. Understood in this historically sensitive way, the theory
of the uncanny has a striking implication for accounts of democracy
and violence, which need to be reformulated thus: the invention and
growth of modern forms of civil society are not synonymous with the
extrusion of violence into the state sphere, where it becomes more or
less invisible. Precisely because the power to define the uncanny is no
longer monopolised by well-defined authorities – churches, communities and professional armies lose their grip on the meaning of death –
the uncanny becomes 'homeless'. There develops something like a
dialectics of civility, in which the visible reduction and practical
removal of various forms of violence from civil society is matched
by their heightened media visibility. Violence reappears in the form
of more or less gratuitous forms of 'simulated' or 'virtual' violence.

CHILD MURDER

The pleasurable experience of witnessing 'virtual' acts of violence is
one thing. The actual violence committed against others within civil
society is another matter. The key point is that within all civil societies there are times and places in which civilians experience psychic
confusion and social fatigue, even the feeling that life (as the Russians
say) is an empty lawless space (*prostranstvo*) founded on humiliation.
Under such conditions, these civilians begin to harbour resentments
and grudges. In desperation, they may be tempted to avenge their
humiliation, confusion and frustration – to expose the hypocrisy they
see around them – by taking it out on others physically. One example should suffice to illustrate the micro-violence hidden away in the
interstices of civil society – the case of child murder within households.

   Although the use of violence as a means of resolving differences with others, like charity, typically begins at home, child murder understandably remains a strange and disturbing phenomenon.
The officially recorded number of child murders in countries such as

Britain, France and the United States has substantially increased in recent decades. Doubts about evidence certainly apply; official statistics are often methodologically vague, heavily dependent upon methods of reporting and categorisation, and politically correct. There is also still no adequate history of modern household violence against children. Yet the latest available figures do present a picture of the patterns of uncivil treatment of children.

During the past forty years in the United States, the recorded number of children murdered during the first year of their lives has doubled; there has been a quadrupling of the murder rate among one-to four-year olds. Each year, more than a 1,000 children are murdered and more than 18,000 are permanently disabled by domestic violence. The micro-patterns are revealing. Four-fifths of children are murdered in their homes, by their parents. Reflecting the amount of time spent with children, women are disproportionately responsible for two-thirds of recorded cases. Almost half of all murders involve children aged less than one year; four-fifths are aged under four. Just over half of the victims are white and female, but among black Americans the incidence of child murder is higher: around 20 children in every 100,000 are slain, around 30 per cent of the total.[19] The trends generate huge media coverage and in consequence child murder, like other forms of violence, appears to move closer to those who previously had heard of, but had never seen, such hideousness. It has come to light that some 60 per cent of those charged with murder are the parents of the child, which casts a lurid light on the cherished term 'blood relations'. Especially anguishing for many commentators are the stories of murderous mothers, trapped in the hell and heaven of contemporary motherhood, who suffocate their children with exhaust fumes, or strap them into safety seats before rolling the family car

---

[19] See the National Clearinghouse on Child Abuse and Neglect Information, *Child Maltreatment 1996: Reports from the States to the National Center on Child Abuse and Neglect* (Washington, DC 1996); R. W. Zalar *et al.*, 'Domestic violence', *New England Journal of Medicine*, 342 (11 May 2000), pp. 1450–3; and Gerald L. Rowles, 'Domestic violence', *http://www.dadi.org/dvca_glr.htm*

into a lake, shake them into unconsciousness or stab their children to death before taking their own lives.

Many shocked commentators have reacted a-politically to such dastardly acts. They talk (in the traditional language of the doctrine of original sin) of 'evil' acts, all the while illustrating their point with spine-chilling, Hitchcockian details of the protagonists' lives; or (a not-unrelated explanation) their commentaries revive Hobbesian assumptions by highlighting the murderous effects of the 'me-first society' (Newt Gingrich) spawned by the cultural politics of the 1960s. Such commentators would do well to pause before they judge so simple-mindedly. They should understand that perceptions of child murder (like all other forms of violence) have a history; that prosecutions of child murder were rare before the sixteenth century; and that, thereafter, for two centuries, a legal clampdown on poor and unwed mothers accused of killing their new-born infants and concealing their remains produced official child murder statistics that were unquestionably higher than they are today.[20]

Keeping the latter figures in historical perspective is vital, and indeed those who rush to condemn child murder as 'sin' and 'evil' are better advised to study the phenomenon with the Spinozist motto at their side: 'Smile not, lament not, nor condemn; but understand' (*Non ridere, non lugere, neque detestari, sed intelligere*). They should as well strive to situate their judgements within the potentially fruitful framework of interpretation that links violence with the dynamics of civil societies. In many recorded cases of child murder, it is clear that both victims and villains are trapped in those high-tension zones of civil society where the conflict-ridden logics of the household (intimacy, sexual desire, identity formation, personal habits, marriage,

---

[20] See, for example, Peter C. Hoffer and N. E. H. Hull, *Murdering Mothers: Infanticide in England and New England, 1558–1803* (New York 1981); René Leboutte, 'Offense against family order: infanticide in Belgium from the fifteenth through the early twentieth centuries', *Journal of the History of Sexuality*, 2 (1991), pp. 159–85; and Keith Wrightson, 'Infanticide in European history', *Criminal Justice History*, 3 (1982), pp. 1–20.

money, the hard work of cooking, cleaning and childcare) interact with, reinforce and often contradict virtually the same list of conflict-ridden logics of both the labour market (with its additional, special stresses and strains of employment, unemployment and underemployment) and the social relations in which it is embedded. Seen within the context of these typical stresses and strains of civil society, the much-vaunted explanation of 'evil' selfishness has no veracity. It fails to acknowledge these stresses and strains. It ignores contributing factors like the experience of humiliation, confusion, fatigue; and it takes no account of the ambivalent feelings of love and hate of mothers and fathers, whose lack of mutuality and social support (the absence of men from parenting, the lack of proper childcare provision, the underprovision of adequate benefits for women who have lost the support of men) push them into a cul-de-sac. Trapped, the only way out is a crazed decision to murder another member of civil society, and perhaps even themselves. At that point, literally, the pressures of civil society kill its own offspring.

Uncivil wars

[T]he dead tree gives no shelter, the cricket no relief and the dry stone no water . .

T. S. Eliot (1922)

In well-functioning, long-established civil societies such incivility is only a mild trend. The tendency of civil society to kill itself, to degenerate into incivility on a grand scale, is normally kept in check by a combination of self-restraint, acts of charity, simple kindness, media coverage and intervention by others, whether families, friends, strangers, social care professionals or the courts and the police. But whenever these mechanisms weaken or break down, civility evaporates, sometimes overnight. Actually existing civil society then begins to resemble an *uncivil society*.[1] There develops a battleground, in which the stronger – thanks to the survival of some social bonds and certain civil liberties – enjoy the licence to twist the arms and clip the ears of the weaker. Under extreme conditions, an uncivil society can haemorrhage to death. Uncivil war looms; then it erupts, with a fury. The distinction between 'good' and 'bad' violence is destroyed. Social and political constraints on vengeance dissolve. Reprisals double, then

[1] When using the old-fashioned adjective 'uncivil', it should be clear that I am not referring to the various forms of action, originally described by Henry David Thoreau's *On the Duty of Civil Disobedience* (1849), as civil disobedience, that is, vigorous acts of deliberate law-breaking, or extroverted acts of disputed legality, whose stated aim is to bring before a public either the alleged illegitimacy or ethical or political indefensibility of certain government laws or corporate or state policies. So understood, civil disobedience is not synonymous with incivility, even though such disobedience is often denounced as 'uncivilised' or 'lawless' or violent by those who fear, or who disapprove of it. Thoreau himself publicly defended a decision not to pay taxes to a government which sanctioned slavery, while Mahatma Gandhi, who did more than anybody in the twentieth century to popularise the strategy of civil disobedience, helped forcibly to obstruct British imperial government. In each case, and in subsequent cases when civil disobedience has been used as a strategy of agitation for change, those who engage in acts of provocation and confrontation are deliberately committed to non-violence, both as a means of contesting illegitimate power and for the purpose of strengthening the institutions of civil society.

triple. Blood appears everywhere: on walls, on the ground, underfoot in deep pools. Victims are shot at, herded at gunpoint from their burning homes. They are summarily executed in nearby houses, or marched in columns to railway sidings, past rotting corpses, to be trucked off to makeshift concentration camps, where they are raped or castrated and then made to wait, with bulging eyes and lanternous faces, for the arrival of their own death.

The problem of uncivil war has already been mentioned, but since (along with nuclear anarchy and terrorism) it poses such a direct challenge to democracy as we know it, its contours are worth examining in more depth. The details are complex, and ugly. The scale and ferocity of violence produced by uncivil wars have fascinated, shocked and sickened the whole world. Words cannot easily describe their cruelty, and their attempted theorisation seems at first glance to be a self-indulgent act of blandiloquence. Those who attempt to reflect on such patterns of violence are easily gripped by feelings of shame that they are uninvited witnesses of events littered by corpses sweet with the smell of doom.

This experience of uncomprehending shame is perhaps one key reason why the kind of modern theorising of bloody conflict famously initiated by Thomas Hobbes's *Behemoth: The History of The Causes of The Civil Wars of England, and of The Counsels and Artifices By Which They Were Carried On From The Year 1640 To The Year 1660* (1668) has been badly neglected of late. There is still too little theoretical reflection upon the wars of our time – which is scandalous considering the sheer volume of armed conflict that has spread to the four corners of the earth. Admittedly, after the end of the Cold War, there is a great deal of confusion about how to interpret these violent conflicts. There is growing agreement that the distinction between war and peace is as questionable now as it was during the Cold War period, but for different reasons. That period, marked by bipolar ideological and geopolitical antagonisms, saw neither war nor peace. While genuine peace, in the sense of the relatively predictable absence of war or threats of war, proved impossible, actual outbreaks of war, even in limited domains, were checked by the serious risks of escalation and of mutual nuclear annihilation; or, to use Raymond Aron's succinct formulation, the Cold War made 'peace impossible, war unlikely'.[2]

By contrast, the crumbling of the Soviet empire and of global East–West confrontations has accelerated the triangulation of violence mentioned at the beginning of this essay. Although it seemed for a time that the end of superpower confrontations would make a Third World War and wars in general rather improbable, in fact localised wars became more prevalent – and more ferocious. If, during the Cold War, the maxim 'neither war nor peace' held sway, then the formula for the post-Cold War period, as Pierre Hassner has put it, is 'both war and peace'.[3] Symptomatic of this enigmatic trend towards uncivil wars and triangulated violence were the garbled developments within Europe itself: while its western regions engaged in a path-breaking politics of integration of territorial states aimed at putting an end to war, a few hundred kilometres to the south-east a bloody conflict with hundreds of thousands of casualties raged.

In the era of triangulated violence, in which both war and peace flourish, bloodshed caused by local wars is widespread. In 1964, it has been estimated that there were active resistance movements within less than a dozen countries – Angola, Cambodia, Congo, Cuba, Cyprus, Guatemala, Laos, New Guinea, Republic of South Africa, Vietnam and Yemen – whereas today the number of such conflicts, according to reliable recent UN estimates, has risen some seven times, which represents nine-tenths of all large-scale armed conflicts around the world.

But not only are local wars on the increase. In some places, their form and content have gone in directions that are not grasped

---

[2] The formulation first appeared in Raymond Aron's *Le grand schisme* (Paris 1948) and was reiterated, shortly before Aron's death, in *Les dernières annels du siècle* (Paris 1984).

[3] Pierre Hassner, 'La guerre et la paix', in *La violence et la paix. De la bombe atomique au nettoyage ethnique* (Paris 1995), pp. 23–61.

by conventional analyses of so-called civil war. In order to clarify this point, some further reflection on the conventional understanding of 'civil war' is necessary. According to the standard social science approach, civil war is violent conflict within a society resulting from attempts to seize or maintain state power and its symbols of legitimacy by extralegal, violent means.[4] Civil war is a violent form of horizontal conflict with vertical aims. It is said to be 'civil' because civilians are engaged in it. It is said to be 'war' because violence is applied by all parties to the conflict. Typically, it is explained, civil war is triggered by the absence of effective formal and informal channels for resolving certain social and political grievances. The consequent sense of frustration, or futility, or fear of reprisals among sections of the population encourage all parties to embrace the assumption or conviction that violence is necessary. There then follows a carefully planned and executed struggle to seize the means of state power by using rational-calculating violent methods.

It is explained that there are usually three phases in any civil war. Phase one sees the building of the structures of a resistance movement, especially order-giving, message-receiving networks. During phase two, the protagonists of civil war directly apply violence against their enemies. Their sabotage, underground and guerrilla units apply terror at intervals, selectively hitting the brain and nervous system of the enemy power structure – the ruling elites, the communication and transportation centres and the most strategically sensitive industries. The final phase of civil war, when the outcome of the conflict is decided, is that of insurrection, in which the conflict explodes into the open, with coordinated uprisings in various parts of the country. There

---

[4] The various works by J. K. Zawodny on 'unconventional warfare' well illustrate this approach. See, for example, his two-volume *Men and International Relations: Contributions of the Social Sciences to the Study of Conflict and Integration* (San Francisco, CA 1966); his essay, 'Unconventional warfare', *American Scholar*, 31 (1962), pp. 384–94; and his edited collection, *Unconventional Warfare*, in *Annals of the American Academy of Political and Social Science*, 341 (Philadelphia 1962).

are probes by the resistance movement to obtain control of either the capital or strategic parts of the country in order to establish some sort of legitimate counter-government which can act openly on behalf of the organisation. This stage is critical, since it compels the resistance to emerge on the streets and to fight until it wins, or is destroyed. At this point, the insurgents act in large units, and street fighting is conducted according to the rules of infantry tactics. The insurgents' objective is a series of uprisings, spreading like brushfire, intended to destroy the enemy's formal power structure and machinery of violence throughout the whole territory. At some point, the conflict comes to an end, and the civil war normally may be said to have ceased when either one faction forcibly subjugates its opponent (as in the American Civil War), or the warring parties establish their independence from each other (as in the civil war that led to the separation of Belgium and Holland), or, mutually exhausted and weakened, the protagonists arrange an at least temporary truce (as in the Wars of Roses).

The orthodox literature on civil war is admittedly summarised here in the briefest terms, but I have done so in order to highlight its inability to grasp the ways in which 'civil war' can easily become, and today often is, a euphemism for the most terrible experience of death and destruction. Orthodox commentators have often failed to question the assumption that civil war by definition must take place at the level of the nation-state. They have not asked whether the concept of a 'civil war' can be extended 'downwards' to the sub-state, or 'micro-level'. What is also striking – to extend an insight of Hobbes – is that so few theorists have enquired whether or to what extent the combatants' violent struggle during a so-called civil war can degenerate into a conflagration in which, in violation of the old moral precepts of rationally calculated 'just war', the means of violence appear to take on a life of their own and violence consequently becomes an end in itself.

Some of these possibilities have been explored fruitfully in the writings of Hans Magnus Enzensberger, Robert Kaplan, Martin van

Creveld and others,[5] according to whom the end of the Cold War has hastened the decay of conventional armies and the classificatory grid of territorial states. Our era sees the plunge towards what Kaplan calls 'a jagged-glass pattern of city-states, shanty-states, nebulous and anarchic regionalisms'. The heartlands of Europe and other metropolitan regions fall under the shadow of 'low-intensity conflict' (van Creveld), or what Enzensberger calls 'molecular civil war' (*molekularer Bürgerkrieg*). This local violence in Solingen, Tower Hamlets, Val–Fourré, Rio de Janeiro, Los Angeles and Marseilles disturbingly parallels the large-scale wars of the former Soviet Union, Africa, Asia and Latin America. Every carriage on a city's underground, says Enzensberger, can become a miniature Bosnia. To that observation could be added other examples; for instance, the shanty towns of Rio de Janeiro's Death Triangle, where drug barons and their gunmen impose curfews, decide when people come and go, who lives and who dies, and generally determine who gets what, when; and violent places like Route 66, a stretch of highway winding from Monticello, Utah, to Gallup, New Mexico, which was bedevilled some years ago by hit-and-run killings, body dumpings and a crazed killer named the Mad Trucker, whom local police suspected ran people over for sport.

When they unfold on a large scale, such conflicts are not understandable through conventional categories like class struggle, youth revolt or national liberation. It would also be a scandalous euphemism to call them civil wars. While conventionally organised bloody civil wars no doubt persist, at least some of today's battle zones are best described as a new type of conflict best called *uncivil war*. These wars display disturbingly new common characteristics. Most striking is the way in which the protagonists of violence practise asymmetric violence. They outwit top-heavy, clumsy and expensively equipped conventional armies by wielding their own reasonably

---

[5] Hans Magnus Enzensberger, *Aussichten auf den Bürgerkrieg* (Frankfurt am Main 1993); Martin van Creveld, *The Transformation of War* (New York and Toronto 1991), especially pp. 1–32, 192–227; Robert D. Kaplan, 'The coming anarchy', *The Atlantic Monthly*, 273, 2 (February 1994), pp. 44–76.

sophisticated means of violence according to no rules except that of destructiveness – of people, property, the infrastructure, places of historical importance and even nature itself. Previous civil wars were undoubtedly bloody. But the blood that was spilled nearly always had an organised and self-disciplined form, as Trotsky, the architect of victory in a civil war in which 9 million people died, recognised when likening Soviet power to organised civil war against the landlords, bourgeoisie and kulaks. Some of today's conflicts appear to lack any logic or structure, except that of murder on an unlimited scale. It is therefore tempting to describe the hyper-destructiveness of these battle zones as a late modern regression into 'tribal' or 'primitive' warfare. Kaplan speaks of the emergence of *'re-primitivized man*: warrior societies operating at a time of unprecedented resource scarcity and planetary overcrowding'. The emerging patterns of violence, predicts van Creveld, 'will have more in common with the struggles of primitive tribes than with large-scale conventional war'.

The temptation to think of contemporary uncivil wars as 'primitive' is itself primitive. It should be resisted, because there is much anthropological evidence that wars among hunting and gathering societies had an entirely different logic. In stateless, egalitarian Muslim desert tribes, for example, order among the various horizontally arranged and vertically nested segmentary groups was maintained without political centralisation by the cohesion-producing effects of permanent feuding at all levels, a pattern expressed in the maxim, 'I against my brothers, my brothers and I against our cousins, my brothers, cousins and I against the world.'[6] In his reflections upon Amerindian societies, Pierre Clastres interpreted the chronic violence among these societies as a reflexive means of guaranteeing their members' autonomy and preventing the emergence of oppressive state institutions. 'Primitive society is society against the State insofar as it is society mobilised for war', he observed, adding the surprising observation that tribal chieftains, who do not exercise power as we

[6] Ernest Gellner, *Muslim Society* (Cambridge 1981), pp. 36–69.

moderns know it, were themselves prevented from exploiting war as a means of empowerment because they were engaged in a journey bound ultimately to end in death. 'Each feat of arms hailed and celebrated by the tribe in fact obligates him to aim higher', until the point is reached where, 'realizing the supreme exploit, he thereby obtains, with absolute glory, death.' The practice of sending lone warriors abroad to attack the enemy camp and to die like a sacred king, 'alone against all', mirrors in inverted form this same principle of 'all against one'; so too does the strange practice of temporarily integrating prisoners-of-war into society, giving them wives, treating them royally, until the day they are ritually sacrificed and eaten by their captors.[7]

Parallel but substantively different rules for apportioning violence in war have been a persistent feature of political thought and practice well into modern times. A wise prince, commented Machiavelli, knows that although 'he will often be necessitated' to act 'contrary to truth, contrary to charity, contrary to humanity, contrary to religion', the maintenance of his government, even in war, requires him to observe 'what is right when he can'.[8] 'Before undertaking war', wrote Johannes Althusius, 'a magistrate should first check his own judgement and reasoning, and offer prayers to God to arouse and direct the spirit and mind of his subjects and himself to the well-being, utility, and necessity of the church and community, and to avoid all rashness and injustice.'[9] Even Clausewitz offered a secular version of the same argument by advising caution in wielding violence under certain

---

[7] Pierre Clastres, *Recherches d'anthropologie politique* (Paris 1980), pp. 206, 232, 237, 234. See also Alfred Adler, 'La guerre et l'État primitif', in Miguel Abensour (ed.), *L'esprit des lois sauvages. Pierre Clastres ou une nouvelle anthropologie politique* (Paris 1987), pp. 98–9, 111–12.

[8] Niccolò Machiavelli, *The Prince*, in A. Gilbert (trans.), *Machiavelli. The Chief Works and Others*, 3 vols (Durham, NC 1965), vol. I, p. 66.

[9] Johannes Althusius, *Politica Methodice digesta atque exemplis sacris et profanis ilustrata* (Herborn 1603), ed. and trans, and with an introduction by Frederick S. Carney as *Politics Methodically Set Forth and Illustrated with Sacred and Profane Examples* (Indianapolis 1995), ch. 35, sect. 10, p. 188.

conditions; of special importance for him was the need to observe the primacy of 'moral forces' and 'the intelligence of the personified state' over the violence of war.

In at least some of today's uncivil wars, large and small, all these sober restrictions covering the ground rules of war are swept aside. Alibis abound, to be sure, but the law of battle is straightforward: kill, rape, pillage, burn, destroy everything that moves, breathes or twitches. Emblematic of this violence without structure and limits – of pure violence operating as both means and end – are grisly inner urban disputes. Youths are stabbed to death in a row over drugs. A couple is murdered, then dismembered. Unidentified victims are dowsed in petrol and set on fire. In uncivil wars, analogously, the summary murder and counter-murder of innocents takes place on a large scale. The systematic hunting down and massacre of people like animals in Rwanda by killers who had emptied their heads and hearts of all thought and all heart-felt morals typify this trend. The Rwandan case shows that when everything is up for grabs, uncivil wars can ultimately degenerate into genocide – organised violence that deliberately aims physically to annihilate a targeted group. For this to happen, uncivil violence must be well organised. It must have access to the organisational means of killing people in large numbers (thankfully, this condition is sometimes undermined by the sheer recklessness of uncivil war). It was not because of its 'primitiveness' or 'backwardness' that the Rwandan people – both Tutsi and opposition Hutu – suffered genocide. Their fate, on the contrary, was helped by the technical preconditions of unlimited murder: a well-organised civil service, a small, tightly controlled land area, reasonably good communications and a self-disciplined population capable under pressure of forgetting the meaning of civility.[10] Given these conditions, the thorns of incivility spread on a frightful scale. A survivor of the *Interahamwe* recalled:

---

[10] Gérard Prunier, *The Rwandan Crisis. History of a Genocide* (London 1998).

Then at about 10.00 a.m. the killing began, with machetes and
masus . . . The whole place was completely surrounded, the
church, the hospital, the trading centre. No-one could escape. If
people fled in a group, they threw a grenade at them. Then they
searched the dead bodies for money. I survived a grenade attack.
I fell though I was not wounded. I hid in a corner. My husband
had already been killed . . . At about 2.00 p.m. the attackers left
to attack the trading centre. The dead bodies were just too many.
The place was red. Blood was flowing like water. I could see
babies suckling the breasts of their dead mothers.[11]

What kind of people can engage in unrestrained killing of this
kind? Uncivil violence seems to feed upon characters without character. The violent have to be capable of denying – even in the face of the
starkest evidence – that violence is taking place. Armed with AK-47
assault rifles, or grenades or machetes or just their bare hands, they
exude all the symptoms of what Hannah Arendt called a radical loss of
self. Purged of religious faith and moral scruples, they certainly lack
idealism. They are banal creatures. Like graffiti on urban walls, their
acts of violence are random and usually mindless. They will serve
anybody, betray anybody, do anything to save their skins. The killers'
faces are blank, their words are cynical. Some of them are rendered
decorticate by drugs. 'I don't think about it', they say. 'All I know is
that they are shit', or 'Either you kill or get killed', they add. Such
remarks, familiar to journalists, who commonly have guns waved
in their faces, reveal the striking degree to which today's guerrillas
are autistic. Unlike the murderous followers of Mussolini, Stalin or
Hitler, today's fighters – skinheads who mindlessly firebomb refugee
homes, for example – act as if they are characters in a Céline novel.
They are often no-hopers who believe in nothing but their own private
fantasies. Like the Tiger paramilitaries in Serbia led by the ex-bank

---

[11] Testimony by Clementina Murorunkwere, 13 June 1994, reprinted in the African
Rights report, *Rwanda: Death, Despair and Defiance* (London 1994), p. 258.

robber Željko 'Arkan' Ražnjatović, their senses are attuned only to violence and, not surprisingly, they are forced to take leave of sense itself. Unafraid of being shot or injured, they are self-destructive gangsters driven by 'anger at anything undamaged' (Enzensberger). If guilt presupposes a clear understanding of what one is doing at the time of a crime, then the violent are best described as innocent murderers.

Today's uncivil wars tend to produce chaos in their wake. They vandalise the threefold division of government, army and civilians once enforced by conventional warfare and the Westphalian and Philadelphian models. Today's uncivil wars ransack the legal monopoly of armed force long claimed by states. They deprofessionalise violence (by dissolving 'soldiers' and 'rebels' into 'sobels', as the gunmen were called in Sierra Leone) and put an end to the distinction between war and crime. They ensure that conflict degenerates into 'criminal anarchy' (Kaplan), into deathly destruction and self-destruction that has terrible symbols: the conspicuous poisoning and torching of food by Renamo fighters in a country wracked by famine; the Serbian gunmen who boasted in front of reporters that they felt nothing but pride after massacring every patient in one hospital, and then smashing up its equipment; and in Rwanda the widespread sexual abuse and murder of women, even the disembowelling of pregnant women, the public display of their foetuses, their killers shouting to husbands and bystanders words like: 'Here! Eat your bastards!'

Waste lands

It is important to try to be clear about the self-destructiveness of the perpetrators of bloody violence – about the ways in which their absurd ventures into the land of violence effectively call into question both the efficacy and the legitimacy of violence as a weapon in power struggles, at least on this scale. Uncivil wars not only take away life in the present, they have life-threatening effects for both those who outlive the conflict and those who are yet to be born. Uncivil wars rule from the grave. Uncivil wars threaten the pact, emphasised by Edmund

Burke, between the dead, the living and the unborn, and they therefore destroy the future possibility of a civil society protected by democratic government. This is true in several ways.

War has often been described as good for business, and there is no doubt that war profiteering remains a chronic feature of armed conflicts around the world – the octopus-like arms trade being the apogee of the whole business. Yet there is a long tradition of modern argument, stretching back well into the eighteenth century, that insists that war is often bad for business, that violence produces decadent forms of investment, and that war tends to destroy the infrastructure of market economies, including the civility that is a basic prerequisite of commodity production and exchange. 'I must confess', wrote David Hume, 'when I see princes and states fighting and quarrelling, amidst their debts, funds, and public mortgages, it always brings to my mind a match of cudgel-playing fought in a China shop.'[12] This old thesis that stagnation or pauperisation is the offspring of incivility arguably remains pertinent in the face of all-out uncivil war, which undoubtedly diverts resources into unproductive, mafia-type activities like corruption and criminality. These in turn weaken or wreck the possibility of developing or sustaining a dynamic economy that can enable 'taxation states' to form, and civilians to live well.

The economic pillaging of war-torn uncivil societies like Sierra Leone, Lebanon and Algeria not only serves as a reminder that markets function well only when they are embedded within a robust civil society. The inverse rule applies with a vengeance. Uncivil war perversely highlights the point that where there is no civil society there cannot be markets, exactly because market economies are directly dependent upon a dense and delicate forest of non-violent civil institutions, whose contingent patterns of social solidarity, norms of reciprocity and civic engagement are vital for ensuring flows of information about technological developments; a general awareness of the

---

[12] David Hume, 'Of public credit', in *Essays, Moral, Political, and Literary*, ed. T. H. Green and T. H. Grose (London 1898), p. 396.

credit-worthiness of would-be entrepreneurs; the dampening of get-rich-quick forms of opportunism; and, through the informal social interactions hosted by cafés, bars, clubs and streets, the cultivation of workers' motivation, reliability and sense of dignity.[13]

Uncivil wars, the most extreme form of incivility, also have long-term destructive effects upon the ecosystem in which battles rage. T. S. Eliot's premonition (in *The Waste Land*) of an ultimate war where 'the dead tree gives no shelter, the cricket no relief and the dry stone no sound of water' is no longer mere fantasy. Whether in Kabul or Vukovar or Grozny or Sarajevo, uncivil war leaves behind a trail of ravaged buildings, whole fields of oil-stained earth and piles of toxic rubble where no flowers or trees grow, and where tired, ill-looking men and women bury their dead, leaving the young to grub around in the ruins, in search of firewood, flour, nettles, lizards, and edible grass. The ecological damage caused by uncivil war seems to be unaffected by the degree to which fighting is conducted by 'high-tech' or 'low-tech' methods. Ecological damage is of course a chronic feature of high-technology battle, as in the 1991 Gulf War, in which the American-led coalition bombing of oil wells and tankers in Iraq and Kuwait, and Iraq's torching of oil wells and dumping of oil into the ocean, left the Persian Gulf area covered for weeks in sulphurous black smoke and permanently polluted from biochemical weapons spillages, oil leaks and oil well fires that took many months to extinguish. Many so-called 'low-intensity conflicts' are long-running wars that produce similar effects. The violence at the famous nineteenth-century battle of Solferino lasted one whole day. Uncivil war in Angola lasted three decades; the violence in Afghanistan has been going on for just as long. Little wonder that these conflicts turn entire regions or whole countries into theatres of war that not only destroy civilians but do long-term ecological damage, helped along (as in the widespread dumping of toxic wastes in Lebanon) by organised crime desperate to

---

[13] Robert D. Putnam, *Making Democracy Work. Civic Traditions in Modern Italy* (Princeton 1993), pp. 152–62.

profit from the general unaccountability of power and the breakdown of law and order.

Uncivil wars also do long-term damage to the ecology of human personality. Since uncivil wars threaten individuals with death, they breed fear. Every living creature is drawn into a permanent state of emergency. The conflict resembles a free-fire zone, a killing ground, in which everything that moves, or impedes free movement, is shot at. Hobbes, who recognised the fundamental importance of fear as a political factor, supposed that during intense experiences of violence individuals ridden with fear would come to their senses. They would vote rationally for a peace contract – as if conquering fear were merely a matter of mind over body. In practice, things are never so simple. The fear produced by uncivil wars can have a warning and mobilising function. It can lift aloft those who fight, or are trapped by fighting. It can enable them to survive, even to act as they never thought they could. Fear can even produce a 'craving for the extraordinary', as Ernst Jünger called the bizarre patterns of reckless solidarity among World War I soldiers hell-bent on destroying the cathedrals at Rheims and Albert, and who thought nothing of attacking even Notre Dame from the air.[14] We have heard much of war 'heroism' of this kind but, beginning with Hobbes, we have heard much less of the paralysing and sometimes auto-destructive effects of the fear induced by violence upon individuals. Edmund Burke's reply to Hobbes remains salient: episodes of prolonged violence 'strike deepest of all into the manners of the people. They vitiate their politics; they corrupt their morals; they pervert even the natural taste and relish of equity and justice.'[15]

For every epiphany produced by uncivil war there is at least the same quantity of psychosomatic wreckage. Fear generated by war is profoundly anti-democratic. Violence eats the souls of civilians. It erodes or destroys their capacity to make judgements and to act in

---

[14] Ernst Jünger, *In Stahlgewittern* (Berlin 1929), pp. 114–15.
[15] Edmund Burke, *A Letter to John Farr and John Harris, Esqrs., Sheriffs of the City of Bristol, on the Affairs of America* (1777), p. 203.

solidarity with, and against, other civilians. The violated are afraid of being frightened. They are gripped with fear of ceasing to be themselves. They experience nightmares in a void. Words often fail them, or burn their mouths when they try to speak about their plight. The afraid are haunted by the ghosts of violence, which appear and reappear as extreme trauma syndromes, or as sickening fears of permanent disablement or probable death (as in the so-called 'Gulf War Syndrome' of weight loss, chronic allergies, seizures and cancers that may have been triggered by the cocktails of vaccinations and anti-nerve gas drugs issued to troops subsequently engaged in Operation Desert Storm). Then there are the long-term inner fears that trouble the individual on a random basis. There is a big body of literature describing the low self-esteem, the self-destructiveness caused by humiliation, and willingness to project violence onto others, of many children who have witnessed violence or who have been beaten during childhood. It is also well known that women who have been raped, or men who have been attacked and robbed on the street, suffer occasional nightmares or daytime fits of panic, or uncontrolled weeping. During and after uncivil war, such symptoms are experienced far more intensely and for longer periods, certainly well after the objective conditions of violence have disappeared. If and when peace comes, individuals carry uncivil war within them. They experience no joy in 'victory' or 'peace'.

Clinical evidence from the war in Bosnia, although still impressionistic, documents some of these effects, some of which are sometimes enigmatic, including many cases of women who have been raped, but who – it sounds unbelievable at first – sometimes find that fact among the most understandable and therefore least troubling of their worries. These women are instead traumatised by their separation from their children, deeply disturbed by witnessing their husbands shot dead outside their homes, or shattered by the experience of queuing several hours for water, carrying buckets of it up flights of stairs to their makeshift apartment in a bombed-out hotel – only to fall victim to the snipers' trick of waiting until the woman arrives at her doorway before shooting a bullet straight through each of her buckets, with flawless precision. Like survivors of holocausts, the violated remain vulnerable to 'deformations, dislocations, and imaginative impediments' in the form of psychic numbing; they suffer guilt generated by the escape from death's clutches, and a fragmentary understanding of the hard-won experience of death.[16] The brush with violent death immobilises them. They are forced to struggle, joylessly, against their own confusions and traumas, their half-articulate, disordered experience of the present, unaided by their damaged expectations of the future, if they are blessed with any.

Landmines

Uncivil strife normally leaves in its trail another deadly legacy: whole populations and vast tracts of land saturated with unused or unexploded weapons that can prove to be far greater killers in times of peace than in times of war. Uncivil wars dissolve the distinction between war and peace; peace becomes smouldering war, full of daily reminders of the persistence of violence. Unexploded mines are a symbol of this persistence of violence long after formal agreements to stop it have been made.[17]

A gift of the twentieth century to posterity, landmines are of course not new. Designed as a response to the tank during World War I, they were used extensively in World War II, especially in Russia and Poland. Yet these landmines were large and heavy objects. They were time-consuming to lay, easily detectable and used mainly against specific military targets. Mines were designed to maim or kill enemy troops, to slow their movement, and to protect military installations, troops, civilians and territory. During the 1960s, technical advances made them smaller, lighter and cheaper – the popular P4 MK2 weighs

---

[16] Robert Jay Lifton, *The Future of Immortality and Other Essays for a Nuclear Age* (New York 1987), p. 24.

[17] The following draws upon the well-documented reports provided by the Arms Project of Human Rights Watch and Physicians for Human Rights, *Landmines. A Deadly Legacy* (New York, Washington, Los Angeles, London 1993) and http://www.icbl.org

less than 3 ounces and costs only a few American dollars. That fact, combined with their delayed-action potential, fostered the perception that they could be used offensively, as inexpensive and efficient means of controlling the movement of populations, terrorising them, emptying the countryside, creating refugee flows and literally crippling the opposing forces. What took a World War II battalion all day to put in place now took a matter of minutes. Laos and Cambodia saw the first large-scale attempts to scatter mines at random; by 1979, when the Soviet Union invaded Afghanistan, landmines had become a standard offensive weapon, distributed as 'scatterables' with ease over wide areas by artillery, rocket or plane.

Mines soon became big business. While accurate figures remain difficult to obtain, by the mid-1990s there were some 50 different models, manufactured by around 100 companies in at least 48 different countries; the principal producers and exporters were the United States, Italy, Germany, China, Egypt, Singapore, and Pakistan. The consequent ease with which landmines could be procured, especially by cash-starved armies, made their use a standard feature of uncivil wars, with macabre consequences. In Kurdistan, more than half of the total expenditure on health still goes on treating and caring for the victims of mines. In Cambodia, there are reportedly more than 30,000 amputees in a population of 8 million. As elsewhere, more than half of the victims are boys and girls blown up while engaged in the rural tasks they have always performed – taking flocks to graze pastures, collecting water and firewood – or while playing. In the early days of the war in Soviet-occupied Afghanistan, playful children, before they knew better, were even attracted to the small, brightly painted, air-delivered mines, nicknamed 'butterflies' or 'green parrots'. During the 1990s, before the American overthrow of the Taliban government, an estimated 10 million unexploded mines littered the country, destroying a good part of its irrigation system and, consequently, the population's self-sufficiency in food. In Angola, where uncivil war raged for more than three decades, famine spread through districts too heavily mined to be cultivated. And in war-ravaged Mozambique, repeated mining and counter-mining by both Frelimo government and Renamo forces paralysed transport systems, permanently severed the country's electricity power supplies, forcibly prevented more than 2 million refugees from returning to their homes, and destroyed the tourist industry by killing large numbers of elephants and other wild life in the contaminated game parks.

Landmines kill and maim citizens. They also choke off the possible future growth of a civil society with a good measure of civility. Landmines can lie dormant for up to two or three decades before being detonated by a child at play, an elderly civilian strolling at dusk or a household pig fattening itself on local fields. The wounds they inflict are ruinous. The shock wave from an exploding landmine often destroys blood vessels well up the leg, forcing surgeons to amputate much higher than the site of the primary wound. Landmines also cause secondary infections by driving dirt, clothing, bacteria, metal and plastic fragments into the body's tissues. Survivors of mine explosions suffer intense physical pain. Their livelihoods are frequently lost. Households are confronted with severe financial stress caused by the substantial costs of treatment and rehabilitation, loss of the victim's earnings, and the long-term costs of supporting an unproductive relative. In areas prickling with mines, especially in rural areas, citizens must either learn to live with mines, working their fields as best they can, risking death each day, or abandon their homes to live safely elsewhere, thereby depopulating the local area and weakening the basis of social solidarity.

Clearing mines is no easy job. Landmines may come cheap, but their average cost of safe removal is somewhere between $300 and $1,000 each – a ratio frightening in its implications for a world in which per capita income is often less than that, and in which there are roughly 100 million uncleared mines, and in which mines are still being laid worldwide far faster than they are being removed. The effective banning of their production, export, stockpiling and deployment is nowhere in sight – a depressing symptom of which is the UN's Landmines Protocol of 1983, which feebly attempted to regulate their use, but not production or sale. Although the provisions of the most recent anti-landmine treaty convention (1997) are intended to diminish landmine use against civilians, it contains no effective enforcement mechanisms and ignores the fundamental problem of temporal randomness inherent in mine warfare: the way in which mines effectively outlast their military utility and place civilians at risk, typically on a long-term basis. In the meantime, mine clearance remains a primitive process, with no 'silver bullets' in sight. Paradoxically, sophisticated anti-handling devices, often with electronic sensors or microchips, increase the risk to de-miners. 'Most mine-clearing tools are glorified farm implements', observes *The Bulletin of the Atomic Scientists*, and 'a man with a stick is still the most common instrument'.[18] Needless to say, the hand removal of mines is dangerous and time-consuming, especially given that the people doing it have little idea of the type or location of the mines. The strong political temptation, especially in regions exhausted by war, is therefore to forget the whole dirty business – and violently to suffer its consequences in so-called peacetime.

[18] Jim Wurst, 'Ten million tragedies, one step at a time', *The Bulletin of the Atomic Scientists* (July/August 1993), p. 20.

Ethics

If you are not prepared to take life,
you must often be prepared for lives
to be lost in some other way.

George Orwell (1949)

SOCIAL PACIFICATION

Is it ever justified to use violence to prevent or to reduce violence? Are there circumstances in which the creation, or defence, of democracy should be attempted by violent means? More generally, is it plausible to speak of a democratic ethic of violence?

Such questions are back on the political agenda, in no small measure because even though all wars are nasty, some wars – uncivil wars like those in southern Sudan and Chechenya, Liberia and the Lebanon – have proved to be nastier than most. Marked by reckless and random killing without either mercy or ruth, they produce a trail of destructive effects that ripple through the wider world. Uncivil wars show just how easily collective strife can erupt in otherwise peaceful and vibrant societies with an impressive history of viable pluralism; and how this strife can degenerate into a random and reckless violence that has a logic all of its own. And – the darkest point of all – uncivil wars show how difficult it is to define and master the arts of social pacification and democracy-building once the unrestricted killing of anybody who can be harmed and killed has broken out.

If uncivil wars were confined to specific zones of the earth, away from the hubs and spokes of the globalising world as we know it, they would be of marginal interest to most people. But uncivil wars are not like that. They are not easily contained within geographic bounds. Uncivil wars are hunting and training grounds for gun-runners, mercenaries, profiteers and terrorists who operate on a global scale. Refugees stream from their infected battle zones; businesses disinvest from their wrecked economies; other non-governmental organisations are also forced to escape their clutches. Re-presented to global audiences by news media 24 hours a day, all these effects help to explain why only the blind, or callous, or foolish still regard them as far-away conflicts in far-away lands; and why military ('humanitarian') intervention and (hence) post-war reconstruction have become chronic global problems of our time.

Intervention and post-war reconstruction are also now among the top items of the global political agenda, thanks to the latest fashions in military strategy. For the time being, the dominant pattern of foreign interventions has been set. Those carried out by American forces in Iraq, Somalia, Afghanistan and Kosovo resemble hit-and-run affairs. Like a metal hammer that pounds a wooden stake into the earth, their aim is to beat the enemy into submission, in the expectation that the earthly elements of time will dissolve the animosity that originally nurtured the local conflict. Such intervention bears a strange resemblance to nomads' strikes against their adversaries. Armed to the teeth, the attackers travel light; they rely on their ability to swoop down on their victims, using weapons like stealth bombers and cruise missiles – the contemporary equivalent of nineteenth-century gunboats – to inflict the maximum harm, then to retreat, all the while supposing that the violated will not or cannot retaliate.

Measured in terms of the power to build democratic institutions and peaceful ways of life, this American-style or Washington-backed strategy of quick intervention is deeply flawed. With the outbreak of 'peace', US troops in Baghdad found themselves forced to conduct high-alert patrols through the streets dressed in full combat gear, pistols in hand. Every short-term occupier was potentially a target, including the young American military officers – in the absence of broad global support for the invasion – who had been left to organise schools, purify drinking water, repair power plants and pick up the rubbish, often without knowing what they were doing. On democratic grounds, American-style military intervention is also easy to shame. The disproportion between military casualties and the violence heaped upon civilians is staggering; so high are the levels of protection of the invading armies that their violence is felt by observers and victims alike to have a terrorist quality about it.

There is another difficulty: the power to force others into submission does not translate spontaneously into the power of the survivors to form stable democratic governments and law-enforced civil societies. The psychic traumas, damaged tissues of sociability and ecological and infrastructural damage inflicted by both the war of intervention and all the senseless sanctification of cruelty that came before it are left untreated. In some quarters of the victors' camp, nobody gives a damn about that; when the job is done, the vanquished are tacitly written off (as Kipling once put it) as 'lesser breeds without the Law'. From the standpoint of the survivors on the ground, however, things look rather different. In the aftermath of uncivil war and outside military intervention, it is as if the worldly power to act stops flowing through people's veins. The content of their worlds disintegrates. People feel numbed. They suffer muted anguish and pain. Reckless, indiscriminate killing saps people's trust in themselves and others; it mutilates their capacity for self-organisation; it frustrates their ability to make short-term decisions and long-term plans through households, partnerships, neighbourhoods and other social associations and networks.

Efforts to build or re-build civil society out of the ruins of war start from this point. So also do the difficulties. The crafting of peaceful social relations is undoubtedly an essential antidote to the ruins left behind by uncivil war. Yet talk of the need for a civil society is no all-purpose magic wand. New constitutions and some rudiments of government can be created within a few months. Standing armies take longer to form, perhaps two or three years, but not quite as long as viable market institutions, which take at least a decade. The most arduous task, which can take many decades, is the creation of other trust-producing civil society institutions, like professional associations, trades unions, neighbourhood organisations and self-help and civil liberties networks – none of which resemble naturally occurring substances. The delicate resource called civility cannot be agreed and written by means of round-table meetings, constitutional conventions, truth commissions or covenants (like the 1989 Ta'if Accord that is credited with marking the rebirth of the Lebanese republic). Civility can neither be planned nor legislated from above, nor produced through rational agreement and public controversy. Nor can it be produced like pizzas and fast foods, or like automobiles or microchips, on assembly lines. It takes time to grow.

Like other democratic mechanisms, the institutional rules and organisations of a civil society are deeply contingent. They presuppose the emotional willingness of actors to get involved with others, to talk with them, to form groups, to change or pluralise their loyalties. Especially in a civil society, the propensity of women and men to associate freely and to interact fearlessly with others is not (and should not be) linked to any one particular identity or group, whether based on blood, geography, class, tradition or religion. Contrary to Marx and others, the middle classes are not the 'natural' carriers of the sentiments of civil society. Pacification, ending the pathos of uncivil war, requires that support and encouragement must be given to any group or project capable of engendering the spirit of pluralism and free association. Civil sentiments best hatch and grow in compact milieux like urban areas, through a variety of apparently 'non-political' strategies: architectural design and landscaping schemes; local health and environmental and archaeological programmes; and through a whole range of cultural initiatives, from the performing arts to competitive sports and university seminars. The qualities produced by such initiatives can never be the offspring of ideological groups, movements and parties driven by nationalism or xenophobic racism or re-tribalisation. A civil society rather supposes that women and men can be mavericks – *makari*[1] – who can live with a variety of others in complex

---

[1] Through a striking and hopeful image, Samir Khalaf's account of the difficulties of regenerating civil society institutions (*Civil and Uncivil Violence in Lebanon* (New York 2002) p. 323) points to the metaphorical importance of the traditional figure of the Lebanese *makari*, the wandering peddler known locally for the tales and tidbits that he brings back from the wider world.

ways. It demands, in other words, that they can control their vengeful impulses, that they are capable of *sociability* and therefore have in their hearts the ability to trust and be loyal to others – to be so loyal, in fact, that they feel strong enough to stand up to others and to organise against them.

Why are civil society institutions so difficult to build or rebuild in the aftermath of uncivil war, we may ask? There are various reasons. Business firms are often reluctant to play the role of economic wizards by taking risks and investing in the social and economic infrastructure wrecked by uncivil violence. When they do invest, quick profits often result in kitsch. The Hard Rock Café and Pizza Hut nestle among the public monuments, mosques and shops ruined by bazookas and cluster bombs, but the resulting bourgeois culture of conspicuous consumption is often paper thin. In the absence of genuine markets and a vibrant middle class, business has no genuinely socialising effects. It merely reinforces the public mood of lethargy and disengagement. And when those requirements are satisfied, business investment often tears at the shreds of the social fabric that somehow survived the cruelty of uncivil war. Fashionable hotels, luxury apartments and other high-rise global hang-outs come to stand side-by-side with squalid backyards and dilapidated homes; threatened by gentrification, poor squatters are forced to defend their ground against rich speculators and squads of police wielding truncheons, tear gas and water cannon, or much more lethal weapons.

Meanwhile, in matters of post-war relief and rehabilitation, non-governmental organisations (NGOs) can and do have mixed effects. Compared with governments, NGOs are often flexible and innovative, low cost and responsive to grass roots pressures. But their 'civilising' effects do not happen *spontaneously* or *automatically*. For one thing, the task of rebuilding a civil society from the ground upwards is no substitute for the parallel task of building effective and legitimate governmental structures, which is why – as the fate of tiny Lebanon in the hands of inter-Arab and superpower rivalries so tragically shows – relief and development work is frequently scuppered by local warlords and armed gangs, private armies and occupying forces. The Washington-style invaders' new method of minimising their own casualties in part by using Gurkhas – native auxiliaries like the Albanian Kosovo Liberation Army or the Afghan Northern Alliance – is also no solution. It succours military force and warlords at the expense of civilian government.

Then there are the socially distorting effects of NGO programmes. Observers usually pay too little attention to this, but a careful examination of many post-war reconstruction efforts clearly highlights another rule: to the extent that the sustained development of civil society relies upon NGOs as conduits for aid money and technical support, it often turns them into hostages of fortune, with mixed dividends. Donor funding can (but not always) overwhelm or distort the goal of creating a civil society. It tends to create local organisations that are self-centred and blessed with power that is publicly unaccountable, partly because they are so heavily dependent on their donors; and partly because the staff of these NGOs (as the South African joke has it) En-J-Oy all sorts of privileges otherwise denied those living in misery around them.

TRIAGE?

Uncivil wars are the quintessence of incivility, and the mind-boggling cruelty they produce highlights the clash between might and democratic right. Democracies (ideally conceived) are polities which cultivate a dynamic plurality of more or less equal forms of life that can be held publicly accountable to others thanks to citizens' access to institutions like independent communications media, periodic elections and a vibrant civil society. Seen in this 'ideal-typical' way, democracies dispense with First Principles. They cultivate a broad variety of morals that in turn suppose and require citizens' commitment to a positive ethic: the mutual obligation to live and to let others live, to regard them as equals, to cultivate institutions of civil society that are protected and nurtured by publicly open and accountable government. Democracy is the friend of *multiple moralities*. It stands for a universe of freedom *from* a singular Universal Ethic. That is why democracy requires individuals and groups to be *civil*: to live with moral ambivalence, to practise moral judgements, to use such techniques as indirection, face-saving and self-restraint in order to demonstrate their commitment, in tactful speech and action and bodily manners, to the worldly principle of a peaceful plurality of morals.

This democratic principle is not only a condition of possibility of freedom from all First Principles. It also implies opposition to violence in all its forms. Violence robs both the violator and the violated of their freedom. It is antithetical to the ethic of plural morals. Yet it is obvious that non-violent democracies without foundations are vulnerable to forces – violent individuals, terrorist networks, bellicose gangs, well-trained armies – that want nothing of pluralism and everything of their own particular way of life. When democracies tolerate these intolerants they contradict and weaken their own spirit of civility, which is why in certain contexts – uncivil war, for instance – violence may be required to put an end to violence. Here there are no hard-and-fast rules for spotting and dealing with the violent opponents of democracy. There is simply no substitute for the task of making difficult political judgements in particular contexts. Judgements naturally raise a fundamental strategic question: given that violence threatens whole local populations and impacts negatively upon democracies as we currently know them, can anything be done to prevent or to stop it?

Some years ago, Hans Magnus Enzensberger, Germany's most outspoken political essayist, responded provocatively to this question with an answer that was as disturbing as it was modest: local fire-fighting is the most that can be done and ought to be attempted. *Hic rhodus, hic salta!* First things first. 'No one would dispute that universal solidarity is a noble goal. Those who are determined to achieve it are to be admired', wrote Enzensberger, who in the next breath strongly criticised the cosmopolitan conviction – nowadays associated with the kind of attitude to be found within the emergent global civil society – that citizens and governments of the

(formerly colonial) metropolitan countries have heaped so much violence on the rest of the world that they have a duty to remedy violence in far-off countries like Afghanistan, the Sudan and Chechenya.
In Enzensberger's view, the belief that European omnipotence has
brought nothing but evil to the world is as suspect as the flip-side
conviction that omnipotent Europeans must now deliver good to the
world; or as monstrous as the UN Bosnia strategy of refusing to fight
the main aggressor, and preventing the victims from resisting, all the
while trying to protect them against total annihilation. Enzensberger's
advice was blunt: abandon the pretentious and guilt-ridden nonsense
of universal ethics ('the rhetoric of Universalism') and work instead
for the practical removal of violence in places culturally and geograph-
ically close to home. The Germans, for instance,

> cannot solve the situation in Kashmir; we understand little of the
> conflict between the Sunnis and the Shiites, between the Tamils
> and the Sinhalese; whatever is to become of Angola must, in the
> first instance, be decided by the Angolans. And before we get
> trapped among warring Bosnians, we ought to mop up the civil
> war in our own country. Our priority is not Somalia, but
> Hoyerswerda and Rostock, Mölln and Sollingen.[2]

Enzensberger was probably right to insist that building more
civility into civil societies is an urgent and tangible goal of democratic politics. Yet his clear-headed iconoclasm was arguably marred
by some wild conclusions that today prompt a string of questions central to any examination of the fate of democracies in a world of triangulated violence: has traditional civil war actually disappeared from
the face of the earth? Is there remaining but a single continuum of
uncivil violence linking Rostock to Aceh? Did the Kurds who resisted
Saddam Hussein or the Palestinian suicide bombers who fought the
Israeli army all act like 'autistic' German skinheads or English football

---

[2] Hans Magnus Enzensberger, *Aussichten auf den Bürgerkrieg* (Frankfurt am Main
1993), p. 90.

yobs on the rampage? If not – as seems probable – then surely violent struggles against domination and genocide, as well as sustained efforts to rebuild civility in former war zones, make sense? And since some of these struggles – in South Africa, Bosnia and Burma, for instance – have wider and sometimes direct implications for democratic countries and for global power politics, can the citizens and governments of actually existing democracies simply turn their backs or shrug their shoulders, muttering something about the need for first things first? Isn't the cultivation and defence of a global civil society backed by representative government possible, and desirable? Or has the problem of cruelty in fact ceased to be a global affair?

Enzensberger anticipated some of these challenging questions, and tried to answer them through the argument that the general containment and reduction of uncivil war is technically impossible, especially in the aftermath of the Cold War. There is just too much violence around to deal with it comprehensively. He mistakenly discounted the possibility that will and force of circumstances might propel the United States, the world's policeman, into playing the role of a global swing power that is capable of fighting against uncivil wars on several fronts simultaneously.

Enzensberger also rejected the alternative ideal of a global civil society and the complementary policy of building up the institutions of the emerging cosmocracy, which would in turn require 'that the many sources of global or regional turbulences be dealt with in ways that would minimize violent conflict among states, reduce injustice among and within states, and prevent dangerous violations of rights within them'.[3] Enzensberger was aware that his own argument was trapped potentially within a performative ethical contradiction (how is it possible to advocate the reduction and tolerance of violence at the same time?), but he insisted that Gödel's maxim that not

---

[3] Stanley Hoffmann, 'Delusions of world order', *New York Review of Books*, 9 April 1992, p. 37. See my discussion of global civil society and cosmocracy in *Global Civil Society?* (Cambridge and New York 2003).

even mathematics can save itself from the quagmire of inconsistency applies also to the problem of uncivil war. The selection of priorities is necessary and inevitable. Where to begin? Where can I engage my efforts most effectively? Which of these options should take precedence? Such questions must be at the heart of governmental and military and civil campaigns against incivility. Fantasies of omnipotence among politicians, diplomats, generals and citizens should be abandoned. They should be replaced by the logic of *triage*: just as field medicine first categorised the wounded into the three categories of the slightly wounded, the terminally injured and the critically ill in need of priority treatment, so today's uncivil wars are not all remediable. Some require light bandaging by outsiders. Others, the ones that are incurable, have to be left to their own deathly fate; the remainder, those with reasonable prospects of resolution, should preoccupy us.

Enzensberger's case for political pragmatism, written as it is in spare, angular prose full of ironic understatement, stands within the modern tradition of Jonathan Swift's *A Modest Proposal for Preventing the Children of Poor People in Ireland from Being a Burden to their Parents or Country; and for making them beneficial to the Publick* (1729). Since its publication in the first quarter of the eighteenth century, that tract has continuously fascinated and shocked its readers with the tongue-in-cheek suggestion that the cruel pauperisation of the Irish within the confines of the British Empire could be alleviated by the farming of Irish babies for the metropolitan meat market. In certain quarters, Enzensberger's proposed strategy of *triage* evoked similar shocked outrage, so confirming his reputation as a sagacious provocateur who knows how to hit his readers where it hurts. That hostile reaction may have been intended by Enzensberger. For as the controversy whipped up in Germany by his earlier claim that Saddam Hussein really was another Hitler shows, one of Enzensberger's recent preoccupations has been to question the dogmatic prejudice of both naive pacifism and crude-minded militarism. As a political writer who assigns a special role to irony in an age inclined to literalness, he writes skilfully, in many voices. He is certainly no protagonist of

parochial apathy or self-exculpation. Nor can he be accused of condon-
ing war, either by neglect or by advocacy, or untoward comparisons. 'It
glistens like the broken beer bottle in the sun/ at the bus-stop outside
the old people's home', he writes elliptically in a poem. War 'rus-
tles like the manuscript of the ghostwriter at the peace conference./
It flickers like the blue reflection of the TV-set/ on somnambulist
faces.'[4]

Civil violence?
The spirit of Enzensberger's reflections on violence arguably continue
where Brecht left off, not with his ideological (Marxian) certainties but
by using a poetic form of the strategy of *Verfremdung*, in which the
observable is poked and prodded and labelled with disturbing and conflicting understatements, always with a feel for the 'torment of choosing' and awareness of the need for making judgements about what is
to be done. That emphasis on *judgement* indicates why Enzensberger
does not assume that his word is the last on the subject of violence,
and why further reflection on the same theme is not only warranted,
but required. There is certainly plenty of room, theoretically and politically, for contesting his claims, especially by widening the scope of
his concerns (as this essay on violence and democracy is attempting)
and by extending, sometimes to the limits, his rather vague proposals
for coming to terms with the problem of the destructiveness of uncivil
war.

From the perspective of democratic politics, Enzensberger's
emphasis upon judgement is important. But while in a democracy
the recognition of complexities, dilemmas and aporia is indeed essential, Enzensberger's defence of the principle of *triage* is only a beginning. His essay gives voice to the working maxim so far adopted in
this essay: that involuntary death by violence is a scandalous violation of the ground rules of any civil society, especially one that

---

[4] Hans Magnus Enzensberger, 'Der Krieg, wie', in *Kiosk. Neue Gedichte* (Frankfurt am Main 1995), p. 8.

enjoys a maximum of democratic freedoms and equalising solidarities. Violence, civil society and democratic government cannot peacefully coexist, this maxim implies. For if violence begins to plague the subjects of any democracy then it loses its civility and (in the extreme case) instead slides towards an *uncivil society*. That much – as those who champion the principle of non-violence emphasise – is clear. But it is important to recognise that the simple ethical equation of non-violence and democracy does not always work. The straightforward commitment to non-violence may well have a distinguished history featuring distinguished writers like Thoreau and W. H. Auden, but today, in the era of triangular violence, our thinking about violence and democracy needs to become more complicated. For there are times and circumstances – the caveat is crucial – when violence functions as a basic, if highly paradoxical, precondition of the pursuit or preservation of a civil democracy. Let us call this the Paradox of Civil Violence and – for the purpose of bringing greater clarity to the field of democratic ethics – explore some of its contours, first at the individual and then at the collective levels.

Consider the contentious matter of self-violation under duress. Although the will to live is usually a brave act of defiance against the violence of captors who would like nothing better than their captives' suicide – as in the annihilation camps during the period of Stalinism – there are sometimes circumstances in which there is no shortage of good reasons to kill oneself, and in which, thus, the act of suicide is not unreasonable. A dramatic example: Jan Palach's brave burning of himself in Wenceslas Square in Prague in January 1969, shortly after the Russian invasion of Czechoslovakia.[5] In his subsequent appeal, issued from his hospital bed as he lay dying, that others resist the invasion peacefully in various ways, Palach demonstrated that violated subjects can be forced by circumstances to choose whether to lose everything,

---

[5] See the interview with Jan Kavan in Michael Randle, *People Power: The Building of a New European Home* (Stroud 1991), p. 153. The background political circumstances are detailed in my *Václav Havel: A Political Tragedy in Six Acts* (London and New York 2000), pp. 200–33.

spiritually speaking, or instead to take their lives, both as a protest against the present incivility and as an expression of the wish that there be a future world freed from the scourge of violence. These are circumstances in which the forces of free will and determinism are mixed together. Palach was convinced that everything had capsized and that his nation was drowning in nothingness. His act of putting himself to death in public was nevertheless *chosen*. His choice cast doubt upon the old prejudice that those who kill themselves, even if they do so spectacularly, simply depart from the realm of the visible and enter a zone of 'malign opacity' (Baudelaire), in which relations with others are forever destroyed. Suicide is not always a synonym for clandestinity. It can be a public affirmation of civility, in which, paradoxically, the courage and principles of the person who has taken their own life ensure that she or he is lifted out of time and – by being remembered – honoured by others with a form of immortality.

Questions concerning the relationship between violence and democracy and civil society are undoubtedly complicated by the problem of whether individuals' choice to suicide, strictly speaking, is anything like a self-chosen act, or whether it is better understood as a desperate act of last resort when the subject concludes that since all other options have been taken away, self-violation is the most 'civil' way of completing one's existence on earth. Steeped in the customs of the civilising process, restrained by religious prohibitions, and encouraged by modern advances in medicine, we tend to blanch at talk of suicide. This reticence persists despite the ironic fact that Christianity, which refuses to sanction suicide, is founded on an act of self-sacrifice (John Donne even contended that Jesus committed suicide); and despite the fact (a bitter pill that some honest liberals have been forced to swallow) that the principle of self-determination of citizens implies, and under extreme duress may well require, an act of self-destruction. Many of us still prefer to regard death as the potentially avoidable entropy of the body. We think of it as the last great barrier to immortality. The age of pestilence and famine seems to be behind us; so long as we are lucky to avoid a brush with fatal accidents or grossly uncivil acts, death for around 80 per cent of citizens in the developed world has been transformed into a more or less distant destination along a long, winding and predictably downhill road called delayed degenerative disease.[6] Death loses its sting, but so too does the perfectly worded suicide note of Charlotte Perkins Gilman: 'I have preferred chloroform to cancer.'

Suicide seems irrational. It gets the cold shoulder. True, the corpses of those who take their own lives are no longer dragged, beaten and mutilated, through the streets by a braying crowd who gather to watch and taunt their ignominious burial alongside a lonely stretch of highway. Yet those who suicide still incur the prejudice of clinicians who think them manic or depressive; the contempt of moralising clergy who judge them evil; and the mercenary processing of life insurance agents who look unfavourably on their heirs, sometimes frustrating their inheritances. Few people seem to understand that, under circumstances that are not chosen, death can be rationally chosen, that one's life can serve to affirm a life well lived before the deterioration of the body sets in, bringing with it physical or emotional damage that appears to the subject as worse than death itself. That at least is the case of those who champion physician-assisted death or voluntary euthanasia in circumstances of terminal illness. Still fewer seem to understand Jan Palach's personal conviction that a noble death is always preferable to an ignoble life. Under despotic conditions, suicide is of course a consciously willed but not freely chosen decision. Those who choose to end their lives would probably not do so in the absence of a conquering power. Yet in such contexts, suicide arguably serves to distinguish a citizen from a subject. As Shakespeare's Antony pointed out, suicide sends a clear message to friends and foes alike: 'I am conqueror of myself.'

Any democratic consideration of the ethics of violence must also confront the possibility that there are times and places when the

---

[6] A good survey of the history and changing attitudes towards death by suicide is Margaret Pabst Battin, *Ethical Issues in Suicide* (Englewood Cliffs, NJ 1995).

deployment of violence by whole groups against their opponents *may* serve as a basic condition of building or developing a civil society marked by tolerance, pluralism and democratic accountability procedures. The links between violence and civil society and democracy are more complicated than most observers imagine. Those who take up the sword, it has often been said, shall perish by the sword. 'Blessed are the meek, for they shall inherit the earth . . . Blessed are they which are persecuted for righteousness' sake, for theirs is the Kingdom of Heaven', others add. Well and good. But, as Simone Weil pointed out, there are times when the meek defenders of democracy, those who refuse to take up the sword, or relinquish it, simply perish on the cross after suffering indescribable hell on earth.

That is why the collective deployment of violence against others, taking up arms against a sea of troubles, *may* sometimes serve, against all odds, as a symbolic moral protest against absolute evil and, therefore, as a signal to future generations that gross incivility will not be tolerated. Examples include the Warsaw ghetto uprising against Nazi occupation; or the effective tactic of Auschwitz prisoners responsible for washing and ironing SS uniforms, who searched for comrades who had died of typhus, picked the racially unprejudiced lice off their corpses, and then slipped them under the collars of the neatly ironed military jackets of their future victims. Collective violence *may* also serve effectively to stop the perpetrators of violence in their tracks, as in the British resistance to Nazism during World War II and in some successfully executed 'wars of liberation', like that waged in Eritrea against the Ethiopian regimes of Hailie Selassie and Colonel Mengistu. Collective violence – actual or threatened – may throw the violent off balance, cause them to act foolishly, even to lay down their arms, to abandon the conflict or (as Clausewitz pointed out) to refrain from using violence in the first place.

Collective violence *may* also have a profoundly transformative effect upon individuals. It can sometimes enable them to shake off fear and servitude and to live as free and equal citizens. One example: the early twentieth-century transition to parliamentary democracy and universal suffrage, it should not be forgotten, was catalysed by (threats of) violence, and not just on the domestic front. War and rumours of war tested the competence of ruling elites, visibly exposed previously hidden inequalities, created new solidarities and swept away monarchic arrogance. Whether today's triangle of violence will produce analogous effects is doubtful, and even the earlier twentieth-century violent transition to parliamentary democracy had immense costs – violence at home and abroad left deep scars upon the body of the newborn democracies. The point being suggested here is that there is no universal rule that war supports democracy. The claim that violence *always* has a liberating, cathartic impact upon the perpetrators, as Fanon famously supposed in his call for revolutionary violence of the colonised against the colonisers, is questionable. Fanon's account (in *Peau noire, masques blancs* (1952) and *Les Damnés de la terre* (1961)) of how the depersonalised colonial subject can violently defeat the system of violence that dislocates and disempowers it demonstrably romanticises the gun and the bomb. It does so by camouflaging the ugliness of violence with a hotchpotch of assumptions – in Fanon's case, a faith in existentialist humanism, a crudely modernist belief in history as progress towards perfection, and a species of psychiatry that suppressed the scraps of evidence within his own clinical reports that showed just how deeply disturbed some individuals are by the agitated hallucinations and terrifying phantoms caused by their own violent acts of liberation.[7] None of these assumptions properly belong in a democratic ethics of violence.

TRENTON

And yet – the qualification is perplexing – there is still plenty of counter-evidence that there are times and places when acts of collective violence serve to lift the spirits of the unfree and unjustly

[7] Jock McCulloch, *Black Soul, White Artifact. Fanon's Clinical Psychology and Social Theory* (Cambridge and New York 1983), especially pp. 93–5.

treated, to give them the courage to stand against those who violate them, even to triumph without proceeding to massacre their conquered opponents. Consider the following example of how character can be positively transformed by civil violence: the American Revolutionary struggle against the British during the 1770s.

The conflict in the American colonies was something of a prototype of the early modern form of collective resistance to despotism, backed by force of arms. True, it was neither a war of national liberation nor a struggle for 'democracy', simply because the revolutionaries thought of themselves as republicans concerned to put an end to popish despotism. And unlike the total wars that followed the French revolution, it is also true that the American struggle for independence was a part-time war. The struggle for territory and military supremacy was subordinated to the battle for the hearts and minds of the population. Soldiers took time off from battle. That is why, even when the American forces were unsure of survival, let alone victory, its troops found time to recuperate from their duties without immediate fear of being dragged away by their British enemies.

Compared with most modern revolutions, it is also true that the American upheaval was self-restrained. It witnessed comparatively small amounts of physical violence, even in the form of threats. The general tactic of smoking out loyalists from the nooks and crannies of civil society by means of purgative rituals such as taking and publishing names, oath taking and threats to confiscate property was widely practised at the local community level, and with considerable success.[8] The tactic of turning suspected loyalists into social outcasts was designed to avoid violence and counter-violence. It effectively confronted loyalists with two choices: to conform, or to leave. No more than one loyalist in eight left the United States, but many more chose to switch localities, most of them unharmed by violence.

[8] John W. Shy, 'Force, order, and democracy in the American Revolution', in *The American Revolution: Its Character and Limits*, ed. Jack P. Greene (New York and London 1987), pp. 78–9.

The Americans' struggle against the British Empire nevertheless relied on the use of civil violence to crush their enemy's will to power, and to build a new federated republic. The point that civil violence was permissible – that it could be used in self-defence for certain foreseen, strictly defined ends[9] – was evidently understood by the underdressed and dispirited American troops preparing for battle at the end of 1776 against the superior forces of the British and Hessian army at Trenton, New Jersey.[10] The battle has since become part of the official American memory of the Revolution, in no small measure because at the time each side grasped, with utter seriousness, that a British victory might well cause the American colonists' struggle to collapse. The Americans, for their part, badly needed a victory to divert the British threat to Philadelphia and to inject new life into their flagging fight for independence. George Washington met the challenge by assembling volunteers from Philadelphia, a regiment of German immigrant units from Charles Lee's command, and a further 500 men sub-commanded by Horatio Gates – about 6,000 troops in all.

In the late-afternoon light of Christmas Day, 1776, officers assembled the American troops into small squads and read to them the text of Thomas Paine's *The American Crisis*. On the eve of battle, its opening sentences must have sounded strangely primeval to the ears of men thinking about death and injury. The words soon became famous and will always remain so until the cause of citizens' freedom is extinguished. 'These are the times that try men's souls', wrote Paine. 'The summer soldier and the sunshine patriot will, in this crisis, shrink from the service of their country; but he that stands it *now*, deserves the love and thanks of man and woman. Tyranny, like hell, is not easily conquered; yet we have this consolation with us, that the harder

---

[9] The ethical and legal issues of whether individuals have a positive right of self-defence and, if so, whether and in which ways there ought to be limits upon the exercise of this right, is explored in Suzanne Uniacke, *Permissible Killing. The Self-Defence Justification of Homicide* (Cambridge and New York 1994).

[10] A fuller account of the background context, details and symbolic significance of the battle for Trenton is presented in my *Tom Paine: A Political Life* (New York and London 1995), ch. 5.

the conflict, the more glorious the triumph.' After nightfall, through a storm of hail and sleet, the American troops were ferried in flat-bottomed boats across the Delaware. They inched towards Trenton. Some of them left trails of blood in the snow from their bandaged or bare feet. Their officers prodded them during halts to keep them from plummeting into an icy sleep from which they might never awake. By daybreak, the troops had reached the outskirts of Trenton. That day, 26 December, had been chosen because, one of Washington's aides remarked, the Hessian mercenaries occupying the town were known to 'make a great deal of Christmas in Germany' and would proba-bly be sick from a surfeit of raucous dancing, schnapps and beer. The American gamble paid handsome dividends. Colonel Johann Gottlieb Rahl, the German commander at Trenton, was caught in his night-shirt. He was later mortally wounded in the heavy street fighting that erupted. By nightfall, the Hessians had been routed; 1,000 men were taken prisoner and, to the Americans' delight, nearly all the enemy stores, including fine German swords and 40 hogsheads of rum, were captured. Trenton was won. Thanks to the musket, the grip of the British Empire on America was loosened – with political and social consequences that are still felt today, in all four corners of the earth.

Violent episodes like the battle of Trenton force a reconsidera-tion of the claim, famously defended by Hannah Arendt, that power and violence have nothing in common. 'Violence can destroy power; it is utterly incapable of creating it', she writes, adding that the category of power should be reserved for peaceful associations of citizens who deliberately speak and act in concert.[11] Violence is by nature instru-mental, Arendt continues. Like all means, it always and everywhere requires guidance and justification, which in turn presupposes a group of people thinking and acting in terms of the distinction between means and ends. Arendt admits that in practice violence and power are commonly intertwined, but her purist insistence on their theoretical

---

[11] Hannah Arendt, *On Violence* (New York and London 1969), pp. 44–56.

division and the primacy of the latter over the former easily lends itself to pacifist misinterpretation; it overlooks those cases (such as the American struggle for Trenton) in which violence and power are *positively* related; and it underestimates the various ways in which the outcome of the violent confrontation of armed power groups acting in concert is often decided not only by power-boosting 'morale', but also by the timing, luck, ferocity and skill with which their weapons are deployed against each other. Violence can indeed destroy power relationships (as happens in despotic regimes, as Montesquieu pointed out), just as power relationships can sometimes stop violence in its tracks. But out of the barrel of a gun violence can also create bonds of solidarity, power relationships in Arendt's sense, where none had existed before.

REVOLUTIONARY VIOLENCE

The propensity, in some circumstances, of violence to raise hopes, to stimulate awareness that things could be otherwise, and to galvanise actors' sense that they are all in the same boat has tempted some modern thinkers to glorify violence. George Sorel's *Réflexions sur la violence* (1908), the classic revolutionary syndicalist recipe for dramatically toppling the state by means of a mass social movement from below, is a striking example of this modern fetish of violence.

Réflexions sur la violence is so intoxicated with the elixir of violence that – in retrospect – it arouses the suspicion that it is wilfully blind to the basic incompatibility between the respective organising principles of violence (the potential annihilation of others) and democracy (the open tolerance of differences).[12] The political context in which the tract was written obviously differs from our own. Amidst the growing involvement of socialist movements in party politics, and

[12] Georges Sorel, *Réflexions sur la violence* (Paris 1908). The following quotations are my own translations from the third edition (Paris 1912), which includes 'Apologie de la violence', first published in *Matin* (18 May 1908). Sorel's earliest sketch of a theory of syndicalist violence appears in *Insegnamenti sociali della economia contemporanea*, written in 1903, but published only in 1906, pp. 53–5.

inspired by a wave of anti-parliamentary activity throughout western Europe after the 1902 Belgian general strike,[13] Sorel's defence of syndicalism was driven by the expectation of a profound crisis of both parliamentary socialist politics and the capitalist system. Drunk on the idea of an 'absolute revolution' of the workers' movement against private property, civil society and the state, Sorel cursed the 'democratic stupidity' of socialist party politics. The parliamentary road to socialism contributes blindly to the growing power and legitimacy of the modern state (Sorel specifically drew upon Tocqueville's account of the rise of democratic despotism). By so strengthening and legitimating the state machinery, parliamentary socialism contradicts its declared aim of eventually abolishing the state. Furthermore, he argued, parliamentary politics masks the contradictory interests of labour and capital. Charmed and seduced by the pettifoggery and chicanery of electoral politics, and especially by promises of social welfare legislation enacted through the state, parliamentary socialism drags the bourgeoisie and the proletariat far from the path assigned them in Marx's theory. Enfeebled classes, Sorel warned, foolishly always put their trust in the protective powers of government.

Sorel also attacked the parliamentarism for indulging the political spirit of Robespierre. Every (attempted) political revolution from the time of 1789, he argued, has strengthened the repressive powers of government. Despite good intentions, a parliamentary socialist government would do the same. There are no greater protagonists of order than victorious revolutionaries. In office – here Sorel anticipated the later argument of Robert Michels – parliamentary socialism would institute a kind of dictatorship of politicians over their followers. Power brokers like Jaurès (a founder of the moderate Parti Socialiste Français) would in practice act no differently than other political revolutionaries, who upon coming to power have always pleaded 'reasons

[13] See Henriette Roland-Holst, *Generalstreik und Sozialdemokratie* (Dresden 1902), especially pp. 53–69; and Phil H. Goodstein, *The Theory of the General Strike from the French Revolution to Poland* (Boulder 1984).

of state' – and accordingly employed repressive legal sanctions and police methods – against their enemies.

Sorel reasoned that dictatorship could be stopped in its tracks only if the socialist movement relied upon the resolute class separatism of the proletariat. Its militant refusal of centralised political leadership, its native sympathy for violent action and its growing belief in the efficacy of strikes – all this exposed the fraudulence of ruling-class attempts to mediate state and civil society through parliamentary politics. The violence of the proletariat, its willingness forcibly to take matters into its own hands, sharply polarises civil society. It comes to resemble a field of battle between two antagonistic armies. Note Sorel's proto-fascist conviction that violence has its charms, that it has a deeply aesthetic dimension, that it needs therefore to be liberated from the chains of means–ends calculation. 'The strike is a phenomenon of war', he wrote. Proletarian violence, 'beautiful and very heroic', has emancipating effects. It is honest salvation from the hypocrisy of bourgeois barbarism. The new middle class of salaried bureaucrats crumbles. Capitalist employers (note Sorel's belief in History) are forced to play the class role ascribed to them by history. Class divisions are deepened and simplified, just when they seemed in danger of rotting in the marsh of parliamentary politics. Proletarian direct action, originating in the small-scale, face-to-face *sociétés de résistance* of the trade unions, lances the boils of violence within the bourgeois property and state systems. Direct action also snaps the chains of bourgeois habit and cowardice, and produces a new culture of solidarity in civil society. No longer blinded by party politics, the proletariat is ever more guided and inspired by myth. Sorel here drew upon Henri-Louis Bergson; when they are believed, clusters of shared, emotionally charged mental pictures, such as the myth of a general strike laced with violence, sharpen workers' determination to work towards a socialist future. The proletariat, initially in but not of civil society, ceases to be acted upon. It becomes a living social movement in possession of itself. It becomes capable of acting against the power of capital and its state apparatus, without the mediation of the party form or the party system. This process crystallises in the actual drama of the general strike, which Sorel, in a telling comparison, likened to a Napoleonic battle that crushes its adversary outright. The general strike of workers makes it clear, Sorel concluded, that only two historical options remain open to the socialist movement: either bourgeois decadence or the violent struggles of the proletariat to seize productive property and (note Sorel's reductionism) to abolish the state.

ANTI-PARTY POLITICS

Parallels have sometimes been drawn between Sorel's revolutionary syndicalism and the strategy of anti-party politics that developed in central-eastern Europe between the Prague Spring and the so-called 'velvet' revolutions of 1989. Notwithstanding their wholly different political vocabularies, it is true that the protagonists of anti-party politics shared with the Sorelian strategy a deep antipathy to party politics and to state power. But there the parallel ended. The differences are not just of historical interest. They are worth examining because they tell us much about how, under difficult political circumstances, democratic ways of life can successfully problematise violence, to the point where it becomes possible to envisage a polity that neither relies upon violence as the ultimate weapon in politics nor considers (in Sorel's words) violence 'beautiful and very heroic'.

To begin with, most public defenders of the strategy of anti-party politics (representatives of groups such as Solidarność and Charta 77) were deeply suspicious of ideological myths. They rejected the Sorelian assumption that a single revolutionary class, arising out of the heart of civil society, could ever embody *la volonté générale*. Anti-party politics – it is summarised here in ideal-typical terms – was a pluralistic and not a monistic type of opposition. That was why – again in contrast to Sorel – it rejected the myth of the abolition or withering away of the state. A democratic society, one containing and openly valuing many different, often tensely related interests, was seen to require a framework of governing institutions, which can help prevent the outbreak of serious domestic conflict, as well as negotiate with other governments elsewhere on the face of the earth. Hence, anti-party politics aimed not to abolish political power, but rather to 'socialise' some portion of it, to create a civil society in order to prevent the encroachment of government upon matters which were considered, simply speaking, none of its business.

The democratic opposition to Soviet-type, one-party systems also rejected Sorelian myths of brave and heroic violence. Sorel some-times tempered his affection for the charms of violence. In less san-guine moments, he supposed that the nature of violence was to serve as a cold-blooded means for the realisation of a world-historical end. 'Proletarian acts of violence . . . are purely and simply acts of war', he wrote, 'Everything in war is carried on without hatred and without the spirit of revenge: in war the vanquished are not killed; non-combatants are not made to bear the consequences of the disappointments which armies may have experienced on the battlefield.'[14] The opponents of Soviet-style totalitarianism rejected this 'just war' line of argument as dangerous. 'Taught by history', wrote Adam Michnik, 'we suspect that by using force to storm the Bastilles of old we shall unwittingly build new ones.' He continued: 'The experience of being corrupted by terror must be implanted upon the consciousness of everyone who belongs to a freedom movement. Otherwise, as Simone Weil wrote, freedom will again become a refugee from the camp of the victors.'[15] Violence consumes and de-moralises the person who uses it. 'Castro wanted a free Cuba', Michnik observed, at a critical moment when Solidarność had its back to the wall:

> But in the revolutionary struggle against Batista, he was corrupted by power. Whoever uses violence to gain power uses violence to maintain power. Whoever is taught to use violence cannot relinquish it. In our century, the struggle for freedom has been

---

[14] Sorel, *Réflexions sur la violence*, p. 161.
[15] Adam Michnik, 'Letter from the Gdansk Prison', *The New York Review of Books*, 18 July 1985, p. 44.

fixed on power, instead of the creation of civil society. It has
therefore always ended up in the concentration camp.[16]

Living under a heavily armed regime that ensured that surveillance, military parades, prison and fears of violence were everyday
companions of the whole population, the democratic oppositions of
central-eastern Europe understandably developed a profound antipathy towards the deployment of violence.[17] They consequently associated bravery not with heroic acts of violence (such as terrorism,
assassinations or kidnappings) against their perceived enemies, but
with the civilised patience of citizens who seek to live decently in an
indecent regime and therefore remain unmoved by acts of violence
directed against them. Writers such as Michnik saw an inner con-
nection between violence and politics. They consequently rejected
the view that violence is the midwife of every old society pregnant
with a new one (Marx). Violence was instead seen as synonymous
with haemorrhages and miscarriages – even the death of the body
politic – caused by the forceps of revolution. Violence functioned as
the enemy of all societies, old and new. Again in contrast to Sorel, the
democratic oppositions developed a fundamentally different sense of
time. They rejected fantasies of apocalyptic revolution because they
sensed that a precondition of democratic government and an open civil

---

[16] Adam Michnik, 'Towards a Civil Society: Hopes for Polish democracy', an interview with Erica Blair (John Keane), *Times Literary Supplement*, 19–25 February
1988, reprinted in *Letters from Freedom. Post-Cold War Realities and Perspectives*
(Berkeley and London 1998), pp. 96–113 (at p. 107).

[17] The experience of omnipresent violence was expressed sharply during this period in a
well-known Polish anecdote, dating back to the early 1950s, when sections of Polish
industry were restructured to produce arms. A father badly needed a pram for his
newborn child. Unable to find one anywhere in the shops of Warsaw, he approached
a friend, who happened to be working in a factory which manufactured prams – or
so he thought. The friend promised to fetch him a pram, piece by piece. Each day,
the pram factory worker brought his friend bits and pieces, carefully smuggled out
of the factory by stuffing them into his heavy winter overcoat. A fortnight later, the
two friends decided that they now had a complete set of parts. But, the anecdote ran,
when they came to assemble the bits and pieces they found that they had actually
built a machine-gun.

society is that citizens acquire a measure of patience. They envisaged a peaceful transformation of the one-party system by means of a slowly ripening development of civil society underneath the edifice of state power.

Prior to the 1989 revolutions, finally, the protagonists of anti-party politics shunned violence because they sensed that the possibility of a civil society and political democracy depends upon shaking off the presence of the one-party system within each and every individual by altering the relations of power 'closest' to them. Those who lived a life of anti-party politics rejected the innocent fiction that power in the one-party system was a thing to be grasped or abolished. Power was not seen to be concentrated in a single place (for instance, in the leading echelons of the Party or, in Sorel's version, within the ruling bourgeois class). The ruling regime was not divided between those who had power and those who were powerless. The one-party system was rather viewed as omnipresent and omnivorous, as a labyrinth of tunnels and caves in which control, violent repression, fear and self-censorship swallow up everybody, at the very least by rendering them silent, amoral and marked by some undesirable prejudices of the powerful. Since the lines of power organised by the one-party system were seen to pass through all its subjects, ran the reasoning, civilians could defend themselves against it only by being different in the most radical sense – by driving the system and its violence out of their own personal lives. Democratic opposition was seen for this reason to be most effective when it keeps its distance from the one-party system. Democratisation was considered not merely a matter, say, of replacing party-appointed officials with a government or head of state elected once every few years. Democratisation rather depended on 'returning to Europe' by successfully cultivating non-violent mechanisms of self-protection, individuation and social cooperation in areas of life 'underneath' the party-dominated state: in the household, among friends, in the publishing initiative, the workplace, the parallel economy, and in the sphere of unofficial culture.

JUDGING VIOLENCE

What is the relevance, if any, of this way of thinking about violence for democratic politics? The principled commitment of the democratic opposition in central-eastern Europe to the strategy of non-violence arguably highlighted the advantages of pacifist strategies, at least under certain conditions. To begin with, principled pacifism, insofar as it complements the plurality of identities that add zest to a democracy, is certainly a legitimate way of life for subjects enjoying a government-protected civil society. Haunted by a world that is full of violence, principled pacifism adds to citizens' sense that they have a choice, that this world contains options – that it is dangerous and, hence, in principle, in need of the democratisation and reduction of *surplus* violence, even the elimination of *all* violence. Partly the non-violent option does this by ringing alarm bells. Pacifism warns against the unpredictable effects and unintended consequences of the strategic reliance upon violent means. And – trapped within a triangle of violence – it heaps doubt upon each and every version, old and new, of the doctrine of the 'final conflict' or 'victory in the war against terrorism'. It rejects as dangerous nonsense talk of 'final solutions', or of wars 'to end all wars' or of violence to 'end violence'. It disbelieves chatter about 'the final revolutionary struggle' to unite humanity – or the contemporary doctrines that certain instruments of destruction are so frightening that they will never be used, or that they are so perfect they are safe to use. The principled commitment to non-violence emphasises that violence is incompatible with democracy – that it is *anti-social*. For this reason, as Martin Luther King Jr often pointed out when defending pacifism as a tension-creating strategy, non-violent resistance also operates as a utopia, signalling to the present or future citizens of any democracy that a world in which there is less violence or no violence is thinkable, perhaps even achievable.[18]

---

[18] See, for example, King, 'Letter from Birmingham City Jail (April 16, 1963)', in James Melvin Washington (ed.), *A Testament of Hope. The Essential Writings of Martin*

The potency of this utopia is always reinforced when peaceful but bold actions win out in circumstances seemingly hostile to the pacifist option. Not only does non-violent collective action often nurture individuals' capacity to overcome their fears and strengthen their courage to act creatively and cooperatively.[19] There are also times when non-violent protest literally disarms violent power. The dramatic victory of Greenpeace against the world's largest oil multinational company, Royal Dutch Shell, in the North Sea in the summer of 1995 – when activists occupied the obsolete Brent Spar platform in order to prevent its sinking – is a remarkable example of collective action guided by principled non-violence. So too is the exemplary boldness of public figures like M. K. Gandhi and Martin Luther King, or the brave action of civil society actors like Aung San Suu Kyi, who defied a cordon of heavily armed Burmese soldiers by walking slowly towards them, silently daring them to disobey orders – shouted three times – to open fire on her, forcing them to look away in disgrace, to lower their rifles, and to allow her to pass gracefully through the cordon, flanked by her stunned supporters.[20] Such episodes of courage serve as a basic reminder of two points: that violence is the scourge of democracy, simply because violence is the intended or half-intended denial of the physical and mental being-in-the-world of an individual or group of (potential) civilians; and that violence can and often does beget violence, that violence is a wild horse, and that those who ride it can end up on the ground, badly hurt and dragging others in their train, towards their death.

Luther King Jr. (San Francisco 1986), p. 291: 'we must see the need of having non-violent gadflies to create the kind of tension in society that will help men [sic] to rise from the dark depths of prejudice and racism to the majestic heights of understanding and brotherhood'.

[19] Ample evidence of these effects of non-violent public action is cited in Gene Sharp, *The Politics of Nonviolent Action* (Boston 1973); and Frederic Solomon and Jacob R. Fishman, 'The psychosocial meaning of nonviolence in student civil rights activities', *Psychiatry*, 25 (1964), pp. 227–36.

[20] M. K. Gandhi, *Non-Violent Resistance (Satyagraha)* (New York 1951), pp. 77–90; Martin Luther King, Jr., 'Letter from Birmingham City Jail'; and Aung San Suu Kyi, *The Voice of Hope* (London 1997).

The fact that those who use violence are often themselves violated, such that violence kills off the potential democrat in both the violator and the violated, is often downplayed by the intellectual critics of pacifism. They prefer instead to point out that the dogmatic commitment to an ultimate goal grounded in a First Principle, of which religious or moral (as distinct from tactical) pacifism is an example, often produces philosophical and political muddles that are incompatible with democratic politics. These critics of dogmatic pacifism have a point, broached in Orwell's jibe that following the war against Nazism there was a question that 'every pacifist had a clear obligation to answer . . . "What about the Jews? Are you prepared to see them exterminated? If not, how do you propose to save them without resorting to war?"'[21] Orwell was right to ask this question – and he was right as well to point out one absurd consequence of Gandhi's particular brand of pacifism, which rested upon the teaching that God exists and that the world of solid objects is an illusion to be escaped from: his recommendation that German Jews should have committed collective suicide in order to draw the world's attention to their plight.

Gandhi found himself trapped in moral tangles more frequently than is usually realised by his latter-day supporters and critics alike. Non-violence (*ahimsā*) was for him required of a world suffused by the eternal Divine. Within this earthly order, each individual is endowed with a unique self (*swabhāva*) and her or his own unique truth (*sat*), which implies that all people are required to respect the truths of other selves. Hence, the principle of non-violence means 'active love' of others: protecting them from harm or destruction and promoting their well-being. Non-violence serves as an absolute and indivisible norm.

[21] George Orwell, 'Reflections on Gandhi', *Selections from Essays and Journalism: 1931–1949* (London 1981), p. 838. Note Orwell's addition: 'If you are not prepared to take life, you must often be prepared for lives to be lost in some other way. When in 1942, Gandhi . . . urged non-violent resistance against a Japanese invasion, he was ready to admit that it might cost several million deaths' (*ibid.*). The best account of Gandhi's richly suggestive but poorly coordinated theory of non-violence is Bhikhu Parekh, *Colonialism, Tradition and Reform*, revised edition (New Delhi 1999), chs. 4–3.

It reminds people of the possibility and desirability of a world liberated from violence (*himsā*). Principled non-violence confronts and shames those who are violent with the evils they commit; and it nurtures creative experiments that aim to perfect the techniques of disarming them with energetic love. Non-violence aims to drown the islands and continents of cruelty in 'an ocean of compassion'. When asked if violence was justified in restraining a lunatic on a murderous rampage, Gandhi was emphatic. 'There must be within you an upwelling of love and pity towards the wrong-doer', he replied. 'When there is that feeling, it will express itself through some action. It may be a sign, a glance, even silence. But such as it is, it will melt the heart of the wrong-doer and check the wrong.'[22]

Gandhi was sometimes less sure that the pure norm of non-violence was indivisible. He acknowledged, with regret, that human existence on earth was impossible without inflicting violence on other living organisms; since each animal, plant and vegetable was alive, the human body was a malevolent 'house of slaughter'. There were times as well when wilfully killing others was justified because it emancipated them from unbearable pain. The avoidance of violence also sometimes required defensive violence, as when (Gandhi reasoned) the Polish resistance committed acts of violence against the Nazis, or when prisoners resisted their torturers, or when women used their 'nails and teeth' and other forms of physical strength to repel men who tried to rape them. Principled non-violence, Gandhi concluded, was one value among others (like truth, self-respect and national independence). That was why violence was 'understandable' and 'infinitely better than cowardice' or 'passive, effeminate and helpless submission'.[23] Gandhi's difficulties suggest that the pacifist struggle for a peaceful world, one that relies on the tactical principle that the use of violence is forbidden, can be self-contradictory. Especially in

[22] Raghavan Iyer, *The Moral and Political Writings of Mahatma Gandhi* (Oxford 1987), vol. 2, p. 432.
[23] Gandhi's remarks are cited in Bhikhu Parekh, *Colonialism, Tradition and Reform*, revised edition (New Delhi 1999), pp. 147–51.

circumstances when the renunciation of violence, or the hesitation to use it, results in the annihilation of its victims – nowadays this might be called the blue helmet (the UN in Bosnia-Herzegovina) syndrome – non-violence succours the violent. It stands accused of ignoring the possibility that the actual or threatened use of counter-violence might have had demonstrably pacifying effects by convincing the aggressor to take the finger off the trigger, or even to lay down arms, and to live and let live. Hence we come to Max Weber's hard-nosed remark: 'No ethics in the world can sidestep the fact that in many instances the attainment of "good" ends is bound to the fact that one must be willing to pay the price of using morally dubious means or at least dangerous ones – and facing the possibility or even the probability of evil ramifications.'[24]

Given the potentially unpredictable ('good' and 'bad') consequences of the decision to use or not to use violence for certain defined ends, democratic politics is well advised to reject both dogmatic pacifism and the fetish of violence. Both indulge the same commitment to some kind of absolute normative principle, and to its implied means. Both approaches therefore cloud and confuse an already complex normative and tactical issue. They can even succour the violent and so increase the probability of violence in human affairs. Democratic thinking and politics should reject all talk of the need for a General Theory of Violence based on formal ethical principles and abstract-general reasoning. It is true that the rejection of such ethical algebra does not resolve anything except the need to be politically aware of what can and must be avoided – like cases of wanton violence perpetrated against others. And it is obvious that the rejection of absolute formulae is unlikely to impress or silence either those for whom violence is by definition anathema or those who are so in love with violence that in certain contexts, like revolutions or a civil society that is crumbling, they are prone to regard violence as an indispensable means or a thrilling end in itself. There are indeed

---

[24] Max Weber, 'Politik als Beruf', in *Gesammelte Politische Schriften*, ed. Johannes Winckelmann (Tübingen 1958), p. 540.

people – crude-minded anarchists, bomb-planting terrorists, fanatical advocates of a version of *jihad* not sanctioned by the Qur'an, deranged members of millenarian cults, murderous street thugs – who would laugh at the suggestion that violence can or should be subject to reasonable talk or considerations of democratic procedure. They believe they have Right or Necessity on their side. If they were to think about the matter at all they would quickly conclude that their own fetish of violence is universal in the sense that it is absolutely justified and applicable to each and every conceivable context. Unconvinced by talk of pluralism and civil society and democracy, they simply want to reach for the trigger, to kill or to maim others.

When confronted by such types, democracies are left with only one option: to arrest the violent or, if they resist arrest violently, to deal with them by using violent means. Violence – publicly accountable and subject in principle to strict limits – becomes an effective remedy against the fetishists of violence, who are themselves trapped in a lethal performative contradiction. By practising their absolutist principle of violence, they imply that violence can or should have no ethical or geographic limits – even when it is directed at them. Thomas Hobbes demonstrated why: if even just a few people in the world accepted or lived according to the absolutists' principle of unrestricted violence, then nobody would be safe. The fetishists of violence would have to live with the consequences of an absolute principle – strictly applied, in the age of nuclear weapons and dirty bombs and other forms of triangulated violence. That would of course result in the termination of their and others' worlds within a matter of minutes or hours. No doubt, the fanatics of violence, for instance Timothy McVeigh (chief architect of the 1995 Oklahoma City bombing) or a suicide bomber like 17-year-old Bilal Fahs, one of the first Lebanese 'martyrs',[25] might accept that outcome. They would do so in the name of some type of earthly absolute or transcendental religious standard that effectively aestheticises violence as both a means and an end. They

---

[25] Martin Kramer, 'Sacrifice and "self-martyrdom" in Shi'ite Lebanon', *Terrorism and Political Violence*, 3, 3 (Autumn 1991), pp. 30–47.

would massacre innocents in defence of 'freedom' or strap explosives to their bodies and go out to die, along with their enemies, treating the outcome as an act of sacrifice or divine duty executed in accordance with some theological principle or higher secular imperative. But if, in a moment of humility, the fanatics of violence were to face up to the possibility that their unswerving commitment to violence, when universally applied, would destroy everybody and everything in the world, then on pragmatic grounds alone they would be forced to recognise that their own fetish of violence is unacceptable to others. If only to preserve their own skins, they would be forced to compromise. They would be obliged to accept that the violence principle has to be limited – that the use of violence must be restricted by regarding it as a *means* of achieving some designated end that is necessarily subject to calculations that highlight the possible contradiction between ends that are desired and the means that are chosen for their pursuit.

It goes without saying that every society and age has recognised the need to tame and restrain the means of violence. The repertoire of symbolic and institutional restraints is remarkably wide indeed, but what is unique about democratic ways of thinking and acting is that full and unembarrassed recognition is given to the vexed relationship between the ideals of democracy and the use of violence. From the perspective of a democratic politics, the systematic, unrestrained use of violence – the total and totalising violence that is unique to modern, European-type societies – is anathema. Democracy involves the democratisation of violence. It demands the perception that the term violence is publicly contestable – and stretchable enough to cover acts that once were not considered violent. Democracy rejects the presumption that violence is 'natural' or God-given or somehow rooted in the way things are. It holds those who use violence or control the means of violence publicly accountable. It rests upon mechanisms that ensure that violence is seen as contingent and removable. And in matters of violence – and all other matters as well – democracy involves the rejection of pseudo-universal First Principles. Its institutions of publicly accountable government and an open and equal civil society provide a viable and potent ethic that treats these institutions as both a necessary precondition and consequence of moral pluralism.[26] That ethical commitment to plural forms of life implies that there is an elective affinity – but not an absolute law-like bond – between non-violence and democracy. From a democratic perspective, violence is 'bad', but not always so. Violence can be deemed 'good' only when it serves as an effective means of creating or strengthening a peaceful civil society secured by publicly accountable political-legal institutions. Democracy requires commitment to the rule that violence is only justified when it serves to *reduce* or *eradicate* violence. The converse rule applies: considered as a means to a designated end, violence can be considered 'bad' insofar as it both contradicts that end, veers out of control or results in growing quantities of *surplus* violence within the specific social context or wider body politic in which it is used. One implication of this rule is clear: the development, stockpiling or use of nuclear weapons is always bad. So too are 'dirty bombs' and biochemical weapons – as are hand-held guns that swarm like locusts through a community.

Formulated in this way, democratic reasoning is not wedded dogmatically to pacifist strategies – despite the fact that democracy thrives on non-violence and points ultimately to a world without violence. This of course begs the question of when and where violence is legitimate under democratic conditions – of how to spot the times when it is justified to use certain forms of violence for particular purposes against one's designated opponents. This question cannot be answered formulaically. It can be answered only tentatively and by means of decisions that are formulated and applied within the unique conditions of specific temporal and spatial contexts.

Such an approach – in effect, the commitment to the politics of democratising violence in all its forms – most certainly does not

---

[26] See the longer discussion of ethics and morals in the final section of my *Global Civil Society?* (London 2003).

mean that anything goes, or that the practical use of violence and considerations about the ethics of violence are subject to the laws of blindness and arbitrariness. On pragmatic grounds alone, a democratic ethic of measured violence is opposed unconditionally to weapons that have 'overkill' effects. Besides, the decision to use or to refrain from using violence is subject to normative restraints. It is a matter of *judgement* in the philosophical sense. Judgement, the learned capacity to choose courses of action in contexts riddled with complexity, is among the chief democratic arts. It relies neither on the rules of deduction or induction nor the conjectural thinking of abduction. Judgement avoids flights of fancy as much as it shuns practical reason in the Kantian sense. Practical reason 'reasons' by telling actors what to do and what not to do. It lays down the law in the language of imperatives, like 'Thou shalt not kill', or 'An eye for an eye'.

Judgement avoids categorical imperatives that instruct those who act always to act in such a way that the criteria of their acts can become a general law. Judgement tacks between the unique and the general. It is neither 'reflective' nor 'determinant' (to use the highly questionable distinction drawn by Kant to describe decisions that derive general rules from the particular, or derive the particular from the general, respectively[27]). Judgement instead involves the recognition that the practical choice of how to act in any context must be guided by the appreciation of its particularity. Another way of putting that recognition is to say that judgement entails the recognition that this context is unique or different from what we are used to, and that therefore we need to compare and to contrast it with previous or contemporaneous situations that more or less resemble the particular situation at hand.

---

[27] The distinction between *die reflektierende Urteilskraft* and *die bestimmende Urteilskraft* is developed in Immanuel Kant's introduction to *Kritik der Urteilskraft*, in *Werkausgabe*, ed. Wilhelm Weischedel (Frankfurt am Main 1974), vol. X, sect. 5.

GEORG ELSER

The need to recognise that we know that we do not know what is to be done, that decisions require judgements, and that judgements lie within the field of force between the particular and the general, are quintessential features of the art of judgement that, paradoxically, rescue it from mere arbitrariness. In matters of violence, from a democratic perspective, we can say that the most plausible working maxim is: the decision to use or not to use violence for political or social ends, whether in the household or on the battlefield, is always risky, and plagued by ongoing confusion and unintended consequences, some of which sometimes quite unpredictably contradict the stated purpose for which violence was considered the appropriate or effective means. Ethical judgements about the utility and effects of violence are therefore necessary. In matters of violence, to be sure, defenders of a civil society and publicly accountable government must recognise that violence normally – but not always – contradicts and erodes civility. But before putting this precept on a pedestal, they must also recognise that the most dangerous thing confronting citizens is not that they will violate or be violated, or kill or be killed. Far worse is their *abstention* from making judgements about violence by surrendering blindly or sheepishly to the prevailing means of violence and extant relationships of armed or potentially armable power. In matters of violence, the friends of democracy should not forget Georg Elser: the humble quarryman who came within 10 minutes of blasting Adolf Hitler to smithereens in Munich's Bürgerbräu-Keller, and who understood well that those who flow with the tide risk ending up on the rocks of the devils' islands.

The delicate and often dangerous process of context-bound judging, exemplified here by the brave action of Georg Elser, is of interest not only to political philosophers. There is evidence that it is of concern as well to citizens who themselves routinely practise judgement calls within actually existing democracies, as has been demonstrated in an early study by Janie Ward of everyday conceptions of violence among American adolescents of mixed ethnic background.[28] A majority of respondents in this sample had themselves suffered or witnessed violence within the household or neighbourhood. Not surprisingly, most displayed a sophisticated capacity to reason morally about the subject. A minority of respondents, those with a reflective understanding of 'care' as the basic principle needed to resolve conflicts in human relationships, typically found violence intrinsically wrong. They reasoned that violence hurt people and was 'unnecessary, since it could have been avoided through dialogue'. When pressed to assess the ethics of the actions of people who felt that they had no other means than violence to protect themselves and others from danger, the same respondents considered violence understandable, but morally wrong.

A majority of respondents, by contrast, judged that judgements about violence were necessary, and that violence was therefore justifiable within certain circumstances. Ward distinguished three different, but related types of moral judgement exercised by her respondents. Those who thought in terms of the principle of 'rule- and rights-governed justice' considered violence appropriate when used to remedy or avenge undeserved punishment or unfair treatment. Those who instead combined 'justice' with 'care' criteria considered that in circumstances when a person was pushed to the limit and left with no other option, a woman using retaliatory violence to put an end to her suffering at the hands of a man, for instance, she or he was justified in resorting to violence, which was usually seen as an act of empowerment. A third group of respondents, those for whom ideas about 'justice' and 'care' were not simply combined but actually inseparable, judged violence – within certain clearly defined boundaries – to be a 'fair', 'tolerable' and 'acceptable' means of protecting the self and others from the danger of irreparable harm.

---

[28] Janie Victoria Ward, 'Urban adolescents' conceptions of violence', in Carol Gilligan *et al.* (eds.), *Mapping the Moral Domain* (Cambridge, MA 1988), pp. 175–200.

Ten rules for democratising violence

> No example is so dangerous as that of violence employed by
> well-meaning people for beneficial objects.
>
> Alexis de Tocqueville (1856)

THINKING REMEDIES

Greater clarity about the ethics of violence is important for democratic politics. So too is the careful consideration of the *means* that can be used legitimately to reduce or to prevent *surplus* violence. Every effort to reduce or rid the world of violence must try to prevent the fetish or 'aestheticisation' of violence. Attention must instead be paid to the degree of compatibility between the chosen means and the end in sight, and to the possible or probable unintended consequences of a chosen course of action. Nietzsche's wise advice should be heeded: 'Whoever fights monsters, should see to it that in the process they do not become a monster. And when you look long into an abyss, the abyss also looks into you.'[1] The democratisation of violence additionally requires greater sensitivity to the repertoire of viable strategies for eliminating violence in the world around us. Their type and number is bewilderingly broad. Towards the non-violent end of the spectrum are all those 'soft' means, including civil disobedience, 'truth and reconciliation' tribunals, psychotherapy and the due process of law backed by the threat of punishment. Harder means include the police use of pepper spray and rubber bullets, secret surveillance and government-enforced amnesties for handing in weapons. The toughest means – the calculated use of violence, sometimes in ferocious quantities, to repel violence through warfare – are the most life-threatening, both for people and democratic institutions. Decisions about whether

---

[1] Friedrich Nietzsche, *Beyond Good and Evil*, trans. Walter Kaufmann (New York 1966), p. 89 (translation altered).

and when any of these methods of pacification are compatible with democracy are controversial. It is clear that a moratorium ought to be placed on the production and use of weapons – nuclear bombs, for instance – that have the technical capacity to kill and maim people and their environment and to do so on a vast scale in a frightening manner. Matters of judgement nevertheless do not disappear in efforts to rid the world of surplus violence. Given that the act of ridding the world of nuclear weapons is desirable, how is this best achieved? What weapons systems, if any, would replace the bomb? How will nuclear plants and weapons undergo de-commissioning, and can legal compensation and something like 'truth and reconciliation' processes help the world come to terms with the long history of suffering and long-term damage caused by the invention of the bomb? Given that apocalyptic terrorism operates like a deadly worm within the entrails of democracies and the institutions of (global) civil society upon which they rest, what activist forms of surveillance, policing and military action are required to defeat it militarily, and thus to reduce the civilian fears that it induces? To what extent are these means compatible with the goal of preserving the institutions and spirit of democracy, which (we know from many historical examples) can suffer implosion and – under extreme conditions – democide when threatened by fear and violence? Can civil society initiatives complement what can be achieved through the counter-intelligence and counter-violence of the police and the armed forces?

In various times and places, under pressure from such questions, 'softer' or 'harder' means may be considered as legitimate and effective ways of defending or promoting democratic ways of life. By definition, their appropriateness depends upon circumstances, and so it cannot be the job of political reflection to legislate in advance the 'right' or 'proper' way of democratically ridding the world of violence. In matters of violence, simple-minded morality plays should be avoided. Far more can be learned (to stick to literary analogies) from the espionage novels of Graham Greene: especially the way they probe complex situations in which appearances are deceptive, ready-made formulae don't work and judgements are as necessary as they are fraught with potentially evil consequences. Yet while detailed policy proposals and political tactics remain ineluctably context-dependent, careful reflection upon the subject of violence and democracy can usefully clarify and highlight their probable advantages and disadvantages. In the dirty business of violence, given just how threatening it can be for democracy, political thinking should especially concentrate on defining what counts as *surplus* violence and what should *not* be done – and on sketching the corresponding ways of thinking and acting that tend to ensure that such mistakes are avoided. For this purpose, efforts to democratise violence can profitably rely on rules that serve as guides to action in specific contexts. Although these democratic rules are by definition prudential rather than providential, they can have positively democratic effects. For citizens and policymakers alike, *ten* such rules are especially pertinent.

The first rule: *always try to understand the motives and context of the violent.* The methods of dealing effectively with incivility in its milder or murderous forms necessarily vary not only according to time and place; the methods need to be tailored as well to the form and motives of the violence to be resisted, or dispensed with. Sometimes distinctions about the forms and motives of the violent are difficult to draw, and not only because motives melt away when violence is bureaucratised. Some violence is so dastardly that motives at first seem irrelevant. Any person with democratic instincts easily feels at least an ounce of empathy with the narrator of Jorge Semprun's *The Long Voyage*: 'There's no point trying to understand the S.S.; it suffices to exterminate them.'[2] Similar blood vengeance impulses – 'flog 'em, 'ang 'em' – reportedly surface among audiences watching prime-time television treatments of violence that is shocking in its cruelty. The instincts aroused by such coverage tend to reinforce the impression of sameness – that it's the same old violence and that those responsible are 'sick' and in need of the cell, or a few seconds on the electric chair.

[2] Jorge Semprun, *The Long Voyage* (Toronto 1964), p. 71.

Kicking the habit of thinking of violence through undifferentiated and motive-less categories becomes difficult. This has unfortunate policy consequences, for as Hans Toch and others have argued, in the field of criminal violence, it is impossible to develop effective sentencing practices and responsive treatment programmes unless the undifferentiated mass of 'violent offenders' is broken down into more meaningful clusters. Only when that is done can more discriminating identifications of causes and effects and more sensitive prescriptions for control become possible. The seasoned mugger is not the disturbed sex offender; the impulsive burglar is neither the professional burglar nor the calculating terrorist nor the chronic disturbed exploder.[3]

The analytic recognition of these different categories is a precondition of understanding the motives of the violent, who are *typically* individuals who have suffered past or present humiliation. James Gilligan summarises well the complexities of the point: even the most apparently 'insane' violence, he argues, has an intelligible meaning to the person who commits it. Among the gifts of psychoanalysis to democracy is its will to explore and explain the motivations of those who are violent. Violence is never the product simply of a *mens rea* – an 'evil mind', as judges are wont to say – nor can it be categorised under the legal concept of 'insanity', which reduces a violent person to the status of an animal, or a thing that is incapable of judgement or responsibility for its own actions.

'Psychoanalytically', argues Gilligan, 'all behaviour, including violent behaviour, whether it is labelled as "bad" or "mad", is psychologically meaningful. But until it is understood, it cannot be prevented – that is, brought under individual and societal self-control.'[4] The roots of face-to-face human violence are always enigmatic, but they are most often traceable to the dispositions of

---

[3] Hans Toch and Kenneth Adams, *The Disturbed and Violent Offender* (New Haven and London 1989).

[4] James Gilligan, *Violence: Reflections on Our Deadliest Epidemic* (London 2000), p. 9.

character first learned in the household, then later confirmed in adult life. A randomly chosen case: Bilal Fahs, responsible for victimising others in Amal's first 'self-martyring' operation in 1984, was himself a victim of early abuse. Born into poverty, he lived his early years in a one-room cinder-block house with slum-standard amenities; his penniless father sold vegetables from a cart. A few months after his birth, Bilal's mother separated from his father, who remarried and had more children. The house was crowded beyond endurance, and Bilal, paralysed by feelings of neglect, was sent off to live in another single-room dwelling, this time with his paternal grandmother.

The case of Bilal Fahs suggests the rule that men of violence are typically victimised during childhood. Physical abuse, sexual exploitation, ridicule, rejection: such experiences can produce humiliation so deep that they begin to feel like decomposing rubbish. They become living dead who turn to violence as the only way of avenging injustice. Seen in this way, the function of violence is to stop others in their tracks, to muffle their insulting laughter, to make them cry instead, so extracting from the world a measure of what is perceived to be justice. It is no accident that most violent, face-to-face crimes in this world are committed against other men by men who are desperate, in the face of humiliation, to shore up their 'manhood' by defending themselves through the most desperate act: violating the body of another.

The rule that violence is always bound up with the context and motives of its agents has an important implication: that descriptions of violence as a timeless substratum of the human condition should be rejected wherever and in whatever form they surface. The 'ontologisation' of violence comes in many guises, ranging from vernacular descriptions of 'human nature' as naturally or essentially prone to violence through to sophisticated philosophical claims, such as Jacques Derrrida's reflections on justice.[5] Derrida warns against

---

[5] Jacques Derrida, 'Force of law: the "Mystical Foundations of Authority"', *Cardozo Law Review*, 11, 919 (1990), pp. 927–45.

the intellectual tendency within some strands of deconstructionism to give 'authorization to violent, unjust, arbitrary force'. He quotes Pascal:

> Force without justice is tyrannical. Justice without force is contradictory, as there are always the wicked; force without justice is accused of wrong. And so it is necessary to put justice and force together; and for this, to make sure that what is just be strong, or what is strong be just

> ['la force sans la justice est tyrannique. La justice sans force est contredite, parce qu'il y a toujours des méchants; la force sans la justice est accusée. Il faut donc mettre ensemble la justice et la force; et pour cela faire que ce qui est juste soit fort, ou que ce qui est fort soit juste].

Derrida draws from Pascal the observation that violence and law are twins, then transforms that proposition into the generative claim that within any context the emergence of systems of law and justice is *always* attended by the exercise of violence; no violence, no legal judgements, no justice. Insinuating that social and political life can never be rid of violence, and that foolish are those who think otherwise, Derrida's deconstructionism ignores its own warnings against the ontologisation of violence. 'The very emergence of justice and law', he concludes, 'the rounding and justifying moment that institutes law implies a performative force, which is always an interpretative force . . . Its very moment of foundation or institution . . . [is] a *coup de force* . . . that in itself is neither just nor unjust.'

Vernacular descriptions of 'human nature' as naturally or essentially violent are equally problematic. Exactly because democratic ways of life inflate and probe the sense that human nature is contingent, the resort to lugubrious accounts of so-called 'human nature' is undemocratic. Such pessimistic ontologies suffer from a short and flawed memory,[6] on which basis they then eternalise what is in fact temporally contingent. Best described as a species of the dogma of original sin, stripped of the fear or mention of God, these ontologies are in practice of little or no help in resolving or reducing incivility in the institutions of either government or civil society. Sometimes they serve as apologias of frightful violence. Consider the ideologies of 'primitivism', which suppose (for instance) that killing on the scale witnessed in Bosnia-Herzegovina or in Rwanda during the 1990s is what one would expect from such regions. For such ideologies, the very words 'Balkans' and 'Africa' reek of violence; they are places on earth where brutish human nature has always clutched at the throats of the living, uncensored by the codes of civility enjoyed by more 'civilised' peoples elsewhere. The ideologists of primitivism often reason inductively. Acts of grisly violence are grist to their mill. They infer that human nature must be evil for it to fire 120mm mortar shells into crowded marketplaces, so producing an almighty explosion, followed by a gentle sound like rain or mountain brooks, then a split-second's silence as shoppers are blasted off their feet with a force they have never before experienced, followed by limbs and flecks of flesh splattered everywhere, the air thick with the screams of the wounded and dying, leaving behind the wails of relatives, friends and witnesses, if there are any.

Ontologists of violence are often confident in their clichés. They speak with conviction and force about how 'people are naturally evil', or 'wicked' or 'creatures of original sin'. But such talk is problematic. Ignorant of its own historical foundations, it suffers from an indiscriminate acceptance of 'the facts' to prove, through induction, its fancies. It is also uninterested in the motivations of those who kill and are killed. It doesn't ask questions. It wants solutions, which explains why

---

[6] Ashley Montagu, *The Human Revolution* (Cleveland and New York 1965), p. 24: 'The violences that have been attributed to his original nature have, in fact, been acquired predominantly within the relatively recent period of man's cultural evolution.'

pessimistic ontologies often function as alibis that meld easily into authoritarian antidotes to incivility. The function of these ontologies, whether intended or not, is to disarm consciences, to persuade others that really nothing can be done, except for the strategy of putting trust in 'war' against 'enemies', or tougher law and stricter order, or opting for a private solution (dealing with car thieves by purchasing a lockable, corrugated iron garage in Moscow; employing security staff in London or Tokyo or Abidjan; paying protection money to a warlord in Rio de Janeiro), all the while hoping for the best, which in practice means offloading violence and its costs onto others.

So we come to a second rule: *wherever possible, exercise caution and heap doubt upon the schemes and plans of those who talk of 'necessity' and call for the harshest possible remedies – 'crackdowns' and 'zero tolerance' and 'war' – against those whose violence is often dismissed as 'evil' or 'pathological'.* During the period of hysteria aroused by Red Army Faction attacks against business and government in the Federal Republic of Germany, Chancellor Helmut Schmidt remarked: 'Those who defend the rule of law must be prepared to go to the limit of what democracy sanctions and permits.'[7] The deep ambiguity buried in this statement serves as a reminder that whenever democracies tackle violence the dangers of hubris and authoritarianism should not be underestimated. Pressured by external violence, democratic governments are sometimes prone to cut back-room deals with the violent, to provide them with safe havens in exchange for reciprocal agreements not to conduct violent attacks within the state's own territory.[8] Suspicion should always be at the ready when the practitioners of violence talk of 'necessity', or 'emergency', or 'classified secrets', or 'defending sovereignty' or 'going to the limit'. Especially when things are not going well for the dominant interests, the old democracies are prone to stir up talk of

---

[7] From the documentary film, *Baader-Meinhof. In Love with Terror* (London 2002).

[8] Michel Wieviorka, 'French politics and strategy on terrorism', in Barry Rubin (ed.), *The Politics of Counterterrorism: The Ordeal of Democratic States* (Washington, DC 1990), pp. 61–90.

this kind. The preoccupation with apocalyptic terrorism in the early years of the twenty-first century is an example of how violence and counter-violence breed official clampdowns that are bad for democracy: arrests without charges or trials; the transgression of data protection laws; armed soldiers in public places; high profile military exercises; constant chatter about tightened security; whispers about torture, and getting tough; new legislation in defence of the realm; the spread of a permanent war mentality.

Meanwhile, in the field of criminal law, there are parallel signs of a strengthening consensus that criminal violence is a growing 'pathology', and that its obscure causes place it beyond realistic hope of remedy. 'The very high crime rate of young black males is an aspect of the pathological situation of the black underclass, but there do not appear to be any remedies for this situation that are at once politically feasible and likely to work', writes the former chief judge in the US Court of Appeals, adding that 'there is no feasible method of preventing parents from beating their children, and also it is unclear whether the beating causes the later violence or the beating and the violence are consequences of the genetic endowment shared by the parents and their children'. These premises lead easily to the conclusion that the old strategies of flexible sentencing, supervised parole, treatment for drug dependency, psychotherapy and job training should be abandoned. 'Decades of unsuccessful experimentation with different types of rehabilitative programmes have demonstrated the practical futility of the rehabilitative approach and, in the process, have largely discredited criminology as a discipline.' It is said that multivariate data analyses conducted by social scientists prove that 'punishment reduces crime both through deterrence and through incapacitation', and it follows that getting tougher is the right course of action. Violence should greet violence. Crime management should be directed almost exclusively at protecting civil society from itself. More prisons – some of them run by profit-seeking 'security firms' – are needed. Tougher policing and swifter arrests should be matched by the streamlining of the court system. Juries should be invited to infer from criminal defendants' refusal to testify that they have something to hide. Evidence obtained by the authorities in violation of the law should be considered reliable. Tough sentencing and extensive incarceration should become commonplace. Consideration should be given to extending the death penalty to crimes other than unusually brutal or wanton murders. And the costly protraction of criminal proceedings, especially in death cases, where (in the United States, whose prison population has quadrupled in three decades to over 2 million people) intervals of ten years between sentence and execution are common and intervals of twenty years are not uncommon, must be stopped.[9]

From the standpoint of democratic institutions and ideals, this type of 'just desserts' reasoning is founded on questionable premises that lead to authoritarian conclusions. It is all very well to talk of stopping crime in its tracks, getting it off the streets, keeping it behind bars. Getting violent with violence is, however, risky. It cultivates the illusion that the violence of imprisonment and capital punishment reduces violent crime.[10] By ignoring more effective *non-violent* remedies for incivility, legalised violence also potentially injures civil society much more than moderate and occasional criminal violence. The key problem is the chain reaction that is triggered when violent power is exercised over others. The power to get others to do what they would otherwise avoid doing, backed by violent means, easily breeds arrogance, the belief that the powerful are immune from responsibility towards others who are meanwhile forced to suffer pain and humiliation. A culture of control spreads. And whenever arrogance mixes with violence and power, the temptation to brutalise the bodies of those who resist is just around the corner. Democracies that use violence

---

[9] Richard Posner, 'The most punitive nation. A few modest proposals for lowering the US crime rate', *Times Literary Supplement*, number 4822 (1 September 1995), pp. 3–4.

[10] See Frank E. Zimring and Gordon Hawkins, *Incapacitation: Penal Confinement and the Restraint of Crime* (Oxford and New York 1995), a well-known study that concludes that California's tripling of its prison population in the 1980s affected the rate of violent crime insubstantially – 0.007 homicides and 0.055 rapes per prisoner-year – if at all.

against either their own or other populations are not exempted from this chain reaction, which often produces a new political division much worse than that between rich and poor: the cleavage between the torturable and the non-torturable classes. 'Every society which feels itself threatened by dissent', Pierre Vidal-Naquet pointed out during the French military campaign against Algerian independence, 'can quite easily, today or tomorrow, tolerate a sporadic or systematic use of torture . . . Whatever its nature, all dissent can push the modern state, however liberal it may be, to the use of torture.'[11]

A third rule: *resist the drift towards authoritarian 'law and order' strategies by firmly reminding politicians, judges, the police and military that governmental efforts to reduce violence cannot succeed unless civility and freedom are cultivated at the level of civil society.* Many activist supporters of democracy understandably worry about the general erosion of civil freedoms that normally accompanies military and police action and the setting up of new security bureaucracies, like the new Department of Homeland Security in the United States. They worry as well about the despotic, aggressive and racist effects of attempts to counter grisly terrorist attacks through clenched-fist military operations, like the Israeli army's 2002 Operation Defensive Shield, a silver-tongued phrase for describing the criminal-like invasion, occupation and destruction of Palestinian cities.[12] Arms and calls to arms breed hubris. Civilian life does not take kindly to the loss of sleep and frayed nerves induced by strip searching; or by helicopter gun ships chopping the air above the heads of frightened urban residents; or the tightening of visa regulations and airport security; or by flag-waving and talk of the need for permanent war against evil. Political power may well grow out of the barrel of guns, but the velvet power of civil institutions thrives on permanent decommissioning of weapons, responsible exercises of power and strategies of social pacification.

---

[11] Pierre Vidal-Nacquet, *La torture dans la Republique: essai d'histoire et de politique contemporaines (1954–1962)* (Paris 1972), pp. 175 and 14.

[12] David Grossman, *Death as a Way of Life. Israel Ten Years After Oslo* (New York 2003).

This is why, for instance, in efforts to break apart the triangle of violence that the world has drawn around itself – a triangle bounded by apocalyptic terrorism, uncivil war and nuclear anarchy – imaginative political leadership, sting operations, prudent military interventions and stiff judgements by courts of law will not be enough. If authoritarian outcomes are to be minimised, anti-violence initiatives that arise out of civil societies themselves are essential. Surgeons speak of enucleation to describe the process of removing tumours from shells. The same term could be used to describe a basic political priority of the friends of democracy: the systematic removal of nuclear weapons and weapons-making systems and materials from the structures of the world's governmental and non-governmental structures. The priority will be hard to realise; new peace and disarmament movements will be required. But not only is a renaissance of militant public campaigns against nuclear weapons and installations overdue; global citizens' campaigns against 'classical' and apocalyptic forms of terrorism will also be needed. They will have to bite the bullet: wrestle with the problem of how and when armed force can be used legitimately to put a stop to violence in uncivil war zones. Citizens' campaigns against uncivil war and political repression and torture (like that of Amnesty International, which has more than 1 million members in 162 countries, or the Catholic Relief Services and the International Network of Engaged Buddhists) will also be needed. Greater support from citizens and business and government will need to be given as well to civil society groups like Saferworld – a London-based research and lobby group that publicises the deadly effects of global arms flows and pressures bodies like the European Union into restricting arms sales to dictatorial states and armies that abuse the rights of civilians.

Rule number four: *wherever and whenever possible, make efforts to repeal or prevent the 'privatisation' of the means of violence.* There are signs, in some regions and many local communities of the world, of a long-term trend towards the 'scattering' and 'privatisation' of the means of violence – either 'outsourced' to business organisations or into the hands of civilians, so turning them into paramilitary or gangster figures. The emergent triangle of violence currently drives this trend. Black market, cut-price deals on weapons exacerbate the problem. Global businesses like Executive Outcomes and Brown and Root Services meanwhile specialise in the provision, for a price, of such military skills as intelligence, risk assessment, strategic planning, training, operational support and combat preparations. The consequence is that the day-to-day defence of civilians against imaginary or actual threats of violence is passing into the hands of a booming security and war-fighting business. The trend is so strong that it is possible to imagine times and places where quite a few states' monopoly of the means of violence will be permanently eroded, or destroyed outright, by new forms of *condottieri*.[13]

We return at this point to the claim (of Umberto Eco, Tanaka Akihiko and others) that late modern ships of state are now marooned and drifting into 'medieval' waters. The claim rests upon some historical fantasies, and should therefore be handled with care, especially since the long and bloody struggle of modern state-builders to monopolise the means of violence within a given territory has constantly been resisted by urban militias, private armies, armed mercantile companies, privateers, fiscal agents, and armies of regional lords and rival claimants to royal power.[14] There are nevertheless plenty of documented cases – including uncivil wars – where the contemporary structures of government and the social relations of civil societies are becoming twisted and deformed into grotesque shapes by gun-wielding gangs and cartels. Fuelled by media and the global networking and 'miniaturisation' of the means of violence, there seems to be a worldwide upsurge of *non-governmental* forms of violence.

Consider just one extreme instance of this anti-democratic trend: the power structures operated in Colombia by the Medellín and Cali cartels, which together with regional groups in cities like Bucamaranga and Santa Maria reportedly controlled 80 per cent of the

[13] See Peter Singer, *Corporate Warriors* (Ithaca and London 2003); Gary T. Marx, *Civil Disorder and the Agents of Social Control* (Irvington 1993), and *Undercover Police Surveillance in America* (New York 1988).

[14] Janice E. Thomson, *Mercenaries, Pirates, and Sovereigns. State-Building and Extraterritorial Violence in Early Modern Europe* (Princeton 1994).

world's cocaine production from the 1970s onwards.[15] Lorded over by such figures as El Alacrán (Henry Loaiza Ceballos, or 'the Scorpion'), Pablo Escobar ('the Robin Hood Paisa') and the Rodríguez Orejuela brothers, no parts of Colombia were left untouched by the structures of narco-violence. Drugs and guns flowed through the veins of its social life, twisting the construction industry, football clubs, the taxi trade, hotels and some newspapers around their violent fingers. As drug traffickers became major landowners, they began to create private militia – MAS (Muerte a Secuestradórs, or 'Death to Kidnappers') was the most notorious – to protect their power and investments. Private guns extended into the military, the police and the judiciary. During the first half of the 1990s alone, more than 1,500 politicians and trade union leaders, 1,000 police officers, 70 journalists, 4 presidential candidates – out of a field of 6 in 1990 – an attorney general and a governor were killed by the armed forces and their drug-running paramilitary allies commanded by such figures as El Alacrán. The Scorpion himself symbolised the whole worldwide trend towards the privatisation of the means of violence. Beginning his career as a *sicario*, a hitman, with a reputation for casual ruthlessness, he travelled up through the drug ranks to lead the military wing of the Cali cartel. He was there implicated in some of its darkest exploits, such as the 1991 massacre of over 100 peasants, whose bodies were dismembered by chainsaws.[16] Faced with violence of that kind, uncorrupted figures who tried to set their faces publicly against guns, drugs and killings were usually provided with rough treatment – or murdered. In 1983, after being accused in the Colombian Parliament of accepting drug money, Rodrigo Lara Bonilla, the then minister of justice, responded with vehement denials. He then redoubled his attacks on the cartels. Hundreds of drug-transport planes were seized. Arrests were made. Whenever the minister travelled, he would pack and repack his own

[15] See Winifred Tate, 'Paramilitaries in Colombia', *The Brown Journal of World Affairs*, 8, 1 (Winter/Spring 2001).
[16] These events are documented in the Amnesty International report, *Political Violence in Colombia: Myth and Reality* (London 1994).

bags, convinced that someone from a cartel somewhere would plant cocaine on him. His efforts came to nothing. The following year, he was gunned down and perished in a puddle of blood on the streets of Bogota.

The Colombian case is an extreme example of the contemporary unpicking of the so-called Westphalian model of territorial states that monopolise violent resources. Within actually existing civil and uncivil societies, the possible forms of *condottieri* are highly variable, ranging from uniformed private enterprise security agents wielding wap phones and walkie-talkies and (where permitted) guns on their hips through to armed gangs operating under the tutelage of rough trade warlords. In every case, private antidotes to violence are self-contradictory, since they bring violence, or threatened violence, into the heart of social and political life. As antidotes to violence, private solutions are also unjust – they serve to offload threatened or actual violence onto others, who are left to cope as best they can, if they can. Private solutions are always private; they have few or no socialising effects. They relegate some to the probability of cruel encounters and bloody deaths; the lucky remainder are free to live in luxury in laagers, behind compound walls, surrounded by armed security guards, balaclavaed soldiers, sniffer dogs, electronic alarms and barbed wire, with loaded guns under the bed.

A fifth rule: *in the search for 'peace' among civilians and their governments be constantly on the look out for impractical proposals and unworkable solutions dogged by means–ends discrepancies.* In matters of violence, prudence is measured by actors' level-headed ability to think in terms of means and ends and to make judgements about whether the preferred means and ends of action are compatible. The need for prudential rules in a democracy should be obvious, so just one negative illustration will suffice: the old tactic of imagining a political community that proves that men and women can live together in harmony.

The utopian fantasy of a new civilised order liberated from an old world of violence is discussed in every undergraduate course

in political thinking, but arguably its tactic of non-violently with-
drawing from the world is contradicted – and rendered obsolete – by
the peculiarly modern pressures of state- and empire-building, civil
society formation, weapons technology, and the more recent growth
of a global civil society and an ensemble of governmental institutions that criss-cross and overlap on a world scale.[17] Despite such
long-term trends, the lure of a country where violence has no place
has a long pedigree and continuing appeal. Its prototype is the vision,
stretching from Plato's *Republic* to Rousseau's *Considérations sur le
gouvernement de Pologne*, of a small political community of patri-
otic and potentially armed citizens, who live in isolation from other
political communities; who have no external military or commercial
ambitions; and whose concern for non-violent perfection is matched
by a certain superiority complex and mistrust of foreigners, which
binds them together into a freedom-loving citizenry of potential warriors emancipated from the curse of war.

Rousseau's advice to Count Wielhorski and his fellow Polish
representatives on the eve of the first of the three partitions which
led, in the period between 1772 and 1795, to the disappearance of that
country from the map of Europe, exemplifies this vision. 'Establish
the Republic so firmly in the hearts of the Poles that they will maintain her existence despite all the efforts of her oppressors . . . avoid the
frippery, the garishness and the luxurious decorations usually found in
the courts of kings . . . Begin by contracting your boundaries . . . devote
yourselves to extending and perfecting the system of federal government: the only one which combines the advantages of large and small
states', Rousseau urged. He went on to insist, while looking back over
his shoulder, that 'our distinction between the legal and the military
castes was unknown to the ancients. Citizens were neither lawyers
nor soldiers nor priests by profession; they performed all these functions as a matter of duty.' The political moral was clear, or so Rousseau
thought:

[17] These various trends are examined in my *Global Civil Society?* (Cambridge and
New York 2003).

preserve and revive among your people simple customs and wholesome tastes, and a warlike spirit devoid of ambition . . . Do not waste your energies in vain negotiations; do not bankrupt yourselves on ambassadors and ministers to foreign courts; and do not account alliances and treaties as things of any moment. If you want to keep yourselves free and happy, heads, hearts and arms are what you want; it is they that constitute the power of a state and the prosperity of a people . . . pay little attention to foreign countries, give little heed to commerce; but multiply as far as possible your domestic production and consumption of foodstuffs . . . Each citizen [including the peasantry] should be a soldier by duty, none by profession. Such was the military system of the Romans; such is that of the Swiss today; such ought to be that of every free state, and particularly of Poland.[18]

The deepening global interdependence of political and economic forces and the spread and interweaving of unarmed civil societies with divided identities has arguably transformed this Rousseau-esque vision of autarkic republican states into an unrealisable utopia. The splendid isolation that it presupposes, and requires, has also been abolished by the spread of weaponry and military prowess that threatens all four corners of the earth with annihilation – along with the extinction of the dictum of von Clausewitz that victory in modern warfare goes to the army that keeps its nerve longer, wills itself to survive, and persuades its adversary by means of the gun to lay down arms. Christa Wolf's talk of 'a bomb induced futurelessness',[19] in which even peace of mind for all peoples has become a thing of the past, may be exaggerated. But there is no doubt that it correctly draws attention

---

[18] The quotations are my translations from Jean-Jacques Rousseau, *Considérations sur le Gouvernement de Pologne, et sur sa réformation projetée* (Geneva 1782). Rousseau had evidently planned a work on a scheme for a partial federation among the smaller states of Europe, and had at one time intended to include it in the *Contrat social*. He handed a fragment to a French friend, d'Antraigues, who destroyed it in a panic; see C. E. Vaughan (ed.), *The Political Writings of J. J. Rousseau* (Cambridge 1915), vol. II, pp. 135–6.

[19] Cited in Robert Pfaltzgraff (ed.), *The Greens of West Germany* (London 1983), p. 4.

to the global obsolescence of peace through autarky. Because we live in an age of growing interdependence, political autarky is no longer a viable political goal. Doubters of that conclusion should ponder four key military developments unique to the last century: American B-29s in 1945 unloading comprehensive destruction from the unprecedented height of 20,000 feet; the counter-detonation by the Russians of their first atomic bomb in 1949; the Americans' deployment in 1956 of B-52 intercontinental bombers capable of flying round trips to Moscow; and the development, by the early 1960s, of intercontinental ballistic missiles capable of reaching their far-flung targets within half-an-hour. The twenty-first century will be remembered for another development: the emergence of a triangle of violence that is capable of wrecking the world through new forms of 'unrestricted warfare' (as two Chinese military scholars, Xiangsui and Liang, have chillingly predicted[20]) based on tightening links among its three deadly sides.

Sixth rule: *cultivate public awareness of political dilemmas, including the most fundamental dilemma of all: that democracies and potential democracies, when faced with violent opposition, must be prepared to use measured quantities of violence if and when non-violent strategies fail, or seem inappropriate – even though the generalised use of violence contradicts the spirit and substance of democracy.* Violence is an accomplice of dilemmas – complex problems whose solutions themselves are problematic – and the two often conspire to stir up troubles in the neighbourhood of democracy. When threatened by armed resistance, for example, unarmed police officers have to consider whether they too need to carry weapons, if only for self-protection. The outbreak of uncivil war – to mention another dilemma – breeds sympathy for distant strangers *and* generates pressures for armed intervention, to kill, to save lives. And a people whose land is militarily occupied and whose identity is threatened with annihilation, understandably dream of democracy, but meanwhile conduct their desperate struggle for survival using weapons: bare hands, rocks, Kalashnikovs, bombs strapped to cars and chests. And so on.

[20] Qiao Liang and Wang Xiangsui, *Unrestricted Warfare* (Beijing 1999).

The subject of violence and democracy is mined with dilemmas. A detailed contemporary example, concerning the politics of Islam, will help to clarify both the problem of dilemmas and the practical rule which it implies: that, in matters of violence, the ability to spot and publicly manage dilemmas is a vital requirement of democracy. Especially in countries in which Islam is potentially a dominant social force, Islamic politics is faced by a strategic problem of how to handle violence. The background setting needs to be understood. In Europe and elsewhere, in recent years, those unsympathetic to Islam have used the problem of violence to demonise it. Especially since the Iranian Revolution, the epithet 'Islamic fundamentalism' and descriptions of Islam as a 'very wicked and evil' religion (Franklin Graham) have been deployed to refer to the violent resistance of those radical Islamic groups and parties – especially networked global organisations like al-Qaeda, which strictly oppose the interventionist policies of the West, especially American military power, and call for the liberation of their lands by using violence against the 'Zionist-Crusader alliance'.[21] The epithet 'Islamic fundamentalist' has also functioned as a catch-all term to refer to any and every practising Muslim – thereby overlooking the fact that there are many contemporary Islamists who are attempting to combat the ideology of Islam-as-Fundamentalism by emphasising Islam's capacity for non-violent power-sharing and, thus, its compatibility with such modern democratic procedures as periodic elections, parliamentary government and civil liberties.[22]

There are those – the Egyptian writer Ahmad Shawqi al-Fanjari and the Tunisian scholar and opposition leader Rachid Al-Ghannouchi have been among the boldest – who deduce every conceivable

---

[21] The emancipation of holy places in Jerusalem and Mecca is a favourite theme of Osama bin Laden. 'The ruling to kill the Americans and their allies – civilians and military – is an individual duty for every Muslim who can do it in any country ... in order to liberate the al-Aqsa mosque [in Jerusalem] and the Holy Mosque [in Mecca]' (*Statement: Jihad against Jews and Crusaders [February 23, 1998]*, in Barry Rubin and Judith Colp Rubin (eds.), *Anti-American Terrrorism and the Middle East* (Oxford and New York 2002), p. 150).

[22] Among the earliest accounts of this recent trend is Edward Said, *Covering Islam: How the Media and the Experts Determine How We See the Rest of the World* (London 1981).

democratic right and duty from the Qur'an, the Traditions of the Prophet and contemporary experience. Al-Fanjari, following the example of Rifa'ah Rafi Al-Tahtawi, the pioneer of cultural westernisation in Egypt, says that every age adopts a different terminology to convey the concepts of democracy and freedom. What is called freedom in Europe is exactly what in Islam is called justice ('adl), truth (haqq), consultation (shura) and equality (musawat). Al-Fanjari says 'the equivalent of freedom in Islam is kindness or mercy (rahmah) and that of democracy is mutual kindness (tarahum)'.[23] He goes on to remind his readers that in the Qur'an the Prophet is instructed to show leniency and forgiveness in the very same verse as he is ordered to consult the believers in the affairs of the community. The Prophet is reported to have said in turn that God 'has laid down consultation as a mercy for His community'. It follows from this interpretation that Islam, contrary to its Orientalist denigrators, is indeed compatible with democracy because there is no place in it for arbitrary rule by one man or group of men. The basis of all decisions and actions of Islamic government should not be individual whim and caprice, but the shari'ah – the body of interpreted regulations drawn from the Qur'an and the Traditions.

Al-Ghannouchi adds that Islam passes another test of democracy, in that it satisfies the requirement that any government should reckon in all its decisions with the wishes of the ruled. In listing the qualities of a good believer, the Qur'an mentions shura (consultation)

---

[23] Ahmad Shawqi al-Fanjari, Al-hurriyat' as-siyasiyyah fi'l Islam (Kuwait 1973), pp. 31, 34, cited in Hamid Enayat, Modern Islamic Political Thought (Austin 1988), p. 131. The following comments on Al-Ghannouchi are drawn from my interview with him on the subject of violence (London, April 2003). See as well 'The Islamic movement and violence', Makalet (1983/4); and 'The efficiency of using violence to establish an Islamic state', in Al-harakah al-Islamiyya wa Manhaj at-Iaghyir (London 2000). His theory of Islamic democracy is further examined in Azzam Tamimi, Rachid Ghannouchi – A Democrat within Islamism (Oxford and New York 2002). See also John L. Esposito, Islam and Democracy (New York 1996). A detailed historical survey of the complex traditions of Islamic thinking about violence is provided in Khaled Abou El Fadl, Rebellion and Violence in Islamic Law (Cambridge and New York 2001).

and *ijima'* (consensus) and in turn places them on the same footing as compliance with God's order, saying the prayers and payment of the alms tax. It follows from this principle of legitimate power, argues Ghannouchi, that even in contexts where the application of *shari'ah* is difficult or impossible, Muslims should work for *shura*, which implies joining with 'secular' forces in opposing corrupt and violent dictatorships everywhere. Standing tall against despotic power, speaking truth straight to its face, aware of the attendant dangers: this is the highest form of *jihad*.

This type of argument about the democratic potential of Islam deserves global attention. Wherever Muslims are living in significant numbers, democratic Islam is a potential force for civility, mutual toleration and power-sharing, exactly because it challenges both the dogma that the teachings of Islam are essentially 'fundamentalist' and its insulting corollary, that all Islamists are gun-wielding power-mongers.[24] Yet arguably Islam can be seen widely as a force for non-violent power-sharing only if it can successfully handle a strategic dilemma: how to craft democratic institutions when confronted with violent opposition, both from within and without its ranks.

Nearly a third of the world's Muslim believers live in countries in which they can never hope to become a numerical majority of the population. In those countries, India, for example, Islamists have certain (overlapping) political options. They can turn their backs upon the world (living apolitically as pietist communities, in accordance with Sayyid Qutb's instruction that there is an abyss between Islam and the world which is spanned not by a bridge enabling a meeting half-way between the two, but one that allows for the 'godless' people of the *jahiliyya* to cross over to the 'true believers' of Islam). Muslims can also live their faith by caring little for the immediate non-Muslim 'unbeliever' society around them and instead bonding with other Muslims elsewhere in the wider world (the strategy of the Jama'at al

---

[24] John Keane, 'Power-sharing Islam?', in Azzam Tamimi (ed.), *Power-Sharing Islam?* (London 1993), pp. 15–31.

Tabligh, the largest transnational Islamic organisation in the world). Or, within their state or locale, these minorities of Islamists can live their faith and espouse the cause of toleration and civil and political liberties for all. If they refuse all of these non-violent options, they are likely to weaken their own socio-political and religious credibility, especially in the eyes of a potentially threatening and threatened non-Muslim majority concerned about 'Islamic fundamentalism'.

Within actually existing democracies, matters are fairly cut and dried: Muslim minorities are either in favour of strengthening democratic institutions, or they are not. Yet in countries and regions in which Islam is potentially a dominant social force, Tunisia or Algeria or Turkey, for instance, Islamic politics feels the pinch of what can be called the *transition to democracy dilemma*. Any Islamic movement that attempts to transform a non-Islamic into an Islamic polity (the latter is often vaguely defined as a political community based upon the revealed and interpreted law of Islam) is forced to choose, or to steer a perilous course, between two incompatibles – the ethical principles of Islam and the potentially violent ways and means of modern territorial state power. Islamic parties that are dedicated to parliamentary democracy – like the Turkish Justice and Development Party (AK) – do so on the working assumption that their enemies are civil human beings, and this in turn limits their range of political tactics. They embrace public discussion, press conferences, vote-getting and parliamentary numbers, rather than terrorism, street violence and dreams of a revolutionary putsch. If and when they are elected to office, it follows that they eschew dictatorship as a means of staying in office. If voted out of office, as Rachid Al-Ghannouchi has urged, they should then leave peacefully, to prepare for future electoral battles.

Of course, an Islamic party or movement that remains faithful to its own principles and to these democratic procedures may never achieve governmental power. Many democratic followers of Islam like to quote the Qur'an: 'O you who believe! stand out firmly for Allah, as witnesses to fair dealing, and let not the hatred of others towards you make you swerve to wrong and depart from justice. Be just, that is next to piety, and fear Allah. For Allah is well acquainted with all that you do' (5; 8). Well and good. But especially in contexts where their opponents do not abide by the power-sharing rules of democracy – violent dictatorships are still predominant within the heartlands of the Muslim world – Islamists find themselves outwitted, censored, beaten up, arrested, executed, or forced into exile. Under such circumstances, which are today the norm for most followers of Islam in the region stretching from Morocco to Malaysia, does this mean that the vision of a democratic government infused with the principles of Islam is both a contradiction in terms and a practical impossibility? Or can an Islamic polity be achieved only if Islamists are prepared to abandon the democratic method temporarily to attain power by violence in the pious hope that an Islamic government so formed will return to the practice of parliamentary power-sharing once Islam has assumed control? Needless to say, this second alternative contains tragic possibilities: a movement for democracy that resorts to despotic methods to achieve its goals will not remain a democratic movement for long. Its chosen means will devour its chosen ends. And yet – here is the painful dilemma – the first alternative, that of clinging to parliamentary democratic procedures under all circumstances, may well doom Islam to a permanent political wilderness: to a land of hostility and war against Islam.

The transition to democracy dilemma sometimes becomes acute. A disturbing example of its failed resolution is Algeria during the 1990s; between 1992 and 2000, more than 100,000 people were killed after the military-dominated High Committee of State voided the country's first multiparty general elections in December 1991, when the Front Islamique du Salut (FIS) won an absolute majority of votes. The military's intervention led to thousands of disappearances, the brutal punishment of its opponents and to the general terrorisation of the rest of society. Its violence was matched by the retaliatory violence of certain Islamist factions, notably the supporters of the Armed Islamic Group (GIA). Specialising in the art of waging hit-and-run attacks against civilians and security forces, GIA militants regarded democracy as a kind of *jahiliyya*, whose violent terror had to be combated, tooth and nail, with bombings, guerilla ambushes, and throat slashings. Whole villages were massacred. Foreigners resident in Algeria were hunted down. An airliner was hijacked. Kidnappings, assassinations and bombings, including car bombs planted in crowded urban areas, became everyday phenomena.[25]

Such savagery, unfolding as it does within a vortex of violence and counter-violence, serves as a warning of the bleak consequences of attempting to resolve the transition dilemma by guns and bombs. Yet the gory details of the Algerian case are not necessarily a cause for general despair. While by definition any dilemma is insoluble, its force can in practice be attenuated in various ways, and it is therefore of interest to note that contemporary political thinkers and actors in countries such as Iran and Tunisia and the Lebanon have begun to set their imaginations loose on the problem of how to maximise the chances of securing a democratic Islamic government in contexts where its bully opponents do not play by the rules of the democratic game.

These democratically-minded Islamists are clear about several matters. First, an Islamic party or government that attempts to come to power and then to rule by terror, force and intrigue is regarded by them as a contradiction in terms. It is (to mention the arguments of Ahmad Shawqi al-Fanjari and Rachid Al-Ghannouchi) anti-Islamic and therefore anti-democratic, even anti-political. The radical voices of Islam repeat the mistakes of the *Kharijit* sect: their conclusion that political change requires bullets and not ballots rests upon the dangerous rejection of politics in favour of the arrogant dualism between true belief (*iman*) and false unbelief (*kufr*). Some Muslims indeed like to speak of the Qur'anic principle that necessities eliminate prohibitions. It is as if they yearn to confirm René Girard's well-known thesis that religious rituals function to offload violence on to the bodies of others, to keep violence *outside* the religious community by scapegoating others.[26] 'If one is faced by necessity', they say, 'wilful

---

[25] Habib Sovaïdia, *La sale guerre* (Paris 2003); Human Rights Watch, *Time for Reckoning: Enforced Disappearances in Algeria* (www.hrw.org/reports/2003/Algeria 0203/)

[26] René Girard, *Le Bouc émissaire* (Paris 1982), especially chs. 3 and 4.

disobedience or the transgression of due limits are guiltless.' But these Muslims also know that 'necessity' (*dharoura*), a jurists' term for what is prohibited, is not a category with a straightforward meaning. They also know that nowhere does the Qur'an sanction permanent violence (*ūnf*) or violence unstructured by a designated end. Passages such as 'Allah does not wish to place you in difficulty, but to purify you, and to complete His favour to you' (5; 6) can hardly be read as an incitement to unrestrained violence. Ibn Khaldun (says Al-Ghannouchi) was firm about this; those who raise their weapons without taking into account their consequences and costs – what Khaldun called 'rashness in war'[27] – must be punished. The Qur'an is not synonymous with the sword. *Jihad*, the fight against godlessness outside or inside the believer, is always to be constrained by the avoidance of discord (*fitnah*), the granting of mercy (*rahmah*), the imperative of justice ('*adl*), and the pursuit of peaceful reform (*islah*).

Democratically minded Islamists insist on another point: that in the struggle for more democracy the methods used strongly condition the tactics and methods of its opponents. The latter are never simply given, and they should not be thought to be so. It follows that successful transitions to democracy are always a learning process in which – as in many of the 'velvet revolutions' of central and eastern Europe, and in the events immediately following the Turkish general election in 2002 – the opponents of democracy can sometimes be convinced to minimise their acts of sabotage and to relinquish at least some of their power democratically. The point for these Islamists is that violence is a wild horse that can ruin its rider. 'Violence cannot be an alternative. If it resolves one problem, it creates many others', notes Fadlallah.[28] 'Violence is an inferior form of *jihad* and is legitimate only in exceptional circumstances, such as self-defence under military occupation', says Al-Ghannouchi. 'Even then it risks stooping to the low practices

---

[27] Ibn Khaldun, *The Muqaddimah. An Introduction to History* (London 1958), vol. II, ch. 3, sect. 35, p. 85.

[28] From my interview with Grand Ayatollah Sayyed Muhammed Hussein Fadlallah (Beirut), 9 December 2002.

of dictators who specialize in the uncourageous art of violence.' Terror breeds fear and armed *jihad* breeds military crackdown or internecine violence – like that which took place between the Shi'ite supporters of Hizbullah and Amal in southern Lebanon. When that happens, the whole political order suffers: 'violence against one part of the body politic is violence against its whole', notes Al-Ghannouchi. Peaceful democratic methods, by contrast, can be politically life-enhancing. Even their opponents can see the vital advantage of non-violence: that by reducing the fear of excommunication (*takfir*) and death it enables *everybody* to sleep peacefully in their beds at night.

Contemporary Islamists who pursue the parliamentary road reinforce their case by refusing to make a fetish of the ideal of sovereign state power. For a variety of reasons that are linked with the contemporary growth of a worldwide system of cosmocratic institutions, certain regions such as the Maghreb and the Middle East are witnessing the decay of territorial state power. Whole areas of this world are beginning to resemble the *form* of the world described by Althusius, in which monarchs were forced to share power and authority with a variety of subordinate and higher powers. The trend has profound implications for the struggle for Islamic government. It renders implausible the revolutionary strategy of seizing state power, if need be through the use of force, precisely because the 'centres' of state power are tending to become more dispersed and subject to (local, regional and global) cross-pressures. Hence governmental institutions are either immune from 'capture' by a single party or government, or (as in contemporary Iran) they are necessarily subject to the push and pull of social forces within and without the country. Not only that, but in so far as 'the state' ceases to be in one place to be 'seized', the struggle by Islamists to monopolise state power, while remaining strategically important, is no longer imperative. The often poorly coordinated and dispersed (if authoritarian and violent) character of state power, whether in Iran, Egypt, Morocco or Malaysia, makes it highly susceptible to the initiatives of social organisations and movements. It becomes possible, even imperative, for Islamists to practise the non-violent art of divide-and-rule from below by mobilising both traditional 'folk' and 'modern' versions of the belief in Islam, and by cultivating their 'grass-roots' networks, above all through professions, in local mosques, clinics and schools. In the view of democratically inclined Islamists, in other words, Islam can attenuate the transition-to-democracy dilemma by seeing that 'violent power is always weak power', and that 'dictatorship is the weakest form of all' (Al-Ghannouchi). Islam, the most socially conscious of world religions, should initially concentrate its energies within the nooks and crannies of civil society. There, in areas of life underneath and outside of territorial states, it can do something violence can never do: empower its followers by stimulating their awareness that ordinary people doing extraordinary things out of simple decency is possible, and that this is the way to win people's hearts. On that basis, it can teach them that large organisations – such as transnational firms and dictatorial states – ultimately rest upon the molecular networks of power of civil society. This teaching has an important corollary; the strengthening and transformation of the micro-power relations of civil society through 'small efforts' (Al-Ghannouchi), like acts of charity and the witnessing of injustice, necessarily affect the operations of large-scale organisations, even when they resort to violence. So these Islamists draw their overall political conclusion: while a more democratic order cannot be built without governmental power, they contend, so it cannot be built *through* political institutions alone. Democratisation is neither the outright enemy nor the unconditional friend of governmental power. It requires government to govern civil society neither too little – nor too much.

Rule number seven: *use every available means of communication to publicise acts of violence so that their causes and effects are subject to public debate and publicly accountable remedies.* Democracies continue to harbour many forms of violence that are suffered in silence. Consider acts of rape, in which sexual intercourse is coerced by violence or its threat. Criminologists concur that this form of violence remains chronically underreported, while some estimate that in countries such as Germany and the United States perhaps only one rape in twenty is officially recorded through a publicly available crime report. The figure may be higher among gays and lesbians. In heterosexual relations, the rape of women by men goes unreported for a variety of reasons, among the most obvious of which is the sense of shame at having been victimised in one of the most personal of crimes and (in the case of rape within marriage) the financial penalties and child-damaging consequences of calling a dastardly act by its right name. But many who suffer the violence of rape complain about other factors that are deemed equally, if not more, important: the loss of privacy and the sense of being humiliated by medical and laboratory procedures designed to establish the veracity of the victim's allegations; the misogyny of criminal justice officials who believe the charge of rape is suspect because the woman herself has dressed or behaved in ways that 'invited' sexual intercourse; and the consequent hell caused to the victim by having to prove legally that she is innocent in the attack that she has suffered.

There are various weapons for breaking down these barriers, including tougher policing, better laws and ridding courtrooms of misogynist judges. But arguably the factor that is most empowering of those who suffer rape – initially encouraging them to do something about their suffering – is greater publicity of the crime of rape itself. Once upon a time, news of unwanted sexual violations of the body was locally confined, and widely ignored by the political authorities, who sometimes went out of their way to remind everybody that in this or that case rape could not have resulted in pregnancy because (so it was widely believed) orgasm was a precondition of conception and orgasm implied consent. Historians tell us that only two rapes in the seventeenth century and six in the eighteenth century were heard by tribunals in Amsterdam; that judges in Frankfurt only heard two such cases between the years 1562 and 1695; that from 1650 to 1815 there were only forty accused rapists in Geneva; and that the *Parlement* of Paris, the French appeals court with the widest jurisdiction in the kingdom, heard on average only three rape cases a decade between the years 1540 and 1692.[29]

The surviving figures are redolent of times when women were considered the chattels of men, who got off lightly for brutalising women, in part because (as one assailant boasted to his victim near the town of Whitby, England) 'no one but the ships will hear your screams'.[30] The figures suggest something else: that on balance the advent of print culture and (during the twentieth century) societies of communicative abundance have helped in the long run to erode the silence and coded symbolism that surrounds rape and other forms of violence. Mediated news of violence can of course be politically dangerous when it touches on governmental or ecclesiastical authority, which is why in Europe the first print representations of violence were heavily censored by state authorities. Broadsheets describing crimes and punishments were usually outlawed. Tongues were cut out and books burned. Certain forms of censorship were later relaxed to allow religious representations of violence that offered readers moral lessons covering such 'wicked' and 'repulsive' crimes as armed robbery and murder (as in the popular *pliegos de cordel* literature in eighteenth-century Spain). During the same century, newspaper, pamphlet and broadsheet representations of violence expanded the repertoire of images of the violent, for instance in descriptions of armed robbers as buffoons or as exotic 'noble bandits', like the Spaniard, Diego Corrientes, who robbed the rich to aid the poor. A trend towards the democratisation of violence – the public circulation of different and sometimes conflicting images of violence and its origins – had begun.

The same trend continues today, albeit in heightened form and by means of different communications media. We live in times in

---

[29] Julius R. Ruff, *Violence in Early Modern Europe* (Cambridge and New York 2001), p. 141.

[30] Cited in Anna Clark, *Women's Silence, Men's Violence: Sexual Assault in England, 1770–1845* (London 1987), p. 25.

which domestic violence, rape, assaults and armed robberies, the violence of organised crime, riots, assassinations and acts of terrorism all seize headlines and serve as 'lead-ins' for television and radio infotainment. To the extent that this coverage convinces audiences that they live in the most violent of times that can be pacified only through tighter surveillance and armed power, the overall effect may prove to be disabling of democracy. That is not a necessary political outcome, however. A strong counter-trend is observable: saturation media coverage of violence nurtures the growth of free-standing public spheres, in which acts of violence and efforts to deal with them are witnessed and monitored non-violently by reading, listening, watching and talking citizens.

How do these public spheres spring up? Their genesis is quite complex.[31] Enveloped within networks of media, most individuals and groups and movements within actually existing democracies get the hang of reacting with or against the stories (news, infotainment, drama, film etc.) that are circulated. Audiences chatter, gossip, make jokes, roar with laughter, swoon, feel sadness, re-tell stories, and complain of indecency, confusion, shock or boredom. All this is quite routine; the audience work of re-working media output is a chronic, everyday affair. It is reinforced by the efforts of journalists, who help to circulate images and stories that suppose that 'the audience' is listening, reading, watching, chatting on- or off-line. The combined effect of these trends is that unusual things sometimes happen, with almost magical effect. Certain stories are whizzed around in the cyclotron called 'the media'; scores or hundreds or thousands and even millions of voices may well join in, and suddenly whole groups or sometimes (it seems) 'everybody' is talking in animated ways about the same figure, event or actual or expected outcome. A big scoop, a blockbuster media event, is born. And then, suddenly, sometimes, something even more unpredictable and quirky happens: a body called 'the public' surrounds the stage. It talks and talks back. There is noise and confusion, some

---

[31] See my *Whatever Happened to Democracy?* (London 2002).

of it caused by tongues that resemble parrots trapped in a cage. But common sense usually has its turn, too. Words, sentences, statements and whole stories begin to count. The story begins to take on a life of its own – with incalculable effects for governors and governed alike. The public keeps the experimental performance going, though not necessarily for long. Media performances, especially blockbuster events, cannot work without publics, who can at any moment heckle, applaud, drift off, or desert the theatre in droves.

Admittedly, these publics for the most part do not resemble the face-to-face gatherings of citizens exemplified by the classical Greek *ekklêsia*, the Roman forum, the New England town meeting, or the rowdy public gatherings sponsored by nineteenth-century Chartism. And although no membership cards or entry tickets are required, they are not realms of universal involvement. All publics – including the global publics that spring up around global media events – tend to exclude others. Yet it is nonetheless important to see that the publics that regularly form under conditions of communicative abundance – the publics who witness or follow stories about bullying or stalking or rape or genocide – are *public* in several important senses that we have inherited from our forebears. These publics are spaces of openness in which controversies break out over who gets what, when and how, and in which things once concealed are now revealed, for the alleged benefit and in the name of many ('all') others.

These publics come in various guises and sizes. Some of them are tiny, like the local circles of newspaper readers who become acquainted with reports (for instance) of a meeting of angry Turkish-speaking Germans, called to discuss what can be done about their verbal and physical harassment in the schools, supermarkets and streets of Berlin. Some micro-publics expand dramatically, like the audiences for early American rap music's clever attacks on police brutality and harassment, evident in KRS One's 'Who Protects Us From You?', a scarifying, cautionary tale of ghetto life, a militant philosophical rap using lyrics like 'Killin' blacks and callin' it the law' and 'Every time you say "That's illegal", doesn't mean that that's true.' The local public spheres that sprang up with the rebirth of women's movements during the 1960s followed a similar logic of expansion; helped along by various means of communication, public spaces created by women appeared within discussion circles, professional associations, clinics, refuges for battered women and publishing houses. On occasion, these publics coalesced and made their impact felt as publicly visible media events, such as demonstrations against rape or in favour of abortion or lesbian rights, or as sit-ins against bigoted judges and government officials.

Some public controversies about violence have a wide reach from the outset. Mediated by national communications systems, they comprise public spheres that dwell upon such matters as urban violence, uncivil war and nuclear weapons – and do so by attracting millions of people who watch, read or listen across vast distances. Sensations are sometimes their offspring, as in the British tabloids' ruthless probing and exploitation of murder, rape and other forms of criminal violence; or in fast-cut, American-style television talk shows that – sprinkled with advertisements for fast food and gadgets – simulate raucous domestic quarrels about matters such as child abuse, cruelty to animals and gay violence, in front of selected audiences who argue bitterly amongst themselves, talk back to the presenter, shout at experts and question the veracity of the interviewees. The largest publics of all – those associated with globally staged media events that dramatise peace conferences, nuclear tests, uncivil wars and military invasions – raise questions about the triangle of violence and are therefore arguably of greatest importance to the whole world. Such global media coverage of violence is often accused of spreading rituals of pacification, of rendering audiences mute by seducing them into fascination with the spectacle of cruel events. That could indeed be legitimately said of the heavily censored coverage of the Malvinas War and the first Gulf War. But there are plenty of counter-examples, like the coverage of the Tiananmen crisis in China during the late spring of 1989, or of the wars in the former Yugoslavia, in which global publics not only form, but are linked to the growth of a 'politics of pity'; by witnessing others' terrible suffering at the hands of violence, millions of people around the world are sometimes so shaken that they speak to others, donate money or time, draw their own conclusions, or support the general principle that humanitarian intervention – the obligation to assist someone in danger, as contemporary French law puts it – can and should override the old crocodilian formula that might equals right.[32]

What is most significant about public spheres and the politics of pity they nurture is that they potentially contribute to the long-term project of democratising violence in its various forms. By portraying uncivil acts as deeply contingent, as 'man-made' events with culprits and victims, they encourage audiences to live for a while in the subjunctive sense, to heighten their sense that the prevailing 'laws' of society and government are far from 'natural', to see with their own eyes that the shape of the world as it is partly depends on current efforts to refashion it violently or non-violently, according to certain power criteria. Understood in this rather old-fashioned way,[33] public spheres are a basic condition of reducing or eliminating incivility and of minimising the chances of its recurrence. Within and among countries striving to become or to remain democratic, they ought to

[32] See my *Global Civil Society?* (Cambridge and New York 2003), pp. 166ff.

[33] To link together violence and publicity is to rediscover and breathe new life into a theme of political thought that is traceable – in the case of Europe – to the Roman legal system, with its emphasis on the inviolability of peacefully negotiated agreements and treaties (*pacta sunt servanda*). Its roots run deeper still, to the Greek conviction that public life and violence had nothing in common, essentially because men distinguish themselves from the animals by virtue of their capacity for speech (*lexis*) and action (*praxis*) and, thus, by their propensity for publicly banding together into a *polis* of citizens protected from physical violence by walls around their city. The presumed tension between violence and public speech and action was a theme subsequently revived and made a prominent feature of the struggle against despotic states in the European region. The language of 'the public', 'public virtue' and 'public opinion' was directed against monarchs and courts suspected of acting arbitrarily, of abusing their power violently, and of furthering their 'private', selfish interests at the expense of the realm. During the seventeenth and eighteenth centuries, the normative ideal of the public sphere – a realm of life in which citizens invented their identities under the shadow of state power – was especially popular among republicans like the 'Commonwealthmen', who simultaneously looked back to the Roman republic (and sometimes to the Greek *polis*) and forward to a world without mean-spirited executive power, standing armies and bloody struggles caused by clericalism.

feature in any discussion of violence and democracy, for at least four reasons. Fed by public inquiries, judicial reviews, funerals and truth commissions, public spheres have a propensity to overcome denials and cover-ups by cultivating shared memories of times past when terrible things were done to people; a powerful example was the symbolic burial (in 2001) of Ken Saro-Wiwa, attended by 200,000 mourners dedicated to remembering the human rights activist who had been executed by the Nigerian junta. Public spheres also heighten citizens' and governments' awareness of the nature and extent of actually existing incivilities. Furthermore, they canvass and circulate to other citizens ethical judgements about whether or not (or under what conditions) a certain form of violence is justified. Finally, public spheres tend to encourage the formulation of remedies for incivility; not only pragmatic proposals that are mindful of the complexity of the whole subject and the troubling implications of violence for democratic institutions, but also uncompromisingly 'utopian' visions of a world no longer cursed by (certain forms of) violence.[34]

An eighth rule: *carefully examine the ethical processes that unfold within publics exposed to symbolic representations of violence; query the commonsense view that actually existing democracies turn violence into pure entertainment.* The growth of publics that worry about violence throws doubt on the customary view that the growing saturation of everyday life with media-driven images, particularly those depicting acts of violence, implicates audiences who know no better in a sado-masochistic relationship with that violence. The customary view is anticipated in Marshall McLuhan's and Quentin

---

[34] Such visions can develop illicitly even in contexts in which levels of violence have reached extraordinary proportions – like those vast areas of occupied Europe in which Hitler's armies had conquered, or his allies were in control. Although during World War II civilian efforts to protect victims and to thwart and sabotage the occupiers' plans were not strong enough to defeat the enemy, the underground public opinion that they cultivated ensured not only that Nazism and its allies were denied legitimacy, in the face of terrible crimes, this public opinion also kept alive hopes for a better future, as has been pointed out by Jacques Semelin, *Unarmed Against Hitler. Civilian Resistance in Europe, 1939–1943* (Westport, CT and London 1993), especially ch. 6.

Fiore's comments on the Vietnam War as the first-ever media war: 'The television war has meant the end of the dichotomy between civilian and military. The public is now participant in every phase of the war, and the main actions of the war are now being fought in the American home itself.'[35] The title of Jean Baudrillard's *The Evil Demon of Images* hardens this thesis; the old adage that war is the continuation of politics by violent means needs to be amended, Baudrillard argues, because media images are now the continuation of war by other means. War, the most concentrated form of violence, has become cinematographic and televisual, just as the mechanically produced image (a film like Francis Ford Coppola's *Apocalypse Now*, for instance) makes war on the world by first devouring everything and everybody in its path during filming, then spewing it out as a mass spectacle of riveting images of napalm, gassed bodies, burned-out tanks, screaming jets, explosions, screaming children, stories of rape and pillage. 'War becomes film, film becomes war.' It is still widely thought that pictures of war bear witness to the world by literally reproducing it 'as it really is'. That is not so, Baudrillard insists. The image, whether photographic, cinematic or televisual, in fact seduces its producers and consumers by promoting spontaneous confidence in its own realism. The dirty reality of war is thereby discursively swallowed up into a black hole of images which extinguish all referentiality. Basic polarities such as subject/object, private/public, good/evil and the imaginary/the real are made to implode. War becomes unquestionable. Images of violence cease to have a transcendent meaning; they are simply violence as it actually exists. Audiences are seduced and captured and held hostage by such images; images of violence fill them with 'a kind of primal pleasure, of anthropological joy in images, a kind of brute fascination unencumbered by aesthetic, moral, social or political judgements'.[36]

---

[35] Marshall McLuhan and Quentin Fiore, *War and Peace in the Global Village* (Corte Madera, CA 2001 [1968]), p. 134.

[36] Jean Baudrillard, *The Evil Demon of Images* (Sydney 1998). Such claims seem to belong less to media analysis than to the world of fictional literature. It is as if

Enzensberger's *Aussichten auf den Bürgerkrieg* replicates the same thesis. Television has become 'a single huge piece of graffiti' which serves up massacre as mass entertainment. Acts of violence in Sarajevo, Kigali, Baghdad, Belfast and elsewhere in effect function as 'a horror movie with its own blood-and-guts productions'. Scenes of broken-hearted refugees, raped and ravaged by pitched battles that rage in distant countries, and footage of desperate violence within the broken-down hearts of sophisticated cities, are not treated with the gravity or sophistication they deserve. They become light entertainment.

Quite aside from its neglect of the growth of variously sized public spheres, the thesis is extravagant – and implausible – for several reasons. If the violence-as-mass-entertainment theory were literally true, then it is unclear how the apocalyptic theory itself could explain how it has emerged unscathed from a world in which all meaning has become enveloped within the mass media. If the theory were literally true, if in other words it was not a deliberately exaggerated provocation, then it is also unclear what should be done about the phenomenon, except, supposing its undesirability, to ban all mass media reportage of violence (a possible recommendation that might well be implied by Enzensberger's call for citizens to forget about the wider world and to concentrate upon the forms of uncivil war closest to home). The thesis also says nothing about the growth of civility associated with what Elias called the modern civilising process; it takes no account of the survival and flourishing of secular forms of the uncanny; and it rests as well upon an unspoken assumption about the nitwit nature of the viewing audience. It supposes that audiences are hapless and gullible idiots. They are presumed to be incapable of interpreting or reinterpreting images of violence, even those which are

contemporary audiences resemble James Joyce's everyman character, Leopold Bloom, who feels he 'must eat' while walking the streets of Dublin, and so enters a restaurant, thinking: 'Hot fresh blood they prescribe for decline. Blood always needed. Insidious. Lick it up, smoking hot, thick sugary. Famished ghosts. Ah, I'm hungry' (James Joyce, *Ulysses* (New York 1934 (1914)), p. 169.

presented with explanations of their origins, causes and ethical implications. At most, audiences are presumed to be capable of catharsis, or gross satisfaction in the misfortune of others.

The presumption that audiences are feeble-minded misanthropes flies in the face of considerable counter-evidence, past and present. Democracies or polities on the road to democratisation have a long history of cultivating works of art and entertainment that often proved painful to audiences because they were *shocking* in their portrayal of violence in all its wrenching and disgusting complexity. Who today does not wince when reading the account in *Huckleberry Finn* of a run-down Arkansas town where the local sport consists in dowsing a stray dog with turpentine and setting it alight? Or feel uncomfortable in the presence of Hemingway's description of putrescent corpses 'in the hot weather with a half-pint of maggots working where their mouths have been'? Or the revulsion induced by reading Jean Giono's account of the 1914–18 trenches:

> The dead lay face down in the mud, or emerged from shell holes, peacefully, their hands on the edges of the holes, their heads resting on their arms. The rats came and sniffed them. They hopped from one to another. They chose the young ones first, those without beards on their cheeks. They sniffed their cheeks, then they settled down and began to eat the flesh between the nose and the mouth, then the edges of the lips, then the unripe apples of the cheeks. From time to time they passed their paws through their whiskers to clean them. As for the eyes, they got them out with little taps of their paws and licked out the eye-sockets; then they bit into the eyes, as if they were little eggs, and chewed them gently, their heads on one side, sucking out the juice.[37]

Today, audiences still often experience moral revulsion at the violent images with which they are confronted. They also take steps to turn away from such images, or they avoid them as far as possible.

---

[37] Jean Giono, *Le grand troupeau* (Paris 1951), pt. 2, sect. 3.

They also often draw their own conclusions, usually by talking with others about the programme format and the 'story' itself, as well as the pros and cons of the violence in question.

The violence-as-entertainment thesis supposes that visual representations of incivility are seamless texts that always overwhelm those who sit still before them – dissolving 'the audience' into a fictional nothingness. That rarely happens, not only for empirical reasons (bitter controversies about violence still abound) but also because the different types of textual representation of violence on offer to audiences guarantee different types of audience response. Some texts about violence are state-centred and subject heavily to censorship; others are more or less journalist-centred or produced from the points of view of the perpetrators or victims of violence; and still others may be an eclectic mixture of some or all of these possibilities. Not only that, but within each of these types of representation of violence there is an observable 'intention of the text' (as Umberto Eco has put it) which tends to codetermine or divine particular types of responses by the audiences who are exposed to the images of violence. There is never just one definitive meaning of any media account of a violent episode, and certainly not that of the author of that account. There are always *plausible or implausible interpretations* of what is communicated, that is, more or less persuasive judgements that are pre-structured by the form and content of the media account itself. Some media narratives, the heavily censored British television coverage of the Malvinas War, for example, encourage flag-waving and the glorification of violence by their audiences. Other narratives, for instance slick televisual news coverage of a rape or murder in the local community, may induce paralysing shock or puzzlement or sickening depression that serves to contain an audience's responses within strictly defined limits. Still other narratives suppose that by so shocking their audiences they can be encouraged to empathise with the violated – to engage not merely in 'understanding' the violated but also to 'overstand' the narratives, that is, to engage in a kind of questioning of the facts behind the facts of the violence that the narratives themselves do *not* encourage audiences to ask.

Media narratives that highlight representations of resistance to violence are a case in point of the latter possibility. Televisual images of uncivil war zones, for instance, never simply highlight the destructiveness of violence. We see not only burning, looting, killing, rubbled buildings and piles of bloodied bodies. We see as well images of the first green shoots of civil society: shoes being fashioned from the tires of a bombed-out car; a woman looking through rubbish tips for rags to use as nappies; a postman who appears from nowhere; a priest gathering around him ragged-trousered, rapscallion youth to set up a car repair workshop in a ramshackle shed next to his war-damaged church.

Less obvious are those diffuse or more subtle forms of resistance evidenced on the screen, including the independent reporter/ journalist, whose face shows sign of stress and whose voice connotes bravery and empathy with the victims. Then there is the silence of the victims of violence, the eerie stillness of those whose violation cannot be spoken of, let alone described; and, linked somehow to their silence, their cries, voiceless cries which are evidently addressed to no one and everyone. The cries of the violated, no matter where they are located on the face of the earth, have never been transmitted so frequently or so widely to such large audiences as they are nowadays. Some of them – like Nick Ut's 1972 photograph of the naked girl screaming while fleeing from her napalmed village in Vietnam, or Kenneth Jarecke's 1991 image of an Iraqi soldier burned to death on the road to Basra – have become iconic. The cries of the violated have uncertain effects, to be sure. Those who break through the silence imposed by violence never know whether their cries will be heard, let alone understood. But, arguably, that is why their cries can be so powerful. Crying exceeds all language, not only in the primeval suddenness with which it breaks the silence surrounding the violence that has been perpetrated, but also in its militant disregard for the grammar of language. Crying never comes to a halt, as if it were reduced to gibberish. It stands outside the boundaries of linguistic sense. It echoes in the ears of those who hear, its meanings infinitely suspended and never fully decipherable. Crying cries out indefinitely to be heard, to be understood, to be remedied.

The crying of those who have been violated sometimes – or often – triggers questions about responsibility among those who see or hear the grief of those who cry. Why and to what extent such a conversion process takes place remains something of an enigma to political analysts, and to publics at large. Empathy with the violated happens, but why and when and for how long remains utterly unpredictable. All that is known is that it happens, and – contrary to the violence-as-entertainment thesis – to the extent that it does happen we can speak of a potentially civilising dialectic hidden within the growing media coverage of virtually all forms of violence. Communications media encourage those who witness violence to have a sense of responsibility for the fate of the violated – to participate in the politics of pity. The act of witnessing violence through the media can be accompanied by several emotions, of which not only denial ('I am not responsible for these horrors') and helpless confusion ('What can I possibly do?') but also *humility* and *guilt* and *shame* are significant possibilities.

Rule number nine: *for the sake of democracy, canvass support everywhere for the civil virtues, the greatest of which is humility.* Understood as a political strategy and as a whole way of life, non-violence is no good unless it is durable. It cannot be so unless the institutions of civil society, in which non-violent power-sharing among different groups is routinely practised, under the protection of publicly accountable government, are lubricated by the 'pre-political' juices of virtue. Those who think that talk of virtues is old-fashioned, or that it is as moralising as a killjoy neo-conservative rounding on those who like sex, and other freedoms, need to think again. Benedetto Croce's well-known warning that those who engage in politics should learn to respect the power of the non-political, applies especially to democracies, which require more than respect for the law, freedom of communication and periodic elections in order to function well. They also need democratically virtuous citizens.

Virtues are the substructure of a peaceable democracy. There are of course many great democratic virtues – among them truthfulness, mercy, tolerance, courage – but the cardinal democratic virtue is humility. Humility is a friend of democracy because it refuses to put itself and other virtues on a pedestal; to be proud of certain virtues, including one's own or others' humility, is to suffer from a lack of it. Although often symbolised by the quiet and boring person of modest upbringing, humility should not be confused with docility or submissiveness. Nietzsche insisted that humility is the morality of slaves, and therefore deserves nothing but contempt. 'Humility [*humilitas*] is sadness born of the fact that a man considers his own lack of power, or weakness', wrote Spinoza, but both he and Nietzsche provide misleading accounts of humility.[38] The humble are not necessarily private, insignificant or inconspicuous individuals – mere subjects who will never become rulers, or who die without leaving any other mark on the world except a few belongings and (if they are lucky) a grave. Humility is neither meekness nor lowliness (what Aristotle called *micropsuchia*) nor servility. Humility is in fact the antithesis of arrogant pride; it is the quality of being aware of one's limits.

Humility has an allergic reaction to the self-satisfied Hobbesian rule *homo homini lupus est* (man is a wolf to men). It does not suppose it to be the starting point for understanding modern politics and international relations. Those who are humble are without illusions. They dislike vanity and have an affinity with honesty; bullshit on thrones is not their scene. Humble human beings feel themselves to be dwellers on earth (*humus*, from which the word humility derives). They know that they do not know everything, that they are not God, or a god or goddess. Humility is a vital resource that strengthens the powerless and tames the powerful by questioning their claims to superiority. It is the opposite of haughty hunger for power over others,

---

[38] Friedrich Nietzsche, *Beyond Good and Evil*, in the *Complete Works of Friedrich Nietzsche*, ed. Oscar Levy (London 1964), vol. XII, aphorism 260, p. 229; and Benedict de Spinoza, *The Ethics*, in Edwin Curley (ed.), *A Spinoza Reader: The Ethics and Other Works* (Princeton, NJ 1994), vol. III, definition 26, p. 192.

which is why humility balks at humiliation. In a world of arrogance tinged with violence, humility emboldens. Unyielding, it gives individuals inner strength to act upon the world. It dislikes hubris. It yearns for its dethronement. Humility detests violence and the violent who, for a time, always suppose that they are right. Humility shuns showy arrogance and all forms of aggressiveness. Humility radiates in the presence of others, calmly and cheerfully – it is a social virtue – enabling them to 'be themselves'. It does not demand reciprocity. It implies equality. It is generous. Augustine wrote: 'Wherever there is humility there is also charity.' Descartes agreed: 'the most generous people are usually also the most humble.'[39] Aimed at the haughty and the bossy, humility implies tolerance, and since it shuns abusive power it anticipates a more equal and tolerant – and less violent – world. The humble live off the simple conviction that the world to which they aspire is better than the world in which they are forced to dwell.

The final rule for ridding the world of surplus violence: *democrats should eschew guilt and instead be prepared publicly to experience shame for the violence that has been perpetrated in past and present struggles to defend or to abolish democracy.* In the English vernacular, these two tiny words – guilt and shame – are normally confused. The markedly different dispositions they signify nevertheless should be distinguished within any account of the tense relationship between violence and democracy.[40]

Guilt, the feeling of culpability for another's misfortune, the emotional obsession with having done something wrong to them, is unproductive of a mature, democratic sense of responsibility for the

---

[39] Augustine's remark is cited in the entry 'Humilité', in Xavier Léon-Dufour et al. (ed.), *Vocabulaire de théologie biblique* (Paris 1970); René Descartes, *Les passions de l'âme* (Paris 1937 [1645–9]), pt. 3, art. 155, p. 102.

[40] I am relying here on the suggestive formulations of Herbert Morris, 'Guilt and shame', in *On Guilt and Innocence* (Berkeley and Los Angeles 1976); Gabriele Taylor, *Pride, Shame and Guilt* (Oxford 1985); and Bernard Williams, *Shame and Necessity* (Berkeley, Los Angeles and London 1993), especially ch. 4.

fate of those who have been violated. Those who are rendered guilty by the act of witnessing (or committing) violence against others are gripped by the feeling that they could easily disappear into a hole, chased by the anger, resentment or indignation of the violated. Even though their actions may not have directly caused the suffering of the violated, the guilty feel as they do because an inner voice tells them that they are indeed responsible. The guilty are haunted by the sound within themselves of the voice of judgement. They feel permanent regret at what they have done to others. That is why they themselves often fear retaliatory punishment, or even inflict it upon themselves, for instance by means of permanently deep-seated guilt.

In practice, the accomplices and witnesses of incivility often mix together the emotions of guilt and shame, but that does not void the distinction between them. Shame understandably arises in both the audiences and perpetrators when witnessing scenes of violence, but not simply because it is an emotion often connected with the process of seeing and being seen. Unlike the experience of guilt, in which the ego is neurotically haunted and paralysed by the cries and blood of the violated, shame is initially the emotion of self-protection, in which the whole being of the shamed person seems diminished, but not obliterated.

When experiencing shame, audiences and perpetrators are struck by their feeling of exposure to the violated, who themselves are often less angry and resentful (as in guilt) than contemptuous, derisive or dismissive of those who witness or inflict their plight. It is as if those who cry out, or bleed, are looking back at those who are watching and can see right through them, even though the audience or the perpetrators themselves are seated in safety, before a control panel, or far away in the comfort of living rooms and theatres. Those who feel shame feel exposed to the wrong people at the wrong time. Consequently, they are gripped by the desire to hide, or to hide their faces, even the desire to switch off their television sets, or (like the first American cinema audiences to witness footage of concentration camp victims and survivors[41]) to skulk from the room.[42] They feel shame not so much because of what they purportedly have done (as in guilt) but because they are gripped by the intuition that the violence they have committed or witnessed falls contemptibly short of the civilised standards they expect of themselves and others in the world around them. Unlike the guilty, who wallow in their own guilt, those who are ashamed, not surprisingly, often yearn to recover or to improve themselves, even to bond or interact with the violated. Caught with their pants down, the ashamed seek to decipher what has happened to the violated and to understand themselves in relation to what has happened – sometimes for the purpose of rebuilding both themselves and the world in which they and their offspring have to live their future lives.

It is of interest that one of the first great twentieth-century novels about power and violence, Kafka's *The Trial*, ends with the theme of shame and not guilt. It might have been expected that the death scene, in which two officials stab Joseph K. twice through the heart in a deserted moonlit quarry, constitutes the pardon, the end of the interminable ordeal for the victim. Kafka refuses that ending by specifying that the shame of it all survives. 'Like a dog', the victim splutters, vomiting out his last words, as if he meant the shame of his murder to outlive him, and to haunt posterity forever. The whole scene is depressing, but here in literary form, surely, is a clue to one of the vital emotional responses required of all thinking, judging, acting democrats to the plagues and images of violence that blight their lives. What will posterity remember democracies for? Propping up dictators and having tea with totalitarians? The invention of concentration camps and escape-proof prisons? Or the napalm bombs they

---

[41] Robert Abzug, *Inside the Vicious Heart: America and the Liberation of the Nazi Concentration Camps* (New York 1985), p. 170.

[42] Compare the remarks of Erik Erikson, *Childhood and Society*, 2nd edn (New York 1963), pp. 252–3: 'Shame supposes that one is completely exposed and conscious of being looked at . . . One is visible and not ready to be visible; which is why we dream of shame as a situation in which we are stared at in a condition of incomplete dress.'

dropped on innocent civilians, the cities they fire-bombed and the nuclear explosions they first triggered? Or will posterity recall how democracies turned rapes and murders into light entertainment? Or the times when they did nothing and turned a blind eye to orgies of genocidal blood-letting? Or terrorised the world by declaring war on world-wide terror? How should democracies today come to terms with all this violence, all this hypocrisy? Should they not feel ashamed of what we and our forebears have done to ourselves and to others – in the name of democracy?

Further reading

The recent history of philosophical and political reflections on violence forms a rich collage of conflicting and converging insights. A number of these remain vital in any assessment of the contours of contemporary violence. Readers who remain unsatisfied with the material cited in this essay, or who are interested in deepening their understanding of the subject, may wish to consult the following additional literature on violence written by specialists in various scholarly disciplines. For her generous help in the preparation of both this list and the index that follows, I wish to thank Maria Fotou.

Adler, Alfred, 'La Guerre et l'état primitif', in Miguel Abensour, ed., *L'Esprit des lois sauvages: Pierre Clastres ou une nouvelle anthropologie politique*, Paris 1987.

Anderson, John K., *Military Practice and Theory in the Age of Xenophon*, Berkeley, CA. 1970.

Besteman, Catherine, ed., *Violence: A Reader*, Basingstoke 2002.

Betts, R. K., 'Nuclear Weapons and Conventional War', *Journal of Strategic Studies* 11 (March 1988), pp. 79–95.

Blok, Anton, *Honour and Violence*, Cambridge 2001.

Bonet, Honoré, *The Tree of Battles*, Liverpool 1949.

Buruma, Ian, *The Wages of Guilt. Memories of War in Germany and Japan*, London 1995.

Buzan, Barry, *People, States and Fear. An Agenda for International Security Studies in the Post-Cold War Era*, 2nd edn, New York, London, Toronto, Sydney, Tokyo and Singapore 1991.

Caffi, Andrea, 'Violence and Sociability', *Politics*, 4, 1 (January 1947), pp. 16–19.

Caillois, Roger, 'Le Vertige de la guerre', in *Quatre essais de sociologie contemporaine*, Paris 1951.

Calvocoressi, Peter and Guy Wint, *Total War*, London 1972.

Campbell, David and Michael Dillon, eds., *The Political Subject of Violence*, Manchester 1993.

Cassese, Antonio, *Violence and Law in the Modern Age*, Cambridge 1988.

Ceadl, Martin, *The Origins of War Prevention. The British Peace Movement and International Relations, 1730–1854*, Oxford 1996.

Cipolla, Carlo M., *Guns and Sails in the Early Phase of European Expansion 1500–1700*, London 1965.

von Clausewitz, Carl, *On War*, M. Howard and P. Paret, eds., Princeton, NJ 1976.

Colas, Dominique, *Civil Society and Fanaticism. Conjoined Histories*, Stanford 1997.

Covington, Coline, *et al.*, eds., *Terrorism and War: Unconscious dynamics of political violence*, London 2002.

Crichton, John, ed., *Psychiatric Patient Violence. Risk and Response*, London 1995.

Duby, Georges, *The Chivalrous Society*, Berkeley, CA 1977.

Dershowitz, Alan M., *Why Terrorism Works*, New Haven and London 2002.

Elias, Norbert, *The Loneliness of the Dying*, Oxford and Cambridge, MA 1985.

Elias, Norbert and Eric Dunning, *Quest for Excitement. Sport and Leisure in the Civilizing Process*, Oxford and Cambridge, MA 1993.

Elshtain, Jean Bethke, *Women and War*, Chicago and London 1995.

Finer, Samuel E, 'State and Nation-Building in Europe: The Role of the Military', in Charles Tilly, ed., *The Formation of National States in Western Europe*, Princeton, NJ 1975.

Foucault, Michel, *Discipline and Punish. The Birth of the Prison*, London 1977.

Freedman, Lawrence, ed., *Superterrorism. Policy Responses*. Oxford 2002.

Gelles, Richard J., 'Physical violence, child abuse, and child violence: a continuum of violence, or distinct behaviours?', *Human Nature*, 2, 1 (1991), pp. 59–72.

Girard, René, *Violence and the Sacred*, Baltimore, MD 1977.
    'Generative violence and the extinction of social order', *Salmagundi*, 63–4 (Spring–Summer 1984), pp. 204–37.

Gray, J. Glenn, *The Warriors: Reflections on Men in Battle*, New York 1970.

Halbrook, Stephen P., *That Every Man Be Armed: The Evolution of a Constitutional Right*, Albuquerque, NM 1984.

Hale, John, 'War and Public Opinion in Renaissance Italy', in E. R. Jacob, ed., *Italian Renaissance Studies*, New York 1960.

Hartogs, Renatus, and Eric Artzt, eds., *Violence: Causes and Solutions*, New York 1970.

Hassner, Pierre, 'Beyond the three traditions: the philosophy of war and peace in historical perspective', *International Affairs*, 70, 4 (1994), pp. 737–56.

Howard, Michael, *War in European History*, Oxford 1976.

Huizinga, Johan, 'The political and military significance of chivalric ideas in the late Middle Ages', in *Men and Ideas. History, the Middle Ages, the Renaissance. Essays by Johan Huizinga*, New York 1959.

Jünger, Ernst, *Im Stahlgewittern*, Berlin 1931.

Kaldor, Mary, *The Baroque Arsenal*, New York 1982.

Keane, John, 'Despotism and democracy. The origins and development of the distinction between civil society and the state, 1750–1850', in John Keane, ed., *Civil Society and the State. New European Perspectives*, London and New York 1988.

Keen, Maurice, *Chivalry*, New Haven 1984.

Kelman, Herbert C., 'Violence without moral restraint: reflections on the dehumanization of victims and victimizers', *Journal of Social Issues*, 29, 4 (1973), pp. 25–61.

Kendrick, Walter, *The Thrill of Fear: 250 Years of Scary Entertainment*, New York 1991.

Leiden, Carl, and Karl M. Schmitt, *The Politics of Violence: Revolution in the Modern World*, Englewood Cliffs, NJ 1968.

Lemarchand, René, *Burundi. Ethnocide as Discourse and Practice*, Cambridge 1994.

Lindqvist, Sven, *A History of Bombing*, London 2001.

McCulloch, Jock, *Black Soul, White Artifact. Fanon's Clinical Psychology and Social Theory*, Cambridge and New York 1983.

McMahan, Jeff, *The Ethics of Killing. Problems at the Margins of Life*, Oxford 2002.

Malcolm, Joyce Lee, *To Keep and Bear Arms: The Origins of an Anglo-American Right*, Cambridge, MA 1994.

Mallett, Michael, *Mercenaries and their Masters: Warfare in Renaissance Italy*, London 1974.

Mansfield, Edward D., and Jack Snyder, 'Democratization and War', *Foreign Affairs*, 74, 3 (May–June 1995), pp. 79–97.

Marx, Gary T., *Undercover: Police Surveillance in America*, New York 1988. *Civil Disorder and the Agents of Social Control*, Irvington 1993.

Mier, Paul, John Keane and Alberto Melucci, 'New perspectives on social movements: an interview', in John Keane and Paul Mier, eds., *Nomads of the Present*, London and Philadelphia 1989.

Minear Larry, and Thomas G. Weiss, *Mercy Under Fire. War and the Global Humanitarian Community*, Boulder, CO, San Francisco and Oxford 1995.

Nancy, Jean-Luc, 'Violence et violence', *Lignes*, 25 (May 1995), pp. 293–8.

Paret, Peter, *Understanding War. Essays on Clausewitz and the History of Military Power*, Princeton, NJ 1992.

Phillipson, Coleman, *The International Law and Custom of Ancient Greece and Rome*, London 1911.

Pick, Daniel, *War Machine. The Rationalisation of Slaughter in the Modern Age*, New Haven and London 1993.

Preston, R. A., S. F. Wise, and H. O. Werner, *Men in Arms: A History of Warfare and its Interrelationships with Western Society*, London 1956.

Robarchek, Clayton A., 'Primitive warfare and the ratomorphic image of mankind', *American Anthropologist*, 91 (1989), pp. 903–20.

Ruff, Julius R., *Violence in Early Modern Europe 1500–1800*, Cambridge 2001.

Schwoerer, Lois G., *'No Standing Armies!' The Antiarmy Ideology in Seventeenth Century England*, Baltimore, MD 1974.

Searles, Patricia, and Ronald J. Berger, eds., *Rape and Society. Readings on the Problem of Sexual Assault*, Boulder, CO, San Francisco and Oxford 1995.

Silberner, Edmond, *La Guerre dans la pensée économique du XVI au XVIII siècle*, Paris 1939.

Singh, Birinder Pal, *Violence as Political Discourse*, Shimla 2002.

Steger, Manfred B., and Nancy S. Lind, eds., *Violence and its Alternatives*, Basingstoke 1999.

Toynbee, Arnold J., *War and Civilization*, London, New York and Toronto 1951.

Vernant, Jean-Pierre, ed., *Problèmes de la guerre en Grèce ancienne*, Paris 1968.

Waltz, Kenneth N., *Man, the State and War: A Theoretical Analysis*, New York 1959.

Walzer, Michael, *Just and Unjust Wars: A Moral Argument with Historical Illustrations*, New York 1977.

Wheeler, Nick, *Saving Strangers. Humanitarian Intervention in International Society*, Oxford and New York 2000.

Whitmer, Barbara, *The Violence Mythos*, Albany, NY 1997.

Wolfner, Glenn D. and Richard J. Gelles, 'A profile of violence towards children: a national study', *Child Abuse & Neglect*, 17 (1993), pp. 197–212.

Wolin, Sheldon, 'Violence and the Western political tradition', *American Journal of Orthopsychiatry*, 33 (1963), pp. 15–28.

Worcester, Kenton, *et al.*, eds., *Violence and Politics: Globalization's Paradox*, New York 2002.

Index

Akihiko, Tanaka 19, 177
Al-Fanjari, Ahmad Shawqi 183, 188
  Al-hurriyat' as-siyasiyyah fi'l Islam 184
Al-Ghannouchi, Rachid 183, 188, 189, 191
  'The efficiency of using violence to
    establish an Islamic State' 184
  'The Islamic movement and violence'
    184
Althusius, Johannes 116, 190
  *Politica Methodice digesta atque
    exemplis sacris et profanis ilustrata*
    116
American Revolution 144–6
  Battle of Trenton 145–6
anti-party politics 150–3
apocalyptic terrorism *see* terrorism
Arendt, Hannah 6, 7, 12, 100, 118, 146
  Correspondence 1926–1969 (with Karl
    Jaspers) 79
  On Violence 6, 7, 100, 146
  The Origins of Totalitarianism 98
Aristotle 38–9, 205
  on violence 38–9
  Politica 38
Aron, Raymond 21, 111
  Le grand schisme 111
  Les dernières années du siècle 163
Augustine 11, 206
Aung, San Suu Kyi 155

Baudrillard, Jean 199
  The Evil Demon of Images 199
Bauman, Zygmunt 65, 82
  Modernity and the Holocaust 65
  on civility 66–7
Benjamin, Walter 12
  Zur Kritik der Gewalt 12
Bergson, Henri-Louis 149
Bin Laden, Osama 11
Brecht, Bertolt 138
Burke, Edmund 119–20, 122

*A Letter to John Farr and John Harris,
  Esqrs., Sheriffs of the City of
  Bristol, on the Affairs of America*
  122

Carmichael, Stokely 11
Castoriadis, Cornelius 88
China 20, 23
civil society 4, 42–3, 96–9
  Ernest Gellner on 43–5
  incompatibility of violence with 38
  its role in American Revolution 144–6
  rebuilding civil society 129, 130–2
civil war 25, 112–13
civilisation *see* 'civilisation' *passim* 42–52,
  53
  civilising process according to Elias
    55–6 *see* civility
civility 3, 56
  Zygmunt Bauman on 66–7
  Samuel Johnson on 42
  and modern state 60–2
  civility politics 82, 90
  civilising process according to Elias 55–6
  dialectics of 105
  rebuilding civil society 129, 130–2
Clastres, Pierre 115
  Recherches d'anthropologie politique
    116
Clausewitz, Carl von 22, 74, 116, 181
Conrad, Joseph 10
Council of Europe 80–1
Croce, Benedetto 204

Darnton, Robert 31, 33
  *The Great Cat Massacre and Other
    Episodes in French Cultural
    History* 33
De Vitoria, Francisco 19
democracy 1
  and Islamic politics 183–91

democratic virtues 204–6
democratic zones of peace 8, 18 (*see also*
    democratic peace, theory of)
means of violence 2
restraining violence 160–2
tendency to democratise violence 2–4,
    30–1, 75–6
democratic opposition in Eastern Europe *see*
    anti-party politics
democratic peace, theory of 17–18
    democratic zones of peace 17, 18
    zones of violent anarchy 17
democratic virtues 204–6
democratic zones of peace 8, 17, 18 *see also*
    democratic peace, theory of
democratisation of violence 2–4, 30–1, 32–3,
    75–88
    ten rules 165–209
Derrida, Jacques 11, 169–70
Descartes, René 206
    Les passions de l'âme 206
détente 85–6
Diderot, Denis 49
Dunbar, James 54
    *Essays on the History of Mankind in
    Rude and Cultivated Ages* 54

Eco, Umberto 19, 177
    'Living in the new Middle Ages' 20
    neo-medieval order 19–20, 102
Elias, Norbert 55, 58–60, 82, 91, 96
    civilising process 55–6, 62
    civilising process and the modern state
        61
    on civility and violence 62
    *Über den Prozess der Zivilization.
        Soziogenetische und
        psychogenetische Untersuchungen*
        55–6
    'Violence and civilisation. The state
        monopoly of physical violence and
        its infringement' 63
Eliot, T. S. 109, 121
Elser, Georg 163
Enzensberger, Hans Magnus 113, 134–5, 165
    Aussichten auf den Burgerkrieg 114,
        135, 199–200
    'Der Krieg, wie' 138
    on uncivil war and intervention 134–5,
        136–7

Erasmus of Rotterdam 56
ethics 128–64
European Union 78, 176

Fadlallah, Sayyed Muhammed 189
Fanon, Frantz 13, 143
    Les Damnés de la terre 13
    Peau Noire, masques blancs 143
fascism 2
Ferguson, Adam 52, 54
    An Essay on the History of Civil Society
        53
    on civilisation 52–3
Forster, Georg 51
Foucault, Michel 37
    *Discipline and Punish. The Birth of the
        Prison* 37, 57
Freud, Sigmund 104
    The Uncanny (das Unheimliche) 104

Galtung, Johan 34, 35
    'Cultural violence' 35
    'Violence, peace and peace research' 35
Gandhi, Mahatma 49, 155
    Non-Violent Resistance 155
Gay, Peter 93
    *The Cultivation of Hatred. The
        Bourgeois Experience, Victoria to
        Freud* 93
Gellner, Ernest 43–5
    *Conditions of Liberty: Civil Society and
        its Rivals* 43–5
    Muslim Society 115
Gilligan, James 168
    *Violence: Reflections on Our Deadliest
        Epidemic* 168
Gingrich, Newt 107
Girard, René 8–10, 11, 13, 26, 188
    La violence et le sacré 8–10, 13, 26
    Le Bouc émissaire 188
    *Violences d'aujourd'hui, violence de
        toujours* 8
Graham, Franklin 183
Greene, Graham 166
guerrillas 27

Hassner, Pierre 21, 111
    *La Violence et la paix. De la bombe
        atomique au nettoyage ethnique*
        21, 111

Hobbes, Thomas 62, 82, 92, 113, 122, 159
    *Leviathan, or the Matter, Forme, and
        Power of a Common-Wealth
        Ecclesiastical and Civill* 93
    *Philosophical Rudiments concerning
        Government and Society* 93
    *The History of The Causes of The Civil
        Wars of England, and of The
        Counsels and Artifices By Which
        They Were Carried On From The
        Year 1640 To The Year 1660* 110
Hook, Sydney 33
Hume, David 120
    'Of public credit' 120

incivility 46–53, 91–2, 97 *and* 'civilisation'
    42–53
India 23
intervention 19, 129 *see also* Enzensberger
Islamic politics 183–91

James, William 94
    'The moral equivalent of war' 94
Johnson, Samuel 42
    on civility 42
Jünger, Ernst 16, 122
    In Stahlgewittern 122

Kafka, Franz 38
    The Penal Colony 38
    The Trial 208
Kant, Immanuel 91
    'Welchen Ertrag wird der Fortschritt
        zum besseren dem
        Menschengeschiecht abwerfen?' 91
Kaplan, Robert 113, 115
    'The coming anarchy' 114
Khaldun, Ibn 11, 189
    *The Muqaddimah. An Introduction to
        History* 189
King, Martin Luther 154, 155
    'Letter from the Birmingham City Jail'
        154, 155
Koselleck, Reinhart 90
    *Kritik und Krise. Eine Studie zur
        Pathogenese der bürgerlichen Welt*
        90

League of Nations 78
Lenin, Vladimir I. 11

Levi, Primo 54
Lévi-Strauss, Claude 64
Logan, John 54
    Elements of the Philosophy of History
        54

Machiavelli, Niccolò 94, 116
    The Prince 94, 116
Mao, Zedong 11
Marx, Karl 10, 95–6
    on civil society 95–6
McLuhan, Marshall and Fiore, Quentin 198
    War and Peace in the Global Village 199
Melville, Herman 5
Michels, Robert 148
Michnik, Adam 1, 151
Miller, Arthur 98
    The Misfits 98
Milošević, Slobodan 26
Mirabeau, Comte de 49, 94
    *L'Ami des Hommes ou Traité de la
        population* 49, 94
Montesquieu, Baron de 147
Muchembled, Robert 31
    on the role of violence 31
    *La Violence au village: sociabilité et
        comportements populaires en
        Artois du XVe au XVIIe siècle* 31

national sovereignty, the end of 15, 19
neo-medieval order 19–20, 102
'new middle ages' *see* neo-medieval order
    and under Eco, Sacco
Niebuhr, Reinhold 6
Nietzsche, Friedrich 205
    Beyond Good and Evil 165, 205
non-governmental organisations 132–3 *see
    also* civil society
Novalis 49
nuclear weapons 15–16
    as a threat to national sovereignty 15
    first side of the triangle of violence
        20–4
    in the post-Cold War world system
        20–4
    Singer and Wildavsky 72–3

Orwell, George 15, 128, 156
    'Reflections on Gandhi' 156
    'You and the Atom Bomb' 15

pacifism 154–8
Paine, Thomas 145
  The American Crisis 145
Pakistan 23
Palach, Jan 139
Pascal 170
Patočka, Jan 87
peace movements 83
  British peace movement 83–4, 87–8
Philadelphian model, the 76–7
Plato 89
  The Republic 89, 180
Polybius 89
  The General History of Polybius 89
post-war reconstruction *see* rebuilding civil
    society
pragmatism 7
public spheres 195–8

Qutb, Sayyid 185

rebuilding civil society 129, 130–2
Rousseau, Jean-Jacques 49–50, 61
  *Considérations sur le gouvernement de
    Pologne, et sur sa réformation
    projetée* 180–1
  'Fragments of an Essay on the State of
    War' 50
Russian Federation 20, 22

Sacco, Giuseppe 19
  neo-medieval order 19–20, 102
Sartre, Jean-Paul 11
Schmitt, Carl 82
  *Der Leviathan in der Staatslehre des
    Thomas Hobbes* 82
Semprun, Jorge 167
  The Long Voyage 167
Shklar, Judith 6, 7
Singer, Max and Wildavsky, Aaron 18, 72–3
  *The Real World Order: Zones of
    Peace/Zones of Turmoil* 18, 72–3
Smith, Adam 52
Sorel, Georges 12, 30
  Réflexions sur la violence 12, 147–50,
    151
Spinoza, Benedict de 205
  The Ethics 205
Starkweather case 101
Suárez, Francisco 19

Sudan 24
Swift, Jonathan 47, 51
  *A Modest Proposal for Preventing the
    Children of Poor People in Ireland
    from being a Burden to their
    Parents or Country; and for making
    them beneficial to the Publick* 51,
    137
  The Correspondence of Jonathan Swift
    48

terrorism 27–9
  apocalyptic terrorism (as the third
    side of the triangle of violence)
    27–9
  classical form 27–8
Toch, Hans 168
  The Disturbed and Violent Offender
    (with Kenneth Adams) 168
Toqueville, Alexis de 148
Torture Committee 81
totalitarianism 67
triangle of violence, the 20–9
  first side of 20–4
  second side of 24–7
  third side of 27–9

uncivil society *see* incivility
uncivil war 24–7, 114–15, 117–19
  as the second side of the triangle of
    violence 24–7
  defining uncivil 109
  destructiveness of 119–20
  uncivil war zones 25–6 *see also*
    Enzensberger
United Nations, the 78
United States of America 20, 22

Van Creveld, Martin 114, 115
  The Transformation of War 114
Vidal-Naquet, Pierre 175
  *La Torture dans la République: essai
    d'histoire et de politique
    contemporaines (1954–1962)* 175
violence 6
  against animals 31
  and civil society 42–3
  and Islamic politics 183–91
  and modern state 60–2
  and public spheres 195–8

violence (cont.)
  as a natural element of human
    nature/affairs 7–11
  as an 'ideal-type' 30
  as entertainment 102–5, 198–200
  collective violence 142
  connections with democracy 1
  democratisation of 2–4, 30–1, 32–3,
    75–88, 165–209
  embodied quality of 36
  ethics of violence 128–64
  fascination in Weimar Germany 103
  global report on 7–8
  humiliation and violence 101–2
  in fascist regimes 2
  in the twentieth century 16
  incompatibility with civil society 38,
    62
  institutional violence 37
  intentional component of 35
  'just violence' 11
  legitimate use of 12
  on defining violence 30–40
  restraining violence 160–2
  self-violence 139–41
  state violence 54–65
  triangle of violence, the 20–9
Voltaire, François-Marie Arouet de 50
Von Kleist, Heinrich 99

Walzer, Michael 13
  Just and Unjust Wars 13
war crimes tribunals 78–80
Ward, Janie 163
Weber, Max 158
  'Politik als Beruf' 158
Weil, Simone 142, 151
Wolf, Christa 181
Wolff, Robert Paul 33
  'On violence' 33